D1539987

PURITANISM IN TUDOR ENGLAND

History in Depth

G. A. Williams
General Editor

Puritanism in Tudor England

H. C. PORTER

LIBRARY
BRYAN COLLEGE
DAYTON, TENN. 37321

UNIVERSITY OF SOUTH CAROLINA PRESS
Columbia, South Carolina

78255

Selection and editorial matter © H. C. Porter 1971

All rights reserved. No part of this publication
may be reproduced or transmitted, in any form or
by any means, without permission.

First published 1971 in Great Britain by
MACMILLAN AND CO LTD
London and Basingstoke

Published 1971 in the United States of America by
UNIVERSITY OF SOUTH CAROLINA PRESS
Columbia, South Carolina

International Standard Book Number
(hardbound):0—87249—222—2
(paperback): 0—87249—223—0
Library of Congress Catalog Card Number: 75—145532

Manufactured in Great Britain

*for David and the
Cambridge Footlights' Club*

Contents

General Editor's Preface

Historical perception demands immediacy and depth. These qualities are lost in attempts at broad general survey; for the reader of history depth is the only true breadth. Each volume in this series, therefore, explores an important historical problem in depth. There is no artificial uniformity; each volume is shaped by the problem it tackles. The past bears its own witness; the core of each volume is a major collection of original material (translated into English where necessary) as alive, as direct and as full as possible. The reader should feel the texture of the past. The volume editor provides interpretative notes and introduction and a full working bibliography. The volume will stand in its own right as a 'relived experience' and will also serve as a point of entry into a wider area of historical discourse. In taking possession of a particular historical world, the reader will move more freely in a wider universe of historical experience.

*

In this volume, Dr H. C. Porter takes the reader into the world of sixteenth-century Puritanism. It is, in part, a process of purgation. The editor warns us against seeing these Tudor zealots in the light of future Dissent and Nonconformity; the shadow of the traumatic seventeenth century lies heaviest of all across us. In this collection the reader is confronted with the discourse of these men in its original force and at adequate length, so that he may directly experience their sensibility. Essays like Cranmer's on the factions in the Church, letters like Calvin's to Edward VI, polemic, measured or fierce, like Barnes's or Marprelate's, take him through a small universe of thought and feeling. There is the extraordinarily vivid record of the interrogation of separatists by Authority, the characteristic, almost archetypal diary of a preacher in Essex, samples of Puritan special pleading and Puritan verse. More familiar documents, Peter Wentworth's speech in the House in 1576 or Richard Hooker's examination of the sectarian mind, set fully in context, acquire new resonance. And the documents are illumined by the editor's highly individual, penetrating and often challenging commentary. A whole world is here recreated, and for its own sake, its own integrity, not as a species of prologue.

The basic theme is the disengagement of a specifically Puritan attitude from the complex world of the English Reformation. In the early days difficult to distinguish with any of that 'precision' its opponents found distasteful, it grew into a major challenge to Establishment. Already in his confrontation with the separatists in 1567, Bishop Grindal was ill-at-ease before a conviction which grew from the same root as his own. . . 'I have said mass: I am sorry for it . . . you see me wear a cope or a surplice . . . I had rather minister without these things, but for order's sake and obedience to the prince. . .' The contest is already sharp. . . .

Canon Watts: You would have us use nothing that the papists used: then should we use no churches, as the papists have used.

Robert Hawkins: Churches be necessary to keep our bodies from the rain, but surplices and copes be superstitious and idolatrous. . . .

Bishop Grindal: Things not forbidden of God may be used for order and obedience' sake: you shall hear the mind and judgement of a well learned man, whom you like of, namely Master Bullinger; (then he read out of a book). . . .

John Smith: What if I can show you Bullinger against Bullinger in this thing?

Bishop Grindal: I think not, Smith.

John Smith: Yes, that I can. . . .'

The editor first sets the scene in Cranmer's definition of 'Parties', Barnes's voicing of a particular spirit and Calvin's urging England to 'go forward to perfection' The thrust of this argument drives on through the dialogue with the separatists and Browne's autobiography, through John Field's trenchancy and the parliamentary discourse of the 1570s; it widens to embrace the Puritan concern for education, the self-analytical *praxis* of Richard Rogers in his Essex parish,

xii

the anti-episcopal invective of Marprelate. The series runs to a climax in the splendid confrontation of Richard Hooker and William Perkins, to close with the latter's imperative Chart of Salvation and Damnation.

Thus, in depth, roundness, precision, colour and life, the Puritan world of the sixteenth century is recaptured in integrity. It is examined in the spirit of Ranke's observation that every generation is equidistant from Eternity. But while Dr Porter's perceptive commentary rigorously excludes deceptive hindsight, it cannot and of course does not avoid the permanencies of contestation. For what emerges from the book is precisely the emergence of that spirit which was to be a formative force in succeeding generations — the 'That I can' of John Smith.

GWYN A. WILLIAMS

Preface

In the extracts, I have modernised the spelling and capital-isation. And (except in the Hooker piece, which reproduces the 1604 punctuation) I have rationalised the punctuation throughout — that is, the original punctuation (often extra-ordinarily erratic) has been emended to allow the argument of the writer to emerge with clarity to the modern general reader.

For permission to use the extracts from manuscript (Numbers 10, 12, 14, 16, 19, 20, 21, 22) I am grateful to the Trustees of Dr Williams's Library, Gordon Square, W.C.1, for allowing me access to the Morrice and Baxter MSS. In the case of material from printed books, I must thank the following: The Archbishop of Canterbury and the Trustees of Lambeth Palace Library (Number 8); S.P.C.K. (Number 11); Thomas Nelson & Sons Ltd (Number 17); the Council of the Royal Historical Society (Number 23). Numbers 2, 7 and 9 are printed from copies in the Cambridge University Library; and Number 24 from a copy in Selwyn College Library.

I am grateful to Professor W. R. Brock for giving me a copy of the 1693 edition of D'Ewes's Elizabethan parliamentary journals; and to Canon Charles Smyth, once my supervisor at Corpus Christi College, Cambridge, from whom I acquired a three-volume folio edition (1612/13) of William Perkins — a copy bequeathed in 1693 by a parson's widow to her four children for three months each in the year, 'that every one may have the use and benefit of it'. Dr Frank Stubbings, Librarian of Emmanuel College, very kindly allowed me to use parts of his own unpublished translation of the Emmanuel Statutes.

The Folger Shakespeare Library, Washington, D.C., awarded me a Summer Fellowship in 1967, and I there began effective work on this book; I am particularly grateful to the then Director, Louis B. Wright.

xiv

No Cambridge student of Tudor matters could refrain from acknowledging the scholarship and inspiration, continuing and humane, of Professor G. R. Elton.

The preparation of my manuscript would not have been possible without the efficient and loyal help of Mr J. M. Tarratt of Jesus College and Mr J. N. Thomas of Selwyn College. Mr Tarratt typed the documents for me, and Mr Thomas typed the editorial material. I am very grateful to them.

Faculty of History   H. C. Porter
West Road
Cambridge
August 1970

An opinion begins to bother me as soon as I can find an advantage in it. Judgement finds its freedom much more seriously compromised when circumstances favour it than when they thwart it, and one suspects one's impartiality much less in resistance than in assent.

André Gide, 'Journal', 8 May 1941

Assist us mercifully (O heavenly father) with thy holy spirit, which knowest the secrets of all hearts, and guide so our doings that thy truth, being boulted out, we may yield thereto according as thy word hath appointed. Let us not swerve from it, neither be withdrawn from the profession thereof, but rather so open our mouths that we may win them to this truth that go about to win us to the liking or bearing with such corruptions and abuses as trouble thy church. Lord, be good and gracious to our sovereign, the Queen's Majesty, that she may both see and do thy will in reforming those things that are amiss, and incline the hearts of all her nobles to the forwarding and perfecting thereof, that thy gospel may have a free course and all superstition an utter overthrow. These things, and all other things necessary, grant unto us for Jesus Christ's sake, in whose name we pray as he has taught us, saying, Our Father, etc.

John Field, 1572 (Dr Williams's Library, Morrice MSS 'B': 'The Seconde Parte of a Register', pt ii, f. 184 v.).

Introduction

'Precisians and godly men that seek for reformation' (1); 'our course to further perfection' (2): two key phrases from Thomas Cartwright in the early 1570s. Cartwright's literary controversy with John Whitgift — one of the best Tudor literary debates in the vernacular — spanned the years 1572 to 1577. Whitgift was especially concerned to draw out the implications of Cartwright's programme (first made public in Cartwright's Cambridge lectures of 1570). Whitgift, like Richard Hooker, thought that, in fact and in theory, the 'precise' imperative, springing from savage indignation against a conforming society, involved a contracting out of that society:

> Why will they not come to our sermons or to our churches? Why will they not communicate with us in our sacraments, not salute us in the streets, nay, spit in our faces, and openly revile us? Why have they their secret conventicles? You know all this to be true in a number of them. I know not why they should do so; except they think themselves to be contaminated by hearing us preach, or by coming to our churches, or by communicating otherwise with us. Which if they do, it argueth that they persuade themselves not only of such an outward perfection, but of an inward purity also, that they may as justly for the same be called puritans, as the novatians were (3).

Whitgift advised the reader to consult Eusebius on the novatians:

> This name puritan is very aptly given to these men. Not because they be pure, no more than were the heretics called cathari; but because they think themselves to be

1

mundiores ceteris, more pure than others, as cathari did; and separate themselves from all other churches and congregations as spotted and defiled; because also they suppose the church which they have devised to be without all impurity (4).

The puritans were like the novatians: third-century schismatics from the western Latin church. Like the cathars (Greek *katharos*, 'pure') — a name applied to several sects, but chiefly to the albigenses of eleventh-century France. Like the donatists — the third-century separatist group in the African church, argued against by Augustine. And they were like the sixteenth-century anabaptists; information about whom Whitgift drew from Zwingli, Calvin, Bucer and Bullinger. Thus the Elizabethan controversy was set in the whole context of the history of western christendom. It is important to remember that the debates illustrated in this volume of documents were seen by contemporaries as part of a story going back at least to A.D. 250: 'This your pretence of cleansing the church from corruptions is but the accustomed excuse of the novatians, donatists and anabaptists' (5): 'that very perfection of an outward platform of a church, which you challenge unto yourselves, is one step to novatianism, and well deserveth the name of catharism' (6).

Cartwright's platform was based on his interpretation of the written word of God. 'I confess that it is no reformation', mused Whitgift, 'except it be agreeable to the word of God. The controversy is, what part of it is agreeable to the word of God. Also, what it is to be agreeable to the word of God' (7). In the 'Second Admonition to Parliament' of 1572, Cartwright set forth 'a platform out of God his book (where it is described at full), according to his will in the same revealed, and the examples of the best reformed churches beyond the seas, as Geneva, France, etc' (8). 'This is no innovation but a renovation, and the doctrine not new but renewed, no stranger, but born in Zion' (9). Whitgift saw the ultimate point: 'Neither would I have men (either puritans, donatists or anabaptists) to dream of such a church, as Plato did of a commonwealth, Aristotle of felicity, and the stoics of their just man' (10).

To Cartwright, 'common reason also doth teach that

2

contraries are cured by their contraries' (11): 'to bring a stick which is crooked to be straight, we do not only bow it so far until it come to be straight, but we bend it so far until we make it so crooked of the other side as it was before of the first side' (12). To tolerate imperfection is 'as if one should be set to watch a child all day long lest he hurt himself with the knife, when as by taking away the knife quite from him, the danger is avoided' (13). How can it be possible 'to fetch chastity out of Sodom, and to seek for heaven in hell'? (14) 'It is not possible, it lieth not in us, to conceal the truth' (15).

Thus the word 'puritan', with its traditional heretical implications, did not please Cartwright. You maintain, he said to Whitgift, 'that those are puritans, or catharans, which do set forth a true and perfect pattern or platform of reforming the church'. The name 'puritan' 'was first by the papists maliciously invented, so it is of you very unbrotherly confirmed'. 'The pureness that we boast of is the innocency of our saviour Christ': 'other pureness we take not upon us' (16). This did not deter the Master of Trinity:

> These men separate themselves also from the congregation, and will communicate with us neither in prayers, hearing the word, nor sacraments. They contemn and despise all those that be not of their sect as polluted, and not worthy to be saluted or kept company with; and therefore some of them, meeting their old acquaintance being godly preachers, have not only refused to salute them, but spit in their faces, wishing the plague of God to light upon them, and saying that they were damned, and that God had taken his spirit from them — and all this because they did wear a cap. Wherefore when they talk of pharisees they pluck themselves by the noses (17).

Cartwright took this rather to heart:

> Whereas Master Doctor compareth us with the pharisees, and saith we do all to be seen of men, and that we hold down our heads in the streets, and strain at a gnat, swallowing down a camel; because they are in all men's knowledge I will leave it to them to judge of the truth of

3

those things. Where he saith we seldom or never laugh, it is not therefore that we think it not lawful to laugh, but that the considerations of the calamities of other churches, and of the ruins of ours, with the heavy judgements of the lord which hang over us, ought to turn our laughing into weeping. Besides, that a man may laugh although he show not his teeth (18).

If you prick us, do we not bleed?

What is our 'straitness of life' any other than is required of all christians? We bring in, I am sure, no monarchism or anchorism. We eat and drink as other men, we live as other men, we are apparelled as other men, we lie as other men, we use those honest recreations that other men do; and we think there is no good thing or commodity of life in the world, but that in sobriety we may be partakers of it, so far as our degree and calling will suffer us, and as God maketh us able to have it (19).

(One has always to beware of assuming that sixteenth-century puritans were like eighteenth-century methodists or nineteenth-century frontier evangelists.)

Whitgift approved of the words of Christ as given by Mark: 'He that is not against us is on our side'. And he characterised the puritans as preferring the Matthew version: 'He who is not with me is against me' (20).

The word 'puritan' was current in England by the late 1560s; taken, perhaps, from the French. Archbishop Matthew Parker did not use it until November 1572, when he discussed the 'Admonitions to Parliament', though he dated the party back to 1565 — he had in those seven years used the words 'recusants', 'precise men', 'precisians' (21). It is difficult, in discussing the history of puritanism, to know where to start: unless one takes as a guide Dr Johnson's thesis (28 April 1778) that the first whig was the Devil. One is immediately lost in the complex contours of medieval heresy and dissent (22). But certainly puritanism is part of the long story of English dissenting radicalism (23). Recent historians have tended to emphasise, quite rightly, the contribution made to the sixteenth-century English reformation by the

4

'lollard' tradition of the fifteenth-century (24). Studies of lollardy and puritanism in Yorkshire reveal many points of coincidence between the phases (25). Difficult, at the grass roots level, to be anything but too general, or necessarily ill-informed. One notes that Dr Leavis, in a typically trenchant essay, has stressed Bunyan's debt to tradition, and to 'that pervasive and potent continuity, a living culture' (26).

What is certain is that puritanism from the 1560s was associated with innovation and subversion. Parker wrote of the puritans in 1573 as 'pretended favourers and false brethren, who under the colour of reformation seek the ruin and subversion both of learning and religion. Their colour is sincerity, under the countenance of simplicity, but in very truth they are ambitious spirits, and can abide no superiority' (27). Whitgift drew attention especially to Cartwright's emphasis on individualism, equality and 'popularity' (government by the majority): 'popularity you cannot avoid, seeing you seek so great an equality, commit so many things to the voices of the people, and in sundry places so greatly extol them' (28). 'Those new men whom we call puritans', wrote Archbishop Sandys of York in 1579, 'who tread all authority under foot' (29). The godly brethren were themselves very sensitive on this point. In 1572 John Field and Thomas Wilcox criticised those enemies who called them 'anabaptists, schismatics, sectaries, and such as went about to pluck the king out of his seat' — those who called them 'reproachfully puritans, unspotted brethren, and such like; those names we abhor and detest' (30). The name puritan was slanderous (31) and odious (32): because it meant schismatic. Let us, went a plea of 1586, hold to 'that preciseness and pureness which God commandeth' — but let us preserve 'true christians from the name of gehennians, precisians, puritans, and all names of heretics; for God's wrath cannot but be marvellously kindled against those that slander, nickname and mock his saints' (33) — a plea from 'we your poor English flock of Geneva (termed gehennians and precisians)' (34), 'reproached to be heretics, anabaptists, donatists, catharists and puritans, and both as schismatics in the church, and as seditious and factious persons in the commonwealth' (35). They were 'true christians': as opposed to 'neuters' (36).

The failure of Elizabethan Authority to comprehend and contain the tradition meant that official abuse became too sharp. William Perkins in the 1590s defended 'those that most endeavour to get and keep the purity of heart in a good conscience' — people almost automatically 'branded with the vile terms of puritans and precisians' (37). Job Throckmorton had made a similar point in the House of Commons in 1587:

> To bewail the distresses of God's children, it is puritanism. To reprove a man for swearing, it is puritanism. To banish an adulterer out of the House, it is puritanism. To make humble suit to her Majesty and the High Court of Parliament for a learned ministry, it is puritanism . . . .
> The Lord send her Majesty store of such puritans (38).

Sir Francis Hastings, speaking in the last week of Elizabeth's last Parliament, talked of the days when he had been an undergraduate at Oxford under Laurence Humphrey (who died in 1589):

> I learned of Dr Humphrey, who was sometimes my tutor, a division of four sorts of puritan. First, the Catholic, which holds that a man cannot sin after baptism. Secondly, the Papist, which is such a merit-monger that he would not only save himself by his own merits, but by the merits of others also. A third sort are the Brownists, or Family of Love; a sect too well known in England, I would they had never so been. The fourth and last sort are your evangelical puritans, which insist wholly upon scriptures as upon a sure ground — and of these I would we had many more than we now have (39).

By that time, the Elizabethan wits had made play with the concept; taking up Whitgift's lead about the pharisees. Marlowe's Faustus (1589) resolved to 'set my countenance like a precisian, and speak thus: the Lord bless you and keep you, my dear brethren'. (In his 1592 'Massacre at Paris' Marlowe used the word puritan to mean huguenot — factious protestant.) The portrayal of the puritan as a hypocrite, or as a self-deluder swayed by ignorant zeal, can be traced through the work (from 1589) of Thomas Nashe and Robert Greene:

6

part of their 'anatomy of absurdity' — praise of folly. Shakespeare in 'Two Gentleman of Verona' (1594) has his Max Miller patter man remark 'even as one would say precisely, thus I would teach a dog'. Never an author to spurn using the same material more than once, Shakespeare repeated the joke in 'Twelfth Night' (1601): 'sometimes he is a kind of puritan' (Maria on Malvolio); Sir Andrew: 'if I thought that, I'd beat him like a dog'. 'The devil a puritan that he is,' quips Maria, 'or anything constantly but a time-pleaser, an affectioned ass'. 'Dost thou think' — Sir Toby to Malvolio — 'because *thou* art virtuous, there shall be no more cakes and ale?' More serious is the characterisation of Angelo in 'Measure for Measure' (1603) — 'a man of stricture and firm abstinence': 'Lord Angelo is precise; scarce confesses that his blood flows' (and eventually revealed as a repressed sensualist). A more mellow Shakespearian comment comes in 'All's Well That Ends Well' (1603): 'if men could be contented to be what they are, there were no fear in marriage; for young Charbon the puritan, and old Poysam the papist, howsome'er their hearts are severed in religion, their heads are both one'.

By the end of Elizabeth's reign the idea was commonplace among intellectuals of the puritan as curious, silly and hypocritical (40). The way was open for Ben Jonson's sharp and well-informed sketches in 'The Alchemist' (1610) and 'Bartholomew Fair' (1614). Elizabethans would have been quite at home with James I's remark that a puritan is a protestant strayed out of his wits; with Macaulay's comment that the puritans hated bear-baiting not because it gave pain to the bear, but because it gave pleasure to the spectator; and with the generalisation of H. L. Mencken — puritanism is the haunting fear that someone, somewhere, may be happy.

But they would have been equally at home with Milton's stress on 'spiritual height', 'temper of purity' and 'native strength of the soul' — perhaps also with Richard Hoggart's defence of 'Lady Chatterley's Lover' as a 'puritanical' book: the distinguishing feature of the tradition of British puritanism being (much to the distress of Mr Justice Byrne and Mr Griffith-Jones) 'an intense sense of responsibility for one's conscience' (41). In the fascinating and distinguished House of Commons debate (1593) on the treatment of separatists

7

(42), most members felt that to proceed too strictly would be dangerous to liberty of conscience in England. Walter Raleigh had a nice compromise: 'In my conceit the Brownists are worthy to be rooted out of a commonwealth' — but wouldn't exporting them be rather too expensive? One mustn't, in dealing with 'disordered Barrowists and Brownists', entrap, by a sort of McCarthyism, 'honest and loyal subjects'. While the debate was in progress, Henry Barrow was executed; 'through the malice of the bishops to the lower house', someone said (43).

Conscience was the crux of the matter; so long as we remember that conscience is the name given by the rigid to their prejudices (which are in turn the product of their social upbringing). But the puritan imperative was severe: it was precisely and exclusively biblical. Nathaniel Ward, an Elizabethan undergraduate at Emmanuel, later an emigrant to Massachusetts, wrote in 1647 that 'the removing of one iota in scripture may draw out all the life and traverse all the truth of the whole bible: but to authorise an untruth by a toleration of state, is to build a sconce against the walls of heaven, to batter God out of his chair' (44). Alarming, but traditional. I think the best quotation to illustrate this basic puritan impetus comes from a document printed in 1572 (45):

It is a common saying, of two evils it is best to choose the least; better it is to have a gospel of Christ joined with a piece of Antichrist than to have none at all. Thus *they* persuade themselves. The *other* do not so. They think it not lawful to join God and Belial together — surely they have some reason, nay they have great reason, for what society hath light with darkness? If all the world might be gained with a little breach of God's word, it were not to be done. Better it were that the whole world should perish, than one iota of God's truth should be over-slipped.

The reference was to St Paul: 'Be ye not unequally yoked together with unbelievers: for what fellowship hath righteousness with unrighteousness? And what communion hath light with darkness? And what concord hath Christ with Belial?' (46)

8

That false antithesis is as good a clue as any to the puritan mind.

It might perhaps help the reader to get his bearings if I give here a statement of what I take to be the four main divisions of Tudor puritan history.

1. It will be obvious from the arrangement of the selections that I find most interesting the tradition of the separatists: those who looked back to the Marian exiles and to the London secret churches under Mary, and continued that London tradition in the 1560s (Part IV: '1567: The London Separatist Congregation'); who were inspired by Robert Browne in the early 1580s (Part V: '1583: Autobiography of Robert Browne'); and who wished, in Browne's words, for 'reformation without tarrying for any': 'let us not therefore tarry for the magistrates', but as 'we hold our liberty' let us 'separate the ungodly' and 'leave our country' (47). This tradition was to be satirised by Richard Hooker (Part XIII: '1593: Richard Hooker's Analysis of the Sectarian Mind') — as it was to be by Ben Jonson: with, in 'The Alchemist' of 1610, the characters of Tribulation Wholesome, the zealous pastor of Amsterdam, and his deacon Ananias; and, in 'Bartholomew Fair' of 1614, the Banbury baker Zeal-of-the-land-busy, and Dame Purecraft, a 'sanctified sister' whom Grindal and Hooker would have recognised as an instance of their conviction that puritanism was of special appeal to females. This tradition was to be one of the foundations of the American experience; as expressed for instance in William Bradford's 'Of Plymouth Plantation' (begun about 1630) which looked back to the godly 'in the north parts' — between Lincoln and Sheffield — at the beginning of the reign of James I.

2. Then we have Francis Hastings's 'evangelical puritans, which insist wholly upon scriptures as upon a sure foundation'. The puritan wing within the church of England, that is to say, those wishing for preciser reformation, but who wished neither to separate from the Elizabethan commonwealth, nor utterly to transform it. Evangelical Plus: as in the material in Part IX on the puritans and education. And of a theological tinge more emphatically Calvinist than official theology could approve of: William Perkins, Part XIV. All

9

this, more or less, within the context of 'the laws of ecclesiastical polity'.

3. More broadly, there is the English tradition of rhetorical and radical indignation and dissent: as expressed here in Part II ('1525: Robert Barnes versus the Prelates'), Part VI ('1572: John Field, 'A View of Popish Abuses' ') and in Martin Marprelate (Part X). A full consideration of this tradition would include William Tyndale, John Skelton and John Bale, and look forward to Thomas Hobbes: for Part IV of 'Leviathan', 'Of the Kingdom of Darkness', is a very Elizabethan document, which happened to be published in 1651. There is no need here to deal only in 'isms': the material can be neater. In 'The Bulletin of the Institute of Historical Research', November 1969, John Fines printed a six-page tract first published about 1590 (the Marprelate period) but based on a lollard manuscript of the 1390s, and, so Fines argues, dating in its revised form from the early 1530s, perhaps from the hand of Tyndale himself. The tract takes up the theme of the 'poverty and wretchedness' of Christ (his followers being 'simple fools' and the New Testament 'foolish writings') compared with the power and pomp of the prelates — a power redressed and ordered, in 'religion and true service', by the Parliament of the 1530s. The tract's appeal to the 'unlearned people', the 'blind lay people', together with passages about monastic 'curious singing and chanting it up', and monastic 'lewd losels', are verbally reminiscent of Field's 'View of Popish Abuses'. The document is a fine example of the continuity of English dissent from the fourteenth to the sixteenth century. Within that continuity, puritanism takes its place.

4. The 'presbyterian' attempt in the 1570s and 1580s to establish the Godly Discipline within the English church: that 'puritan classical movement' ('classis' being an assembly or synod) which Patrick Collinson took as the main theme of his book 'The Elizabethan Puritan Movement'. That movement appears in Part XII of my selection, in the material relating to Richard Rogers in Essex in 1587. And official disapproval of it accounts for much of the opposition to the puritan parliamentary manoeuvres in Parts VII, VIII and XI. The magistrate felt himself threatened. And with reason. The political theory of Robert Browne is due for a fresh consider-

ation; but he was at any rate sure of the duty of the magistrates 'to abase themselves unto God before the face of the church' (48). On this point he appears to be at one with the Thomas Cartwright of the 1570s, who quoted Isaiah, chapter 49: 'kings shall be thy nursing fathers and their queens thy nursing mothers: they shall bow down to thee with their face towards the earth, and lick up the dust of thy feet'. To Cartwright this meant that the civil magistrates, as 'servants unto the church', are bound to 'subject themselves unto the church, to submit their sceptres, to throw down their crowns, before the church, yea, as the prophet speaketh, to lick the dust of the feet of the church'. And, as tapestries are designed to fit a house, and not the house to fit the tapestries, the 'commonwealth' must be 'fashioned and made suitable unto the church', 'made to agree with the church and the government thereof with her government': 'Otherwise God is made to give place to men, heaven to earth' (49). Whitgift — in the tradition of 'the necessity of obedience' (50) — noted that these words of Cartwright should be specially 'well considered, for they contain the overthrow of the prince's authority both in ecclesiastical and civil matters' (51).

The implications of such arguments were to become apparent in the seventeenth century, in both Old and New England. So many writers on puritanism are experts on the seventeenth century, whether in History or English studies, and tend to see the sixteenth century mainly as a prelude to their own concerns, that in this selection I have erred in the other direction, and let the Tudors speak only for themselves. For those still in danger of losing their way, the best available textbook is now Patrick McGrath, 'Papists and Puritans under Elizabeth I', published in 1967, and available in paperback.

A final quotation to illustrate the potential relevance of the material; from an essay on vocation by a modern undergraduate, whose voice would have been recognised by Tudor puritans: 'There are two possibilities for the radical/creative/principled student to take in order to remain relevant, not just to the political movement but to his own ideals. The first is the tortuous path of maximising the good to be achieved by use of one's personal skills, without mortgaging these to the side of oppression. The second possibility remains gearing

11

one's life towards committed action, defined in whatever terms reflect political beliefs.' ('The 1/- Paper', Cambridge, 4 December 1969.)

1. 'Second Admonition to Parliament,' printed in W. H. Frere and C. E. Douglas (eds), 'Puritan Manifestoes', (1907, 1954) p. 105.

2. In Whitgift, 'Works' (Parker Society) i 43.

3. Ibid., i 172.

4. Ibid., i 171.

5. Ibid., i 55.

6. Ibid., i 74. See also: for novatians, i 174; cathars, i 174; donatists, i 112; anabaptists, i 76-83. For the anabaptists, see E. A. Payne in 'New Cambridge Modern History', ii: 'The Reformation 1520-1559', ed. G. R. Elton (1958); and Gordon Rupp, 'Patterns of Reformation' (1969).

7. 'Works', i 93.

8. Frere and Douglas (eds), 'Puritan Manifestoes', p. 94.

9. In Whitgift, 'Works', i 17.

10. Ibid., i 23.

11. Ibid., ii 441.

12. Ibid., ii 442-3. Cf. Francis Bacon, essay 38 ('Of Nature in Men'): 'Neither is the ancient rule amiss, to bend nature as a wand to a contrary extreme, whereby to set it right; understanding it, where the contrary extreme is no vice.' (Everyman ed., p. 117).

13. In Whitgift, 'Works', ii 42.

14. Ibid., ii 123.

15. Ibid., i 39.

16. Ibid., i 171-2.

17. Ibid., iii 522-3.

18. Ibid., iii 523.

19. Ibid., i 110.

20. Ibid., iii 509-10.

21. Parker, 'Correspondence' (Parker Society) pp. 410, 272, 279, 377.

22. For an example of how not to get lost, see C. N. L. Brooke, 'Heresy and Religious Sentiment 1000-1250', 'Bulletin of the Institute of Historical Research', xli 104 (Nov 1968).

12

23. See Erik Routley, 'English Religious Dissent' (1960): one of a series of 'English Institutions' — earlier volumes were on the Constitution and Shipping.

24. A. G. Dickens, 'Heresy and the Origins of English Protestantism' (a lecture given in 1962); J. Fines, 'Heresy Trials in the Diocese of Coventry and Lichfield', 'Journal of Ecclesiastical History' (Oct 1963); Margaret Aston, 'Lollardy and the Reformation', 'History' (June 1964); A. G. Dickens, 'The English Reformation' (1964; rev. ed. 1967); J. A. F. Thomson, 'The Later Lollards 1414-1520' (1965).

25. A. G. Dickens, 'Lollards and Protestants in the Diocese of York 1509-1558' (1959); R. A. Marchant, 'The Puritans and the Church Courts in the Diocese of York 1560-1642' (1960).

26. 1964 essay on 'The Pilgrim's Progress': in 'Anna Karenina and other Essays' (1967).

27. Parker, 'Correspondence', p. 434.

28. 'Works', i 42.

29. 'Zurich Letters' (Parker Society) i 332.

30. 'The Seconde Parte of a Register', ed. A. Peel (1915) ii 84-6.

31. Ibid., p. 224.

32. Ibid., p. 251.

33. Ibid., p. 55.

34. Ibid., p. 60.

35. Ibid., p. 80.

36. Ibid., p. 50.

37. 'Works', iii (1613) p. 315.

38. J. E. Neale, 'Elizabeth I and her Parliaments' (1953-7) ii 151.

39. Simonds D'Ewes, 'Journals' (1693 ed.) p. 683.

40. See for instance 'Diary of John Manningham of the Middle Temple 1602-3', ed. W. Tite (Camden Society, O.S. 99, 1868); Manningham saw a performance of 'Twelfth Night' at the Middle Temple. Also W. P. Holden, 'Anti-Puritan Satire 1572-1642' (1954, 1968).

41. C. H. Rolph (ed.), 'The Trial of Lady Chatterley' (1961) p. 100.

42. D'Ewes, 'Journals', pp. 517-19.

43. Neale, 'Elizabeth I and her Parliaments', ii 291.

44. From 'The Simple Cobbler of Aggawam in America'

13

(London, 1647): Perry Miller and T. H. Johnson (eds), 'The Puritans' (1938); Harper Torchbook ed., 1963 p. 229.

45. 'Exhortation to the Bishops': Frere and Douglas (eds), 'Puritan Manifestoes', pp. 76-7 (my italics).

46. 2 Corinthians ch. 6.

47. Browne, 'A Treatise of reformation without tarying for anie' (Middelburg, 1582): in A. Peel and L. H. Carlson (eds), 'The Writings of Robert Harrision and Robert Browne' (1953), quotes from (in order) pp. 164, 158, 169, 152.

48. Ibid., p. 166.

49. In Whitgift, 'Works', iii 189.

50. Ibid., p. 587: notes of Whitgift's sermon at St Paul's, 17 November 1583 — the anniversary of Elizabeth's accession.

51. Ibid., pp. 189-90.

PART I

1549: Cranmer on the Two 'Parties' in the Church

'Amongst ourselves, there was in King Edward's days some question moved by reason of a few men's scrupulosity touching certain things' (1). Thus Richard Hooker on the origins of Elizabethan Dissent. The present extract is an essay written by Archbishop Thomas Cranmer in the early spring of 1549 — two years after the death of Henry VIII. In it, Cranmer asserted that there were in the English Church two 'parties': the conservative — those 'so addicted to their old customs' that they 'think it a great matter of conscience to depart from a piece of the least of their ceremonies'; and the radical — those 'so new-fangle that they would innovate all thing, and so despise the old that nothing like them but that is new': the sort who within twenty years would be attracting the uncomplimentary adjective 'puritan'.

In his Book of Common Prayer (common to the whole realm) Cranmer wished, he here stated, exclusively to 'please and satisfy' no one party; but to 'profit them both'. Some ceremonies (ceremonies being what John Jewel was to call 'the scenic apparatus of divine worship') (2) had been abolished in England because they had been abused — 'they did more confound and darken than declare and set forth Christ's benefits'; and we must serve God 'not in bondage of the figure or shadow, but in the freedom of spirit' (a characteristically Erasmian emphasis). Other ceremonies 'serve to a decent order and godly discipline', 'stir up the dull mind of man to the remembrance of his duty to God'; and here one must 'have reverence unto them for their antiquity'. Such remaining ceremonies can be 'altered and changed' 'upon just causes' (for they 'are not to be esteemed equal with God's

15

law'): but for the moment they are 'retained for a discipline and order'. The main thing is 'the true setting forth of Christ's religion'. That being assumed, 'unity and concord' override 'innovations and newfangleness': newfangleness, in fact, 'is always to be eschewed'. (This short essay tells us more about the — much misunderstood — mind of Cranmer than do many modern lengthy tomes (3).) We may also note that in the 1549 Liturgy certain pious observances (such as kneeling, crossing oneself, etc.) 'may be used or left as every man's devotion serveth, without blame' (4).

There was a sermon in the 1549 Communion Office — later (unfortunately?) omitted — allowing private confession to the priest if requested: 'requiring such as shall be satisfied with a general confession, not to be offended with them that do use, to their further satisfying, the auricular and secret confession to the priest', and vice versa, 'but in all things to follow and keep rule of charity, and every man to be satisfied with his own conscience, not judging other men's minds or consciences' (5) — sentiments later to be echoed by Elizabeth I, Francis Bacon and Thomas Hobbes (6).

This Cranmerian line had been first publicly expressed in 1536 in the first 'Confession' of the Church of England, the so-called 'Ten Articles' (7). Abuses, it had been there stated — the document was drawn up and debated by a clerical committee headed by Cranmer — must be 'moderated' (a word which Hugh Latimer had been using for a decade) (8). A similar defence of 'laudable ceremonies' was also made in the Royal Injunctions of the summer of 1536 (9). Cranmer further expounded his obsessive theme of the 'middle way' in his 1540 preface to the Bible (10). By 1540 the Archbishop had become aware of the necessity of appealing to 'two sundry sorts of people' (the same point as in 1549): 'some there are that be too slow, and need the spur: Some other seem too quick, and need more of the bridle' (Cranmer was an accomplished horseman); 'some lose their game by short shooting, some by overshooting: some walk too much on the left hand, some too much on the right'. In sum, the 'two sorts, albeit they be most far unlike the one to the other, yet they both deserve in effect like reproach'. (This image of the spur and bridle had been similarly used by Erasmus in an essay, 'Make haste slowly', published in 1508) (11).

16

Cranmer's 1540 biblical preface developed into a warning against excessive idolatry of the written word of God. Pagans defiled themselves with idolatry in worshipping sun, moon and stars; 'there is nothing so good in this world, but it may be abused'; thus in offering the scripture to 'all sorts and kinds of people, and in the vulgar tongue' (Erasmus again!) one must be careful, in reading or hearing, to use modesty and 'due reverence'. Cranmer's brief notes here were to be developed by Hooker in book ii of 'Of The Laws of Ecclesiastical Polity' (1593): fifty or so pages concerning the 'drift, scope and purpose of Almighty God in Holy Scripture' (12), pages which today form the best introduction to Hooker. A similar plea against false 'gospel bearers' had been made by Erasmus in a dialogue of 1529 (13); first published in English at Canterbury in 1550, probably at the request of Cranmer, or of Bishop Nicholas Ridley (then involved in controversy with the arch-newfangler John Hooper, recently back from Zürich).

Note also the defence of the Cranmer line by Elizabeth's first Archbishop, the insular Matthew Parker, who in the early 1560s represented the virtues of English moderatio, mediocrity, compared with the 'preciseness' of Zürich and Geneva (14). Indeed, the French Ambassador, chatting with Parker in the garden of Lambeth Palace in 1564, 'noted much and delighted in our mediocrity, charging the Genevians and Scottish of going too far in extremities'. (The ambassador and his interpreter having departed, Parker noted with relieved delight that none of his archepiscopal spoons had been stolen!) (15) Parker's aim until his death in 1575 was that 'mediocrity shall be received amongst us' (16). To such returned Marian exiles as John Jewel in the summer of 1559 this mediocritas *seemed a leaden, not a golden mediocrity (17). (He changed his mind when he was nominated Bishop of Salisbury in July).*

Such tensions, as the following document illustrates, had become common form in England so early as 1549.

1. Hooker, 'Of the Laws of Ecclesiastical Polity', preface, ch. 2: 1604 ed., p. 10; Everyman ed., i 92.

2. 'Zurich Letters', i 22.

3. I think the best book on Cranmer is still Charles Smyth's 1925 Thirlwall and Gladstone Prize Essay, 'Cranmer and the Reformation under Edward VI' (1926; reprint, with preface by Gordon Rupp, 1970).

4. 'Certain Notes', following the essay 'Of Ceremonies': Everyman ed., p. 289.

5. 'Exhortation' to the Parishoners, before the Offertory: Everyman ed., p. 217.

6. For Elizabeth, see W. P. Haugaard, 'Elizabeth and the English Reformation' (1968) p. 324; for Bacon, ibid., pp. 329-30; for Hobbes, 'Leviathan', ch. xxxii.

7. No. 112 in C. H. Williams (ed.) 'English Historical Documents, v: 1485-1558' (1967).

8. For instance, in a 1532 letter to Archbishop Warham: 'Remains' (Parker Society) pp. 351-6.

9. No. 113 in Williams's 'Documents'.

10. Most conveniently available in 'Cranmer's Selected Writings', ed. C. S. Meyer (S.P.C.K. paperback, 1961) pp. 1-11.

11. 'Erasmus on His Times', trans. M. M. Phillips (Cambridge University Press paperback, 1967) p. 17. For 'Erasmianism' in the English Reformation, see J. K. McConica, 'English Humanists and Reformation Politics under Henry VIII and Edward VI' (1965); and the review by G. R. Elton in 'Historical Journal', (x 1) (1967).

12. Hooker, bk ii, ch. 8, 1604 ed. p. 121; Everyman ed., i 280.

13. 'Cyclops, or The Gospel Bearer', trans. Craig R. Thompson, 'The Colloquies of Erasmus' (1965) pp. 416-22.

14. Words of a French Professor of Civil Law, reported by Jewel 1562: 'Zurich Letters', i 119.

15. Parker, 'Correspondence', p. 215.

16. Ibid., p. 173.

17. 'Zurich Letters', i 23.

1 Essay 'Of Ceremonies' at end of 1549 Prayer Book

Essay 'Of Ceremonies: why some be abolished and some retained'; at the end of the First Prayer Book of Edward VI; reprinted in modern prayer books. Parker Society, 'Liturgies of Edward VI', ed. J. Ketley (1844) pp. 155-7; Everyman's Library no. 448: 'The First and Second Prayer Books of Edward VI', 1949 ed. (with a new historical note by E. C. Ratcliff) pp. 324-6.

Of such ceremonies as be used in the church, and have had their beginning by the institution of man, some at the first were of godly intent and purpose devised, and yet at length turned to vanity and superstition; some entered into the church by undiscreet devotion, and such a zeal as was without knowledge, and for because they were winked at in the beginning they grew daily to more and more abuses, which not only for their profitableness, but also because they have much blinded the people and obscured the glory of God, are worthy to be cut away and clean rejected. Other there be, which although they have been devised by man, yet it is thought good to reserve them still, as well for a decent order in the church (for the which they were first devised) as because they pertain to edification, whereunto all things done in the church (as the Apostle teacheth) ought to be referred. And although the keeping or omitting of a ceremony (in itself considered) is but a small thing, yet the wilful and contemptuous transgression and breaking of a common order and discipline is no small offence before God. Let all things be done among you (saith St Paul) in a seemly and due order. The appointment of the which order pertaineth not to private men; therefore no man ought to take in hand nor presume to appoint or alter any public or common order in Christ's church, except he be lawfully called and

19

authorized thereunto.

And whereas in this our time the minds of men be so diverse that some think it a great matter of conscience to depart from a piece of the least of their ceremonies (they be so addicted to their old customs); and again, on the other side, some be so new-fangle that they would innovate all thing, and so do despise the old that nothing can like them but that is new: it was thought expedient not so much to have respect how to please and satisfy either of these parties, as how to please God and profit them both. And yet lest any man should be offended (whom good reason might satisfy), here be certain causes rendered, why some of the accustomed ceremonies be put away, and some be retained and kept still.

Some are put away because the great excess and multitude of them hath so increased in these latter days that the burden of them was intolerable; whereof St Augustine in his time complained that they were grown to such a number that the state of Christian people was in worse case (concerning that matter) than were the Jews. And he counselled that such yoke and burden should be taken away, as time would serve quietly to do it. But what would St Augustine have said if he had seen the ceremonies of late days used among us, whereunto the multitude used in his time was not to be compared? This our excessive multitude of ceremonies was so great, and many of them so dark, that they did more confound and darken than declare and set forth Christ's benefits unto us. And besides this, Christ's Gospel is not a ceremonial law (as much of Moses' law was); but it is a religion to serve God, not in bondage of the figure or shadow, but in the freedom of spirit, being content only with those ceremonies which do serve to a decent order and godly discipline, and such as be apt to stir up the dull mind of man to the remembrance of his duty to God, by some notable and special signification whereby he might be edified. Furthermore, the most weighty cause of the abolishment of certain ceremonies was that they were so far abused, partly by the superstitious blindness of the rude and unlearned, and partly by the unsatiable avarice of such as sought more their own lucre than the glory of God, that the abuses could not well be taken away, the thing remaining still.

But now, as concerning those persons which peradventure
20

will be offended for that some of the old ceremonies are retained still. If they consider that without some ceremonies it is not possible to keep any order or quiet discipline in the church, they shall easily perceive just cause to reform their judgements. And if they think much that any of the old do remain, and would rather have all devised anew; then such men (granting some ceremonies convenient to be had), surely where the old may be well used, there they cannot reasonably reprove the old (only for their age) without bewraying of* their own folly. For in such a case they ought rather to have reverence unto them for their antiquity; if they will declare themselves to be more studious of unity and concord than of innovations and newfangleness, which (as much as may be with the true setting forth of Christ's religion) is always to be eschewed. Furthermore, such shall have no just cause, with the ceremonies reserved, to be offended; for as those be taken away which were most abused and did burden men's consciences without any cause, so the other that remain are retained for a discipline and order, which (upon just causes) may be altered and changed, and therefore are not to be esteemed equal with God's law. And moreover they be neither dark nor dumb ceremonies, but are so set forth that every man may understand what they do mean and to what use they do serve. So that it is not like that they, in time to come, should be abused as the other have been.

And in these all our doings we condemn no other nations, nor prescribe anything but to our own people only. For we think it convenient that every country should use such ceremonies as they shall think best to the setting forth of God's honour and glory, and to the reducing of the people to a most perfect and godly living, without error or superstition; and that they should put away other things which from time to time they perceive to be most abused; as in men's ordinances it often chances diversely in diverse countries.

* Exposing.

PART II

1525: Robert Barnes versus the Prelates

Of the rhetoric of dissent in England during the reign of Henry VIII, I know no better example than the sermon preached in St Edward's Church, Cambridge, on Christmas Eve 1525: by Dr Robert Barnes, aged 30, prior of the extensive Augustinian friary behind Corpus (the memory of which survives now only in the name of the Friar House restaurant). Or, as the original text of the sermon has not survived, one should say the account of the sermon first given by Barnes six years later, expanded in 1534, and edited by John Foxe in 1572/3; in an edition of the works of Tyndale, Frith and Barnes which made available to Elizabethans the writing of these 'chief ringleaders in these latter times of the Church of England'. Foxe put the three in the tradition of Wyclif, and felt that there was more simplicity and true zeal in their work than in England in the early 1570s. He also felt that Barnes was of especial comfort to the elderly. (One of Barnes's Cambridge pupils, Christopher Colman, appears to have been a member of the Plumbers' Hall separatist conventicle in London in the late 1560s.) Certainly Barnes's mar-prelate rhetoric could stand as a model for later puritans. The savage indignation was similar.

Barnes became prior of the Cambridge Augustinian house in about 1520; having been a member of it (and a friend of the Cambridge Carmelite John Bale) for the previous six years. In the first half of the 1520s he lectured in Cambridge on the letters of St Paul, spread his own taste for good letters and good learning, and made the priory a focus for the Cambridge 'godly brethren' — Latimer, for instance, preached in the chapel. 'If they be poor, they may be buried among

23

the friars.' Barnes's feeling for 'the common people', 'the simple', 'the brethren' — part of the tension between himself, as a regular, and the secular clergy — taps a tradition which the puritans were to exploit: 'your poor brother, whom Christ hath redeemed by his precious blood, dieth in prison, and openly in the street, and hangeth himself for necessity, and yet will you not bestow on him so much as one of your precious stones. Tell me of one bishop that ever brake his mitre to the helping of a poor man'. The feeling emerges most dramatically, in my extract, in the story of the Cambridge copper kettle, which Barnes first told in 1534; a story of a 'naughty lewd kettle', and the exploitation of poor laymen — 'whom God visited with poverty to prove your charity' (a typically trenchant and sobering remark). Later, Barnes was to say that the profits from the dissolution of the English religious houses should have been devoted to the care of the poor. In his own estimation, he was the 'simple poor wretch', the upholder of the 'order of charity', the man daring to speak the truth, who is saved by the mercy of God from the fury of the prelates; the satirist of the 'liberties of holy church'. The man who appeals to plain words, and finds Wolsey's casuistry 'far fetched'.

'I damned in my sermon the gorgeous pomp and pride of all exterior ornaments': the mitres, the gloves, the precious stones, the houses and horses, servants and dogs. They were 'damnable and pompous'. They were also unscriptural: 'Tell me where you find but one prick in holy scripture of your mitres.' He elaborated upon covetousness, as John Colet had done in the sermon to Convocation at St Paul's cathedral in 1512 (1). 'I can see them follow none but Judas,' said Barnes: 'Judas sold our master but once; and you sell him as often as he cometh into your hands.' The prelates are they — 'inordinate butchers', uncharitable, idle, shameful: tyrants. Their law, the canon law, should be compared to the 'holy words of scripture': 'look whether the interpretation of the word do agree with the nature of your laws'. The prelates deceive the simple, and diminish the authority of the nobility and the prince. This appeal to the prince as a liberator from the practice of prelates was, in the 1530s, to be upheld; effecting Colet's fear that, if the spirituality did not quickly put its own house in order, the 'people' would turn decisively

24

against the traditional church. 'Put the case', advised Barnes, 'that this were a lie. . . .' The church in England was unable to survive the harsh test of that imperative.

There is in Barnes, too, a strong sense of the truth under persecution: 'now dare no man preach the truth and the very gospel of God'. The truth revolving round 'devotion', not 'form'; the spirit rather than the letter. So, on the eve of Christmas, remember that 'Christ is every day born, every day risen, every day ascended up'; 'this you must sanctify in your hearts daily, and not one day'. Unfortunately for his Cambridge career, the elegant, witty and sociable friar was liable to be carried away by his own exuberance. In his sermon (preached from the pulpit which is still used in St Edward's) he touched upon points of purgatory and the pardon of sins (with examples from St Edward's and St Benet's), of papal power and of the virgin Mary. Barnes had many enemies. And he had given them their chance.

Adversaries gathered a collection of objections to the sermon (2). Barnes offered to preach again, clarifying his position, on the following Sunday. But the vice-chancellor, Dr Edmund Natures, Master of Clare, forbade that. The vice-chancellor was a drearily predictable establishment cleric, dominated by fears of offending against the 'average'. Instead, Barnes was called to a meeting with the vice-chancellor and a few other authorities to discuss the objections. Barnes said that the opposition points were an inaccurate summary of what he had preached: the compilers pressed them, as seditious, slanderous — and heretical. 'Will you be content to submit yourself?' asked Natures. Barnes: 'Wheresoever I have spoken against God's word, or against the exposition of holy doctors, I will be content to be reformed.' Will you not add to the word and the doctors the phrase 'the laws of the church'? No: this is 'too large, for I knew not what they meant by the laws of the church, nor I was no doctor of law. Wherefore I judged it sufficient for me to be reported by God's word and by the exposition of holy doctors; for that was my faculty.' This meeting was in the Old Schools. And it was ended by a sit-in. During the discussion 'was the whole body of the university gathered together, and knocked at the School doors, and said they would hear the examination'. Natures sent the esquire bedell to talk to

25

the demonstrators, 'but they were the more moved, and knocked sorer'. Natures then, ineffectively, talked to them himself: 'they would not depart, except they might hear this matter judged, and, as they said, it appertained to learning'. Natures washed his hands for the moment of the affair. 'We must give over this matter, for the university is in a rumour.'

Three days later, Barnes was called to the vice-chancellor's chamber in Clare. He wanted impartial witnesses to be called. 'If I shall thus die, I shall be content': 'I am no better than our master Christ'. There followed a discussion about the wisdom of summoning any witnesses; and eventually Barnes agreed to stand by the decision of the vice-chancellor, hoping that charity would override the 'law'. Here again, 'the university gathered together', demanding representatives at the hearing, as there had been at the sermon.

Four weeks passed. A revocation had been written for Barnes, to be read in St Edward's. He had got, by a leak, a copy of it. 'I called into my chamber an eight or ten of the best learned men that were in Cambridge' — a tantalisingly brief and isolated reference to the Cambridge reformers of the 1520s. Barnes mentioned by name only the two who had died by the autumn of 1531: Thomas Bilney and George Stafford. This 'conference' agreed 'that it was neither right nor conscience that I should agree to the revocation'. (Foxe, writing of the year 1526 in Cambridge, was to say that some thirty dons were suspected of owning copies of the works of Luther; and to claim that seven colleges contained 'godly and learned in Christ' — Pembroke, Peterhouse, Queens', Corpus, King's, Gonville Hall and St John's).

Natures decided that the revocation must be read. Barnes refused; and was given a week to think it over. 'I said I would appeal from the vice-chancellor to the whole body of the university.' Then London stepped in. Barnes was taken from Cambridge on 6 February 1526, and on the seventh was interviewed by Wolsey 'in his gallery at Westminster'. Wolsey was quiet and kind, Barnes adamant (foolishly so, he later thought). On 8 February Barnes's trial for heresy began in the Chapter House of Westminster Abbey: by two bishops (plus Fisher, who arrived late), two abbots and three doctors of law. The questioning was general, not merely on the sermon. On 10 February the 'articles' from the sermon were *condemned as heretical — and as slanderous, erroneous, contentious and foolish. On Sunday, 11 February, Barnes did penance at St Paul's. Wolsey was there, 'with all the pomp and pride that he could make'. Fisher preached; 'and all his sermon was against Lutherians, as though they had convicted me for one'. Barnes was in prison in London for a year, then under confinement in Augustinian friaries, first in London, then in Northampton. Then, after a feigned suicide, he escaped to Antwerp, returning to London in the mid-1530s, to become a popular preacher in the City. An upholder of the carnal marriage of the 'fond frantic friar' Luther, wrote Thomas More in 1533: 'run out of religion, abjured of heresy, perjured by relapse, and roiled about like a layman, railing against religion, and all the known catholic church, in contempt of his vow, and his oath too, and of all good christian people on earth, and withdrawing their honours from all the saints in heaven' (3).*

Barnes was burnt at Smithfield in 1540.

1. I had originally intended to print in this book the (contemporary) English version of Colet's 1512 sermon; but C. H. Williams reprinted it in 1967, in 'English Historical Documents 1485-1558' (being vol. v of the series 'English Historical Documents'): no. 79, pp. 652-60 (Williams mistakenly dates it as 1511).

2. My account here is from Barnes, 'Works' (1573) pp. 217-25.

3. More, 'The Confutation of Friar Barnes' Church', being the eighth (and final, and liveliest) book of 'The Confutation of Tyndale's Answer', published in two parts (1532, 1533): the quotation is on pp. cccccxi-xii of part two. The whole 'Confutation' runs to 900 pages, and has never been reprinted since the sixteenth century.

2 Barnes's Defence of his Cambridge Sermon, Christmas Eve 1525

Robert Barnes: 'The Cause of my Condemnation', from 'A Supplication unto the most gracious Prince Henry VIII' (Antwerp, November 1531; enlarged ed. London 1534, 1550): as edited by Foxe on pp. 205-17 of 'The whole Works of W. Tyndall, John Frith and Doct. Barnes, three worthy Martyrs and principal Teachers of this Church of England, collected and compiled in one Tome together, being before scattered, and now in print here exhibited to the Church' (printed by John Day, London, 1573; preface by Foxe). See W. J. Cargill Thompson, 'Sixteenth Century editions of Barnes' 'Supplication' ', in 'Transactions Cambridge Bibliographical Society' (1960).

Barnes's other works include: 'Sententiae': collected from the Fathers (Wittenberg, 1530) preface by Johann Bugenhagen. Barnes wrote as 'Anthonius Anglicus'. German translation by Bugenhagen: Nuremberg, 1531. Latin text reprinted Wittenberg 1536. 'Vita Romanorum Pontificium' (to late twelfth century) (Wittenberg, 1536) preface by Luther. Translated into German 1545, Czech 1565. 'Confession' (1540). German translation printed three times in 1540: Augsburg, Leipzig, Wittenberg (this last with preface by Luther).

Two extracts in 'Fathers of the English Church', ed. Legh Richmond (1807); modernised snatches in 'Reformation Essays of Barnes', ed. N. S. Tjernagel (paperback, 1963); material on Barnes (and Frith, Tyndale and George Joye) in W. A. Clebsch, 'England's Earliest Protestants 1520-35' (1964).

Most gracious Prince, that your grace should know what cause of heresy the bishops had against me, for the which they so uncharitably and so cruelly have cast me away.

28

Therefore have I set out the articles that were laid against me. And as they were laid against me, as I will be reported by their own acts and books. The which articles doubtless were uncharitably and falsely gathered against me in a sermon that I made in Cambridge, in Saint Edward's Church. Wherefore I will beseech your grace with all meekness and lowliness to be my gracious Lord and Prince. And not to suffer me thus shamefully and cruelly, against all law and conscience, utterly to be undone and cast away. But of your most high goodness to suffer me to come to mine answer, and then, if I cannot justify my cause I will be at your gracious commandment, to be punished after right and conscience.

THE FIRST ARTICLE

If thou believe that thou art more bound to serve God tomorrow which is Christmas day, or of Easter day, or of Whitsunday, for a holiness that is in one day more than in another, then art thou no faithful Christian man, but superstitious, and Saint Paul is against thee, saying: You do observe days, years, months, and tides. For unto a faithful Christian man, every day ought to be Christmas day, Easter day, and Whitsunday. The which thing the fathers considering that thou didst not observe, yea, and that thou wouldst never observe if it were left to thy judgement, because thou art given so much to worldly businesses, for that cause they have assigned thee certain days to come to the church to pray together, to hear the word of God together, and to receive the blessed sacrament together.

What fault find you in this article? Because I say that one day is not holier than another? I pray you what is the cause, or what nature is in one day that is not in another, whereby that it should be holier than the other? Because (you will say) that we hallow the remembrance of Christ's birth and of Christ's resurrection in one day, and not in another. This thing I say must you do every day, for Christ is every day born, every day risen, every day ascended up. And this must you believe every day steadfastly. This must you sanctify in your hearts daily, and not one day.

Now vary we but in this thing. You say that we are bound

29

to sanctify but one Christmas day in the year; and that is superstitious and heresy say I, not that I condemn your one day, but that you set it to one day all only that we are bound to do every day. Briefly, my Lord of Rochester* allowed this article, saying he would not condemn it for heresy for an hundred pounds (this was a great sum of money) but it was foolishly said (quoth he) to preach this afore the butchers of Cambridge, as who say, they were all butchers that were at the sermon and not the most part of the university. But the Bishop of Bath† asked me whether we might labour on the holy days or not, seeing it is written: Thou shalt observe thy holy day. I answered that Christian men were not bound to abstain from bodily labour by that commandment, for it was so given to the Jews. And if we were bound to abstain from bodily labour by that commandment, then was the king's grace and all his council, my Lord Cardinal and all his council, in the way of damnation, for they cause men to carry their stuff on the holy day, what day soever it be when they will remove. At this reason all my Lords were astonished, and wist not what to say. They were loath to condemn my Lord Cardinal's grace, seeing he was so holy a prelate of Christ's church, and that fact they could not deny. Wherefore at the last, my Lord of Rochester remembered himself and objected in this manner. A goodly reason, I will make you a like reason, the Bishop of Winchester+ suffered the stews, ergo the stews be lawful. At this reason I marvelled much, for I perceived that it was as lawful for our noble Prince to carry stuff on the holy day (which is not against the word of God) as it is for an harlot of the stews to live in open whoredom, which is against the word of God. And yet my Lords the Bishops, of their great charity and of their innumerable spiritual treasure, suffereth against their conscience both to be done.

Briefly it were too long to recite all the uncharitable manner that they did use with me. And yet earnestly I must be condemned, poor man, for an heretic. But I will recite the saying of doctors for me, that men may see how shamefully I have erred.

St Jerome saith: Therefore be certain days assigned, that we should come together, not that that day in the which we

* John Fisher.   † John Clerk.   + Wolsey.

30

come together is holier than another, but all days be like and equal, and Christ is not alonely crucified in 'Parasceven', and risen only on the Sunday, but the day of resurrection is always, and always may we eat of our Lord's flesh. Here St Jerome saith the self words that I spake; and of these words was I moved to speak, as God does know. Also St Augustine saith: We must observe the Sabbath day, not that we should reckon ourself not to labour, but that all thing that we do work well must have an intention to the everlasting rest; wherefore we must observe the holy day, not by corporal idleness, and unto the letter, but spiritually must we rest from vices and concupiscences, wherefore among all the ten commandments that of the Sabbath day is alonely commanded to be figuratively observed. Also Tertullian: The carnal circumcision is put away, and extincted at this time. So like-wise the observation of the sabbath day is declared to be for a time, for we must keep the sabbath day not alonely the seventh day but at all times, as Isaiah saith.

But here my Lord of Rochester said, first, that I understood not Tertullian, secondarily, that he was a heretic. But I pass over mine answer; for this is but a Lordly word and he could none otherwise save his honour, but yet standeth my scripture fast. And St Jerome, and St Augustine, and also their own law, whose words be these: It is come unto me that certain men which be of an evil spirit have sown certain evil things among you, and contrary to the holy faith, so that they do forbid that men should work on the sabbath day. The which men, what other thing shall we call them but the preachers of Antichrist; the which Antichrist shall make the sabbath day, and the Sunday be kept from all manner of work. This law clearly declareth you to be Antichrists, this is more than I said.

I have great marvel that the Bishop of Bath, being so mighty a lord in condemning of heretics, was not learned in this law, seeing it is his own faculty.

THE SECOND ARTICLE

Now dare no man preach the truth and the very Gospel of God, and in especial they that be feeble and fearful. But I

31

trust, yea, and I pray to God that it may shortly come, that false and manifest errors may be plainly showed. There be certain men like conditioned to dogs; if there be any man that is not their countryman, or that they love not, or know not, say anything against them, then cry they: an heretic, an heretic, *ad ignem, ad ignem*. These be the dogs that fear true preachers.

What heresy find you in this article? I do think that you do feel my prayer to be heard. For doubtless there be many shameful errors now manifestly opened, that at those days had been heresy to have touched them.

THE THIRD ARTICLE

We make nowadays many martyrs. I trust we shall have many more shortly. For the verity could never be preached plainly but persecution did follow.

Here did my Lord of Bath inquire of me if I reckoned them for martyrs that were burnt at Brussels. I answered that I knew not their cause wherefore they died, but I reckoned as many men to be martyrs as were persecuted and died for the word of God. But he said he would make me to fry for this. How think you by this holy prelate? Was not this a charitable argument to retell mine answer with? But this was the strongest argument, that ever they used. And peradventure I may see the day that this argument may be made against them.

THE FOURTH ARTICLE

These laws, these lawyers, these justiciars, that say that a man may lawfully ask his own good afore a judge and contend in judgement, have destroyed all patience, devotion and faith in Christian people.

On this article hangeth also the next.

This pleading in judgement is manifestly against the Gospel. Luke 12: *homo quis constituit judicem*; and contrary to Saint Paul: *iam omnino delictum est*, etc.

Mine adversaries most uncharitably laid these two articles against me, as though I had condemned the lawmaker, law and execution thereof; when I only spake against the uncharitableness of some men which rather seek vengeance of their brethren, than any right or help of the law. For I speak not against all lawyers, or against any for pleading justly after the form of the law; but only against those which taught men that they were bound to prosecute the uttermost of the law under the pain of deadly sin, were the man never so poor and unlike to pay the debt. Against these two persons spake I, and against none other. For it is not, nor never was, mine intent to forbid suing at the law; for I do know very well that *majestratus* is of God. *Ergo*, it must needs follow that all laws, having probable reasons of nature, made to conserve a commonwealth, must also be allowed of God, for laws be a part of the power that is instituted of God.

Moreover, Saint Paul doth appeal to the emperor, which is also *pars litis*. And that he could not do if suing were, *simpliciter*, forbidden. Also, God's laws be God's gifts. Wherefore it must needs follow that we may lawfully use them. But as men may misuse cunning and beauty, so may men also misuse the excellent gift of the laws. Not that laws be evil, but because we use them not to the intent that they were ordained for. No man doubteth but in using of all God's creatures there must be an 'epykya', that is a mean, a measure, and an order; so that no man may thereby destroy his neighbour against the order of charity, which is a guide and a ruler in using of all creatures. As for men to make a rumour in a whole country for a trifle, or else for a man to sue his neighbour which is not able by no means to pay his debt, and so utterly to undo him and to take none end with him but after the extremity of the law — I say that this manner of suits do not become Christian men, *ubi transgreditur equitatis, et charitatis limites*.

And that all men may clearly perceive that these only were both my words and intent, I shall rehearse the occasion that moved me to speak of the lawyers and suitors. The cause was this.

There was a poor man dead, and had made another poor man his executor, and bequeathed in his will to a church in Cambridge a kettle worth 2s. 4d, the which kettle was afterward required by the church-warden. But this executor being a poor man and not able to give this bequest at that time, therefore he desired the church-warden of longer respite, but he could not be heard, for the church-warden would have the uttermost of the law and sued him before the commissary, and at the last condemned him unto prison, where he lay and neither was able to pay his debt, nor to help his wife and children. Now, because I might do something with the church-warden, therefore the poor man's wife came weeping and wailing to me, desiring me in the way of charity to speak to the church-warden for to be good to her poor husband. Whereby I was moved to send for this my friend (his name is called John Drake, a man well known in Cambridge) unto whom I spake in this manner.

'Countryman, I am very sorry to hear of your uncharitable demeanour. Here hath been with me a poor woman weeping and wailing, and crying out how you have undone her, her poor husband and her miserable children, for all they have not one bit of bread towards their food, neither is she able to labour. Wherefore I marvel sore at you, that you will be so extreme unto poor men; whom God visited with poverty, to prove your charity. What mercy will you have at Christ's hand, the which is so extreme unto your poor neighbour, whom He hath bought with His precious blood?

Unto this he made me answer on this manner, how that thing pertained not to him but unto the Church, wherefore he said that all Doctors of Law did say that they must sue therefore, under the pain of deadly sin. And if it were wrong, why did they learn so? Now, I had many words with him, between him and me, as concerning this manner.

But the next day, when I preached, by the reason that the self same man stood afore me in the church, was I brought to remembrance of the case that he and I had commoned of. And because I had not clearly converted him, therefore I recited the case in a parable, that no man knew what I meant but he and I. And of this thing I was moved (as God knoweth) to speak of suitors, the which I think in this case no Christian man can allow. And therefore I say in mine article, 'these lawyers'.

Now is there utterly sin among you (saith Paul) because you go to law one with another; why rather suffer you not wrong, why rather suffer ye not yourselves to be robbed? Also, our Master saith: If any man will sue at the law, and take thy coat from thee, let him have thy cloak also.

May not I say these words? Wherefore were they written by the Holy Ghost, but that they should be learned? Here our master Christ and St Paul speaketh against suitors; no man can deny it, the text is so clear. Now, what suing can be unlawful if this be not unlawful against the which I did speak? Here is a poor man, wife and children destroyed, and no charitable ways taken with the poor man whereby he might make restitution. And my learning saith that *summum ius summa iniuria est*. Wherefore I will be judged by all Christian men, if I ought not in this case to give my friend counsel, not for to sue. Or whether I be worthy to be condemned for an heretic, because I counsel my friend and brother rather to suffer wrong than for to undo a whole household for a naughty lewd kettle.

But let us see how the holy doctors that have written over these places of scripture do expound them. First Athanasius, on this text of St. Paul that I bring: There is utterly sin among you; that is to say, it is to your condemnation and to your ignominy that you do exercise judicials among you; wherefore do you not rather suffer wrong? Also St Jerome: It is sin unto you that you do against the commandment of Christ, that you have judgements among you, the which ought always to keep peace, yea, though it were with the loss of your temporal goods; wherefore do you not rather suffer wrong?; whereas ye ought by the commandment of the Gospel, and by the example of the Lord, patiently to suffer, there do you the contrary, not all only not suffer, but you do wrong unto them that do no wrong. Mark how St Jerome calleth it a precept and a commandment, and no counsel;*

* The question whether certain biblical texts, taken 'literally', represented a divine command or were merely 'counsel' — avoidable advice — was much disputed; especially in the sixteenth century, when the humanists and the Reformers had made more pressing the whole question of the primacy of the written Word of God in the Bible.

and also calleth it sin to do against this commandment. Likewise Haymo saith: It is offence and sin in you that you have judicials; for accusation engendereth strife, strife engendereth discord, discord engendereth hatred. And lest peradventure they would say, this is no sin, to require mine own, therefore saith the Apostle: Truly it is sin unto you, for you do against the commandment of the Lord, the which saith, he that taketh away thy good, ask it not again; wherefore do you not rather suffer loss that ye might fulfill the commandment of the Lord? Mark how he calleth it the commandment of God; and it is sin to ask our own with contention. Now, what have I said in mine article that holy scripture and also holy doctors do not say?

But after this came a doctor of law (whom I knew not) and said that their law had condemned this opinion, and declared those scriptures to be but counsels. But I denied that, and said I knew no such law. And suddenly Doctor Stephen, now Bishop of Winchester,† showed me their law, whose words be these: *illud evangelii, si quis abstulerit, etc, non est praecipientis sed exhortantis.* Now let every Christian man judge whether that these words of their law be of sufficient authority to retell the holy words of scripture or no? But then came Doctor Wolman,+ and he brought this text: If thy brother do offend thee, thou tell the church. What is that (said he), tell the church? To whom I answered that this place made not for his purpose, alleging St Augustine for me. For it speaketh of the crimes that should be reproved by the congregation, and not of the correction of the temporal sword. It also followeth: If he hear not the church, count him as an heathen and as a publican. This is the uttermost pain that our master Christ assigneth there, the which is no pain of the temporal law. But at this answer was he sore moved and said if I did abide by it, I should be burnt. This was a sharp sentence of so great a man as he is. Appelles was a jolly wise fellow, that said once to a shoemaker, *ne sutor ultra crepidam.** But nevertheless let him and them burn as many as they can, yet it is plain that I have spoken never a

† Stephen Gardiner, consecrated December 1531.
+ Richard Wolman, Cambridge canon lawyer, Vicar-General of the Diocese of Bath and Wells.
* 'Let the cobbler stick to his last' (proverb from Pliny).

word but the holy scripture and holy doctors say the same both in sentence and in words. Wherefore I cannot see how they can condemn this article for heresy; yea, and I dare say for them that they reckon it none heresy, nor they did not condemn me for this article.

THE SIXTH ARTICLE

I will never believe, nor yet I can never believe, that one man may be by the law of God a bishop of two or three cities, yea of an whole country, for it is contrary to Saint Paul, which saith: I have left thee behind, to set in every city a bishop. And if you find in one place of scripture that they be called *episcopi*, you shall find in diverse other places that they be called *presbiteri*.

I was brought afore my Lord Cardinal into his gallery, and there he read all mine articles till he came to this, and there he stopped and said that this touched him, and therefore he asked me if I thought it wrong that one bishop should have so many cities underneath him. Unto whom I answered that I could no farther go than to St Paul's text, which set in every city a bishop. Then asked he me if I thought it now unright (seeing the ordinance of the church) that one bishop should have so many cities? I answered that I knew none ordinance of the church (as concerning this thing), but St Paul's saying only. Nevertheless, I did see a contrary custom and practice in the world, but I know not the original thereof. Then said he, that in the Apostle's time there were divers cities, some seven miles, some six miles long, and over them was there set but one bishop, and of their suburbs also. So likewise now, a bishop hath but one city to his cathedral church, and the country about is as suburbs unto it. Methought this was far fetched, but I durst not deny it, because it was so great authority, and of so holy a father, and of so great a divine. But this dare I say, that his holiness could never prove it by scripture, nor yet by any authority of doctors, nor yet by any practice of the apostles; and yet it must be true, because a pillar of the church hath spoken it.

But let us see what the doctors say to mine article. Athanasius doth declare this text of the Apostle, I have left thee behind etc. He would not commit unto one bishop a whole isle, but he did enjoin, that every city should have his proper pastor, supposing that by this means they should more diligently oversee the people, and also that the labour should be more easy to bear. Also Chrysostom on that same text. He would not that a whole country should be permitted unto one man, but he enjoined unto every man his cure, by the means he knew, that the labour should be more easy, and the subjects should be with more diligence governed if the teachers were not distract with the governing of many churches but had cure and charge of one church only. Me thinketh these be plain words, and able to move a man to speak as much as I did. But grant that you may have all these cities, yet can you make it none heresy. For my Lord Cardinal granted that it was but against him, and against you, which be no gods. But I, poor man, must be an heretic, there is no remedy, you will have it so. And who is able to say nay? Not all scripture, nor yet God himself.

THE SEVENTH ARTICLE

It cannot be proved by scripture that a man of the church should have so great temporal possessions.

But they will say, if they had not so great possessions, they could not keep so many servants, so many dogs, so many horses as forty or fifty, and maintain so great pomp and pride, and live so deliciously. What heresy find you in this? Is it heresy to speak against your horses, and your hounds, and your abominable living? And doubtless, I did not say but that you might have possessions; all only I spake against the superfluousness and the abuse of them, for the which all the world wondereth on you. What mischief is there in the world used that is more clearly and openly known than that you do abuse the goods of the church? And yet must I be condemned for an heretic for speaking against it. Alas, do you think that God will suffer this violence that you do use against poor men? I will stand in the danger, and prove how his godly majesty shall judge this matter between you and me. I dare trust him with it.

38

THE EIGHTH ARTICLE

Sure I am that they cannot by the law of God have any
jurisdiction secular, and yet they challenge both powers,
which if they have, why do they not put them both in use?
For they must say, as the Jews said, we may kill no man.

This is the article that did bite you, for you cannot be
content with the office of a bishop, but you will be also
kings. How that standeth with God's law, and with your
oath, I have declared it to our noble prince. I doubt not, but
he will put you to the trial of it. Have not you this many
years condemned many a poor man, and then delivered him
to the temporal power to be put to death, which knew
nothing of his cause? And if he would that ye should put him
to death yourself, then answered ye how you might kill no man.
So that they were always your hangmen.

THE NINTH ARTICLE

They say they be the successors of Christ and of his apostles,
but I can see them follow none but Judas. For they bear the
purse, and have all the money. And if they had not so great
possessions, I am sure an hundred would speak against them,
where now dare not one, for loss of promotion.

As for this article, I will overcome you with the witness of
all the world. You may well condemn it for heresy but it is as
true as your *Paternoster*. Judas sold our master but once, and
you sell Him as often as He cometh into your hands. But I
would it were that ye could prove me a liar, and that you
followed any of the apostles saving Judas only. Yea, I would
that ye were in certain points as good as Judas was. It had
been better for you that you had not meddled against me in
these matters. For now I am compelled to speak many things
which I would for shame of the world never have spoken. But
now that you will have it so, take it to you, and make the
best you can of it.

THE TENTH ARTICLE

There is not the greatest pharisee in this church but I am sure I prick him with these words, and he knoweth that they be true, though he say the contrary, and that do I well know.

This article did I speak because of Doctor Ridley,* which on a time granted in master Doctor Butt's house,† that the bishops were clean out of order. And therefore I say that I know it.

THE ELEVENTH ARTICLE

The ordinary bishops and prelates do follow that false prophet Balaam. For they would curse the people, but by the provision of God they were compelled to bless them, that is to say, to teach them to live well, though they themselves live most mischievously. And so the asses which they ride upon — that is, the common people — have their lives in abomination. This is the heinous heresy. For it speaketh against the holy fathers, which be almost as holy as Balaam's ass, that did once speak the word of God to a good purpose; and so do they never. But I grant that I did offend in calling you ordinary bishops, for I should have called you inordinate butchers. And as for that, that I compared you to Balaam, it is your own law (2, question 7: *secuti sunt;* and chapter, *Nos si*). And as for your living all the world knoweth it. I could tell here many holy points of bishops' living, as keeping of men's wives, and daughters, but I will not; for I should be reckoned uncharitable. But you may do them, breaking not your holy charity.

THE TWELFTH ARTICLE

They set up an idol to deceive the people withal, which is called Baal-peor, or Baal-phegor; that is, interpreted, gasping,

* Dr Robert Ridley, a Cambridge man, Preb. of St Paul's (uncle of Nicholas).
† William Butts, Doctor of Medicine, Fellow of Gonville Hall, and physician to Henry VIII, was principal of St Mary's Hostel, Cambridge (on the site of the present Senate House).

as their laws and constitutions, the which gasp and gape to maintain their wordly honour. They cause us to do sacrifice by fair women, that is by their carnal affections and sweet words, so that God of Israel is forgotten. And thus by their sweet words and benediction they deceive the simple. These be the false masters that St Peter speaketh of. These be the fountains without water, for they give no good doctrine to the people.

Where is the heresy in this, because I compare your laws to Baal? But look whether the interpretation of the word do agree with the nature of your laws or not? What do all your laws but minish the authority of princes, and of all other lords, and exalt yours only? Call you not that a gasping idol? Let this article stand till you be able to prove it heresy.

THE THIRTEENTH ARTICLE

Now they sell us, they sell the people, they sell holy orders, they sell church hallowing, there is no better merchandise in Cheapside. Wilt thou know what is the price of a church hallowing? No less than 40 shillings. They sell pardons, and remissions of sins, as openly as a cow and an ox is sold, for they never grant them without money. The Suffragan of Ely did ask of Master John Purgold 40 shillings and the offering for hallowing of Saint Edward's in Cambridge.* Yea, and he would not do it so good cheap (quoth he) but because he had a god-daughter buried in the churchyard. But this may be proved by examples enough. For bring ye forth one church in all England that you have hallowed without money, or without hope of money, and I will grant my conclusion false. And as for your pardons, all the world knows your handling. I dare say it is the best merchandise in the world, as you handle it.

But was it not a marvellous blindness and a great presumption, so cruelly to handle me for these articles? Was there no middle to have punished me for speaking against you, but that I must needs be an heretic? I dare say there is not one

---

* Purgold was a prominent lawyer practising in Cambridge, sometime Fellow of Trinity Hall: he died about 1527 and was buried in St Edward's.

among you so shameless, that dare come forth now at this day and prove these articles heresy against me. But doubtless as long as I live, and am not restored to my name and fame again, which you have violently taken away from me, will I be unto you a devil, and a pestilence. I require nothing of you but my good name and fame, to the which I have right, and to the which you ought of your charity restore me, though I never required you. I thing you have punished me enough for speaking of a foolish word or twain against you.

THE FOURTEENTH ARTICLE

Wilt thou know what their benedictions is worth? They had rather give thee ten benedictions than one halfpenny. Is not this a sore heresy? You ride through streets and towns, blessing man and stone, but you never give halfpenny to man nor child.

THE FIFTEENTH ARTICLE

Now is come a pardon, whereby they say that they have power to send an hundred souls to heaven. And if they may so do without any further respect, then may they likewise send another hundred to hell. For it followeth in the text, *Quodcunque ligaveris*, that is, whatsoever thou bindest. Is not this a sore heresy, to say that you may not rule this matter at your judgement? But this is a marvellous text, *Quodcunque ligaveris*, for it bindeth in hell and looseth in heaven, and openeth men's purses and coffers in earth, it deposeth princes, it interditeth lands, it looseth a man out of his coat; yea, and oftentimes it looseth a man from his wife, yea and the horse out of the cart. And all is done by this text, *Quodcunque ligaveris*. Is not this a marvellous text, that has so great a power? I know not such another in all the Bible.

THE SIXTEENTH ARTICLE

It is abominable to hear how they preach and teach that they may absolve *a poena* and *a culpa*, which I am sure is

42

impossible, as they understand it. Make of this what you can, and look of your own scholastical doctors, the which learneth boldly that the keys of the church hath none authority over sin, nor yet over eternal pain. But all only hath authority to change everlasting pain unto a temporal pain; and that the pope may change, and take away at his pleasure. And among all temporal pains, you reckon purgatory the greatest, over the which the pope hath full power. This is your own doctrine. Look in Alexander of Hales, in Duns, and in Bonaventure, in the fourth book of the 'Sentences'. Now if you will condemn me, then must you first condemn this your own doctrine.

THE SEVENTEENTH ARTICLE

What is the cause that they forbid us that we should not discuss how great their power is, but because that they would make all men fools, and hold us in ignorance? Your own schoolmen say, the pope's power is so great that no man can nor may discuss it. Also your law commandeth that no man be so hardy as to ask the pope, Lord why do you so? But put the case that this were a lie: yet it is far from heresy. Yet my Lords say that I shall be an heretic, and why, say I? Because we will have it so, say they. Yea, and thou be-est not so content, that shalt be burnt. Marry, I thank you heartily my Lords. *Pro bona vestra informatione*.

THE EIGHTEENTH ARTICLE

They have a law most abominable and contrary to God's law and charity, to excommunicate the people four times in a year. That is to say, those men that raise the rent of an house. (That must you understand, if it belong not to the church. For if it belong unto the church thou mayest raise it in every month once, and no man shall curse thee.) Also they curse them that be not buried in their parish church. That must be understanded, if that they be rich men; for if they be poor they may be buried among the friars.

The bishop of Bath said there was no such manner to curse

43

men. And all the world knoweth the contrary. Moreover I read these articles in the book of the general curse that belongeth to St Benet's church in Cambridge, and there did I mark it with mine own hand, and yet the bishop was not ashamed to deny it. And why? Because I must be an heretic, there is no remedy, the holy fathers have so determined it.

THE NINETEENTH ARTICLE

They have mitres with glistering precious stones, they have gloves for catching cold in the midst of their ceremonies. They have rings and ouches,* and other ceremonies, so many that there is in a manner now nothing else in the church but all jewish manners.

Will you make this heresy, because I speak against your damnable and pompous mitres? I think such ornaments were to be condemned even among heathen men, I will not say among Christian men. But this dare I say, that there was never no God among heathen men that ever delighted in such ornaments. And yet you will serve the God of Heaven by them. And your poor brother, whom Christ hath redeemed with his precious blood, dieth in prison, and openly in the street, and hangeth himself for necessity, and yet will you not bestow on him so much as one of your precious stones. Tell me of one bishop that ever broke his mitre to the helping of a poor man. Was there never man in necessity in England? But all the world may see what you be. These things be sensible enough.

THE TWENTIETH ARTICLE

These mitres, I cannot tell from whence they do come, except they take them from the Jews' bishops. And if they take them from the Jews, then let them also take their sacrifices and their oblations from them, and offer calves and lambs as they did, and then have we nothing to do with them for we be Christian men and no Jews. I pray you tell me where ye find but one prick in holy scripture of your mitres?

* Ornamental brooches.

44

ur master did institute bishops, and St Paul settet.
what is their office, and also what is their ornament, anc
speaketh never a word of your mitres. But I dare boldly :
that if you be put to the trial, you shall be fain to run to th
old law. But can I be an heretic if I condemned clearly your
mitres, and said they were of the devil? When you prove
them to be of Christ's institution, then will I be an heretic. Is
not that enough? I pray you let me so long be taken for a
Christian man. And if you be not content with this, truly
then do ye me wrong.

THE TWENTY-FIRST ARTICLE

These mitres with two horns, I cannot tell what they should
signify, except it be the horns of the false prophet, of whom
it is spoken: With these horns shalt thou blow afore thee all
Syria. And so did he mock their rings, and all their ornaments, and ecclesiastical ceremonies. It will come to my
saying that you be bishops of the old law, for you have
nothing to defend your rings, your ornaments, and your
ceremonies but very tyranny. Wherefore to maintain these,
depose you kings and princes, interdite lands, and burn man,
wife and child. And when you have all done, you have
defended but a devilish token of pride.

The Doctors that would favour your proud tokens, and
expound them to the best, have declared that the two horns
of your mitres did signify the new and the old testament,
that is, how you should be learned in them both. Now I saw
that this exposition did not agree with that thing (for no man
could be less learned in them than you be; I speak of a great
many). Wherefore methought it was but a vain exposition,
and therefore I compared them to the two horns of the false
prophet, because (as you know) this false prophet said unto
the king that he should with these two horns blow afore him
all Syria. And yet he lied, for the king was the first man that
was slain. So likewise you say unto kings, if they follow your
counsel and maintain your authority and be ruled after you,
then shall they overcome all their enemies, as sin, death and
hell. And yet (*Salvo ordine vestro*) you lie, for you have no
word of God for you. Wherefore you must be false prophets.

...ere have I compared with a similitude your mitres to th...
...o horns, and you to false prophets. What if this be false?
...hat if I cannot prove it? Yet can you make me none
...eretic, for then must you make those men heretics that have
compared the forks of your mitres to the new and to the old
Testaments, and you to the true apostles, for they have made
a greater lie than I have done, and they are never able to
prove it. And as for me, I will prove my saying true (if ye will
stand to scripture) or else will I be taken for an heretic.

THE TWENTY-SECOND ARTICLE

They have *baculum pastoralem* to take sheep with, but it is
not like a shepherd's hook, for it is intricate and manifold
crooked and turneth always in, so that it may be called a
mase,* for it hath neither beginning nor ending, and it is
more like to knock swine and wolves in the head with, than
to take sheep. They have also pillers and pollers† and other
ceremonies, which no doubt be but trifles and things of
naught.

I pray you what is the cause that you call your staff a
shepherd's staff? You help no man with it; you comfort no man;
you lift up no man with it; but you have striken down kings
and kingdoms with it, and knocked in the head dukes and
earls with it. Call you this a shepherd's staff? There is a space
in the shepherd's staff for the foot to come out again, but
your staff turneth and windeth always inward, and never
outward, signifying that whatsoever he be that cometh within
your daunger+ that he shall never come out again. This
exposition your deeds do declare. Let them be examined
that you have had to do with. And let us see how they have
escaped your shepherd's hook. But these be the articles, for

* Barnes intended a pun here: with 'mace' and 'maze'.
† Another pun. Barnes was probably thinking of the 'great pillars of
  silver' and 'the gilt pole axes' which were carried before Wolsey
  (together with the Great Seal, the Cardinal's Hat, a silver mace and
  two silver crosses). 'Pillers and pollers', in Tudor usage, meant
  robbers and despoilers. The pun can also include an allusion to the
  clerical round hat, known as a 'pillion' (*pileus*).
+ Power.

which I must needs be an heretic. Nevertheless, all the rld may see how shamefully that I have erred against your linesses in saying the truth.

My Lord Cardinal reasoned with me in this article; all the other he passed over, saving this and the sixth article. Here he did ask if I thought it good and reasonable that he should lay down his pillers and pollers, and coin them. Here is the heresy that is so abominable. I made him answer that I thought it well done. Then said he, how think you, were it better for me (being in the honour and dignity that I am) to coin my pillers and pollers, and to give the money to five or six beggars, than for to maintain the commonwealth by them as I do? Do you not reckon (quoth he) the commonwealth better than five or six beggars? To this I did answer that I reckoned it more to the honour of God, and to the salvation of his soul, and also to the comfort of his poor brethren, that they were coined and given in alms. And as for the common-wealth did not hang of them, for as his grace knew, the commonwealth was afore his grace, and must be when his grace is gone, and the pillers and pollers came with him and should also go away with him. Notwithstanding if the commonwealth were in such a condition that it had need of them, then might his grace so long use them, or any other thing in their stead, so long as the commonwealth needed them. Notwithstanding, I said, thus much did I not say in my sermon against them; but all only I damned in my sermon the gorgeous pomp and pride of all exterior ornaments. Then he said, well, you say very well.

But as well as it was said, I am sure that these words made me an heretic, for if these words had not been therein, mine adversaries durst never have showed their faces against me. But now they knew well that I could never be indifferently heard. For if I had got the victory, then must all the bishops, and my Lord Cardinal, have laid down all their gorgeous ornaments. For the which they had rather burn twenty such heretics as I am, as all the world knoweth. But God is mighty, and of me hath he showed his power, for I dare say they never intended thing more in their lives than they did to destroy me, and yet God of his mercy has saved me against all their violence; unto his godly wisdom is the cause all only known.

47

The Bishop of London that was then called Tunsta[l]* after my departing out of prison, said unto a substantial m[an] that I was not dead (for I dare say his conscience did n[ot] reckon me such an heretic that I would have killed myself, a[s] the voice went, but yet would he have done it gladly of his charity) but I was (said he) in Amsterdam; where I had never been in my life, as God knoweth, nor yet in the country this ten years; and certain men did there speak with me (said he) and he fained certain words that they should say to me, and I to them, and added thereunto that my Lord Cardinal would have me again, or it should cost him a great sum of money (how much I do not clearly remember). I have marvelled that my Lord is not ashamed thus shamefully and thus lordly to lie, although he might do it by authority.

And where my Lord Cardinal, he would spend so much money to have me again, I have great marvel of it. What can they make of me? I am a simple poor wretch, and worth no man's money in the world (saving theirs) not the tenth penny that they will give for me. And to burn me, or to destroy me, cannot so greatly profit them. For when I am dead the sun and the moon, the stars and the element, water and fire, yea and also stones, shall defend this cause against them, rather than the verity should perish. But if they be so charitable to do good works and to spend their money so well, they have prisoners and poor men enough in the land, let them bestow their money of them. And as for me, I do promise them here by this present writing, and by the faith that I owe to Christ Jesus, and by that fidelity that I owe to my prince, that if they will be bound to our noble prince, after the manner of his law, and after good conscience and right, that they shall do me no violence nor wrong, but discuss and dispute these articles, and all other that I have written, after the holy word of God and by Christ's holy scripture with me. Then will I (as soon as I may know it) present myself unto our most noble prince, there offering myself to his grace, that I will either prove these things by God's word against you all, or else I will suffer at his grace's pleasure. Whom the father of heaven preserve in honour. Amen. And if you refuse this condition, then say that you are neither good nor charitable. For I dare say you can desire no more of a Christian man.

* Cuthbert Tunstall, Bishop of London 1522-30.

48

THE TWENTY-THIRD ARTICLE

Priests do mumble and roar out their dirges and masses in the church and churchyards for their founders, curious to speak their words distinctly. But I ensure them that their prayers shall do them no good, but only *acceptatio divina.**

As for this article, the bishops did not make much of, for they perceived that it was gathered without any sentence. For my saying was, that men should make their prayers in such a faith, and with such a devotion, that God might accept them, and not so idly and without all devotion babble and say their dirges, alonely of bondage and of custom, and not of devotion. I brought the saying of the Apostle for me, which saith: Let your petitions and prayers appear before God. And also: He that asketh, let him ask in faith, nothing doubting.

THE TWENTY-FOURTH ARTICLE

There is no prayer acceptable to God, except it be fetched from the fire of the altar.

This article was also gathered without any sentence, for my adversaries did not greatly care what they made of such articles as pertained to learning and edifying. And therefore they never erred so much as they did in them. For in those articles that were against the bishops, they did great diligence, and in a part of them gathered they my very true sentences, and mine own words, though in those things they left out, uncharitably, those words that made for my declaration and also for the probation of my saying, the which I have also here left out, alonely adding the articles as they laid them against me, that all men may see the worst that they had against me. For all men may think that they will neither lay the best, nor yet the truth against me.

But this article did I thus preach: That men should not in their petition and prayers put to their good works, nor their good deeds, and their merits (as, O Lord, I do fast; I do pray; I am no thief; I am in charity with all the world) and for them desire God to be merciful unto them. But they should

* 'Divine favour'.

desire the father of heaven to be merciful unto them alonely for Christ's merits. For they were the things whereby both we and our prayers are accepted in the sight of the father. And to prove this I brought certain scriptures. As this: whatsoever ye shall ask the father in my name, he shall give it you. And also the figure of the old law, where there was no sacrifice done but with the fire that was taken from the altar. Now did I say that Christ is our altar. But this mine adversaries understood not. But I marvel what this article doth among the other heretical articles. I think they do not reckon it heresy.

THE TWENTY-FIFTH ARTICLE

He did not pray for the three estates of holy church, neither made he his prayers in the beginning of his sermon, according to the old custom, but at the last end, and for the true knowledge of all Christian men; making no prayer to our Lady, nor for the souls in purgatory, nor for grace expedient.

If the bishops had had any indifferency in them, or any charity, they would have been ashamed that such articles should have been brought afore them. What is this to the purpose of heresy, that I did not pray for the three estates of holy church? And yet they grant that I prayed for all true Christian men, and that men might come to the true knowledge. Is not all the church contained in this? But they be uncharitable men, without all consideration; they be so blinded in their worldy honour. That I did not pray to our Lady, nor for the souls in purgatory, what is that to heresy? For then were the apostles heretics, for they did not pray in their sermons to our Lady, nor yet to the souls in purgatory. And as for praying for grace expedient, that is not the preacher bound to do openly.

But methinketh by these articles, that God gave me a great grace, that I durst so boldly reprove their abominable living, not fearing the danger that should come thereof; but this I leave to other men's judgement. And I dare boldly say that if I had spoken ten times as much against the authority of our noble prince and against all his noble dukes and lords, and

50

had taken all power, both spiritual and temporal, from them, and given it to our idle bishops, then had I been a faithful Christian man, for I had defended the liberties of holy church. But God send them his grace, and space for to convert. Amen.

PART III

1550-1552: Bucer and Calvin Urge Further Reformation in England

The Newfangled Party gained ground in England in the second half of the reign of Edward VI. In 1550 John Hooper argued that 'ceremonies' (vestments, he especially meant) cannot be used without breaching God's law: and prophetically brought to his support the imperatives of Conscience and Liberty (1). Hooper had lived from 1547 to 1549 in Zürich, becoming the first of the thoroughly Swiss-orientated English Reformers, well versed in Zwingli, Bullinger and Calvin; and giving in 'Declaration of Christ and His Office' (Zürich, 1547) (2) a blunt, brief summary of advanced English opinion shortly after the death of Henry VIII. Nicholas Ridley, Bishop of London, replied to Hooper. His reply circulated in manuscript (Whitgift was to have a copy) (3). And the controversy now seems a pre-echo of Elizabethan debate. Ridley's ideas on use and abuse, things indifferent, public order, the power of the magistrate, the value of historical circumstances, the adding to God's word ('to forbid and make that sin which God never forbade' is 'bringing in bondage the christian liberty, and ungodly adding to God's word') (4) — all these points were to be developed by Whitgift and Hooker: together with his warning against sedition and his comparison of Hooper to the fourth-century 'donatists' and modern anabaptists. Ridley voiced the opinion of Cranmer. Which is probably why Milton was to condemn them jointly as 'halting and time serving prelates', who put England in schism from the Reformation — the exact and scriptural Reformation (5). Even so, Milton acknowledged the reign of Edward as 'those times which are on record for the purest and sincerest that ever shone yet on the Reformation of this island' (6): a point which had been made in the reign of Mary by the martyr John Bradford (7).

The following section — a letter of Bucer from Cambridge to Calvin, and three letters of Calvin to England — show the stresses in the relationship of the English Reformation to Europe: Europe stressing the necessity of further and purer Reformation.

Bucer's letter is a pessimistic report on the state of the game in 1550: a time of 'desolation and betrayal of churches', of unevangelical pastors and uncomprehending people, of the difficulties of Reformation within the framework of the Tudor Constitution; and he includes a gloomy survey of Oxbridge. Martin Bucer (1491-1551), of Strasbourg, had been offered a 'safe harbour' in England by Cranmer in October 1548: a country where 'the seeds of true doctrine have happily begun to be sown' (8). Bucer arrived in England, with his wife and family, in 1549, and became Regius Professor of Divinity at Cambridge until his death in March 1551. He was to be a hero to Elizabethan puritans: a 'deep, learned, politic and experienced soldier in God's Church', who 'observed' and 'forewarned' — that antichrist was at hand if discipline and doctrine were not reformed and received (9). What was the hope in 1550? It lay, so Bucer informs Calvin, in the boy King.

Cranmer had written to Calvin in March 1552 hoping for a universal Protestant Synod to rival the Council of Trent — and which might meet in England (10). Calvin's reply to Cranmer is here given. A reminder that Cranmer was 'regardful of the world at large'; a desire for a 'definite form of doctrine' (Cranmer was especially concerned with the Lord's Supper); references to Bullinger and Melanchthon; praise of Edward; — and a refusal to come to England. Cranmer had written twice to Melanchthon in 1548; and he wrote to Bullinger, as well as to Calvin, in March 1552. Bucer, in the event, was his only top-star acquisition. But it is important to emphasise this European Protestant side of Cranmer. He had spent eight months abroad in 1530, visiting France and Italy (he knew Italian). And in 1532 he spent nearly a year as ambassador to the Court of Charles V, visiting Nuremberg (where he married), Regensburg, and sailing down the Danube to Vienna. He toured a battlefield in

54

south-east Austria, and saw 2000 corpses (the Turkish flag had been raised outside Vienna in 1529) (11). Memories of the Danube remained always with him (12). In his European outlook Cranmer had strong similarities to some Elizabethan puritans. I have called Matthew Parker 'insular'. Parker never left England, pitied foreigners, (13) and thought in terms of a universe 'where almighty God is so much English as He is' (14). Latimer, celebrating the birth of Edward in 1537, had made a similar point: 'our Lord God, God of England! for verily he hath shewed Himself God of England, or rather an English God' (15). It was not until Milton that we get an effective combination of the insularity and the urge to preciser Reformation.

Katherine Parr had compared Henry VIII to Moses, leading England from the bondage of Rome. The work must be completed. In a letter to his godson Edward (aged 10) in 1548 Cranmer declared that Henry VIII had 'diligently travailed for a true and right reformation', and had indeed 'brought many things to a godly purpose and effect'; it was now the duty of the son 'to finish and bring to pass that your father did most godly begin' (16). Edward was to be another Constantine (17). He also was to be a second Josiah: an analogy made by Calvin in the first of his two letters to Edward reproduced here. Josiah was the seventh-century B.C. King of Judah, who became King at the age of eight, and went on, as a youth, to 'make a covenant with the Lord', and become a great Purger and Putter Down of Abominations: clearing the Lord's Temple of vessels made for Baal, putting down idolatrous priests, breaking down the houses of the sodomites — and indulging in other such pious activities (18). The image, to Calvin, of an 'exellent prince'. Cranmer, in his speech at the coronation of Edward, had invoked a 'second Josiah, who reformed the Church of God in his days' (19). And the invocation was common. Thomas Becon in 1550 used it, and went on (20): 'if anything be left behind that is not yet brought into perfection . . . I doubt not but that the King's most excellent majesty' and the Council 'will see it reformed, and never leave off their godly purpose . . . till they have stablished all things in this realm according to God's word, and made this Church of England a worthy spectacle and notable exemplar for all fornications (21) to

55

behold'. (Becon lived till 1567.) That was, so to speak, the Myth of the Protestant Edward. (Edward himself was a pious but attractive boy, whom we seldom directly see: mainly through the distorting lenses of his Prophets.) There was, further, to be a Myth of the Puritan Edward. Appropriately, it was expressed by John Hooper, who urged the King in 1550 to 'purge this Church of England to the purity and sincerity of God's word' (22), and to become a 'fear and terror to foreign and strange nations' (23) (words reminding us of Lear's urge to do things which 'shall be the terrors of the earth'). The Reformation was about to be accomplished, so the argument ran . . . when Edward died: not yet sixteen.

Bucer in his Cambridge letter had drawn Calvin's attention to the danger of Mary. And the reign of Mary was to be the traumatic experience from which much of later puritanism springs. Some of the godly remnant at home found comfort in Augustinian themes of election, reprobation and assurance. John Bradford, especially, in 'the very dungeon of despair' (24) — though his exposition was moderate by the standards of later Calvinists such as William Perkins. Can *God be mutable? We may note that Calvin's 'Institutes' was a popular book with English undergraduates in the second half of the reign of Edward. John Whitgift of Pembroke, Cambridge, read it in the 1553 edition; with 'reverence', he later said, without being 'wholly addicted' (25). The subject of election and reprobation seemed to be in the air by 1550: the year of the publication of the shortest theological work of Tudor England, 'Of Predestination and Election', sixteen small pages by one John Lamberd; of an English translation of one of Augustine's last works, 'De Praedestinatione Sanctorum'; and of English versions of Italian sermons of the late 1540s by Bernardino Ochino, originally published at Geneva. (Ochino was now a prebendary of Canterbury, and is said to have discussed the subject with the Princess Elizabeth.) In 1552 came Calvin's detailed and cantankerous 'De Aetera Dei Praedestinatione': although it was not to appear in English till 1856, a group of English theologians at the time swallowed it whole, and by the end of 1552 they were attacking 'compromisers'. (Cranmer's Article of Predestination (26) was intended as such a 'compromise'.) All this was intensified by the Marian Shock. Anthony Gilbey's 'Treatise of Election and Predestination' was published in Geneva in 1556; and John Knox's longer work on the subject in Geneva, 1560.*

At home, again, in the perilous time, there gathered secret churches of the godly: a precedent to be cited by Elizabethan puritans (and seventeenth-century New Englanders). There was the shock of the burnings, and the memory of the butchers. And, as Richard Hooker rather blithely put it, the 'smaller contentions' of the reign of Edward were, among these exiles who fled from England to Germany and Switzerland, 'somewhat increased' (27).

Hooker was referring to the debates (especially at Frankfurt) about the merits of the Book of Common Prayer — could it be used by the saints or not? Here, as in the Hooper—Ridley debate, Elizabethan arguments were anticipated. Over 470 males left England for Europe in the reign of Mary: about 400 of these (the Newfangled?) went to the centres of Reformation — 125 to Geneva: the most radical haven from Babylon. The exiles included two future Archbishops (Edmund Grindal and Edwin Sandys of York); nine future Bishops (including Jewel); and five future Deans (including Alexander Nowell) (28). There were a dozen or so returned exiles in the first House of Commons of Elizabeth's reign (about 3 per cent — Sir John Neale's 'vital core') (29); and the important 1563 Convocation had twenty-seven returned exiles in the Lower House (total membership, about 105) (30). There was in the 1560s a sense, at least, of hope thwarted, amongst many of these men. A sense, too, that they were 'strangers in our own country' (31); a feel of the 'little flock' (32), of us — 'He was with us at Zurich' (33).

Elizabeth's crucial decision was to ignore the exiles in her choice of an Archbishop; and to appoint Parker, who had lived privately for five years under Mary, enjoying 'delightful literary leisure' (34), translating the psalms into English doggerel, and composing a book proving that the marriage of parsons was lawful 'by the eternal word of God'.

Calvin had reminded Edward of his royal duty 'in maintaining the kingdom of Jesus Christ in England'. How would Parker interpret that duty? How would Elizabeth?

1. Hooper presented his treatise to the Council in October 1550: it has not survived, and most of our knowledge of it, apart from a portion printed in 1763, is deduced from Ridley's reply. See M. M. Knappen, 'Tudor Puritanism', app. I: 'Hooper's lost Argument on the Vestments'.

2. In Parker Society, 'Early Writings of John Hooper' (1843).

3. Ridley's reply was first published in 1853: in Parker Society, 'Letters, Treatises and Remains of John Bradford', pp. 375-95. From Sir Thomas Phillipps MSS.

4. Ibid., p. 382.

5. Milton, 'Of Reformation in England' (1641) bk i.

6. Milton, 'Tetrachordon' (1645): final para.

7. Bradford, 1555 examination. In Parker Society, 'Bradford', i: 'Sermons, Meditations, etc.', p. 471: cf. p. 488.

8. Cranmer, 'Miscellaneous Writings and Letters' (Parker Society) p. 424.

9. Dr Williams's Library, Morrice MSS 'B': 'The Seconde Parte of a Register', f. 201; Peel (ed.) 'The Seconde Parte of a Register', ii 7. François Wendel has published a two-volume edition, with introduction, of Bucer's 1550 'De Regno Christi': one volume of the Latin text, the second a critical edition of the 1558 French translation (1954-5).

10. 'Miscellaneous Writings and Letters', pp. 431-3.

11. Ibid., p. 235: letter to Henry VIII.

12. Ibid., p. 404.

13. Parker, 'Correspondence', p. 420.

14. Ibid., p. 419.

15. Latimer, 'Remains', p. 385.

16. 'Miscellaneous Writings and Letters', p. 419.

17. Bartholomew Traheron to Bullinger, June 1550: 'Original Letters Relative to English Reformation', ed. H. Robinson (Parker Society) i 324.

18. 2 Kings 22-3.

19. 'Miscellaneous Writings and Letters', p. 127.

20. Preface to 'The Flower of Godly Prayers': Parker Society, 'Becon', iii: 'Prayers, etc.', p. 4.

21. The Parker Society editor suggested that 'foreign nations' was possibly the true reading!

22. Sermons on Jonas: Parker Society, 'Hooper, Early Writings', p. 542.

23. Ibid., p. 558. Cf. Hooper to Bullinger, 1550: 'he will be a terror to all the sovereigns of the earth', 'Original Letters Relative to English Reformation', i 82.

24. Parker Society, 'Bradford', i: 'Sermons, Meditations, etc.', p. 308: 'Defence of Election'. Written in prison.

25. Whitgift, 'Works', i 436.

26. Article 'Of Predestination and Election', 'Liturgies etc of Edward VI' (Parker Society) p. 530. The Articles (basis of the Elizabethan 39) were drafted by 1551; argued in 1552 Convocation; printed March 1553. Edward died in July.

27. Hooker, preface, 'Of The Laws of Ecclesiastical Polity': Everyman ed., i 92.

28. Calculations from biographical information given in Christina Garrett, 'The Marian Exiles' (1938, 1966).

29. Neale, 'Elizabeth I and Her Parliaments'. Neale tended to accept Miss Garrett's thesis that the exiles formed a deliberate migration and then, in the 1560s, a cabal: 'one of the most astute manoeuvres that has ever carried a defeated political party to ultimate power' (Garrett, p. 1). So did Michael Walzer in 'The Revolution of the Saints : a study in the origins of radical politics' (1966): 'modern politics begins in England with the return of the Genevan exiles' (p. 113).

30. Haugaard, 'Elizabeth and the English Reformation' app. I.

31. Jewel to Peter Martyr, summer 1559: 'Zurich Letters', i 22.

32. Ibid., p. 27: letter of Richard Cox, May 1559.

33. Ibid., p. 255: letter of 1571.

34. 'Correspondence', p. 483, though it had a bad psychological effect on him: see letter to William Cecil, 1563, in 'Correspondence', pp. 199-200.

3 Cambridge Letter of Bucer to Calvin, 1550

Translation from Parker Society, 'Original Letters relative to the English Reformation', ed. H. Robinson, ii (1847) pp. 545-8: letter ccliii.

Cambridge, Whitsunday, 1550

I greatly stand in need of the consolation of your letters. For though there are not wanting to me in this country faithful friends and brethren in the Lord, yet I know not how it is, but I am most anxiously desirous to learn what my old friends and long tried colleagues are doing, how the work of the Lord is making progress among them, and also that they may advise, comfort, and exhort me. Accounts are from time to time sent me from my native place and other parts of Germany, which greatly distress my mind; and the cause of Christ too is likewise so conducted in this country, that unless the Lord look upon our most innocent and religious king and some other godly individuals with his special mercy, it is greatly to be feared that the dreadful wrath of God will very shortly blaze forth against this kingdom also. The bishops have not yet been able to come to an agreement as to Christian doctrine, much less as to discipline, and very few parishes have pastors qualified for their office. Most of them are sold to the nobility; and there are persons, even among the ecclesiastical order, and those too who wish to be regarded as gospellers, who hold three or four parishes and even more, without ministering in any one of them; but they appoint such substitutes as will be satisfied with the least stipend, and who for the most part cannot even read English, and who are in heart mere papists. The nobility too have, in many parishes, preferred those who have been in monasteries, who are most unlearned and altogether unfit for the sacred

60

office; and this, merely for the sake of getting rid of the payment of their yearly pension. Hence you may find parishes in which there has not been a sermon for some years. And you are well aware how little can be effected for the restoration of the kingdom of Christ by mere ordinances, and the removal of instruments of superstition.

Each of the universities in this country has many excellent colleges, furnished with such large endowments and useful statutes, as are possessed by no university in the world. For not only are very many persons exceedingly well educated in these colleges, in most of which there are above a hundred students, but they afford also honourable exhibitions for clothes and books. It is from these colleges that the swarms of faithful ministers ought to have been sent forth from time to time; for all masters of arts are required to become students in theology, with the exception only of four in each college, two of whom are expected to study medicine, and two law. But such connivance has so long existed, and is especially so prevalent at this time, that by far the greater part of the Fellows are either most bitter papists, or profligate epicureans, who, as far as they are able, draw over the young men to their way of thinking and imbue them with an abhorrence of sound Christian doctrine and discipline. And even our friends are so sparing of their sermons, that during the whole of Lent, which nevertheless they still seem to wish to observe, with the exception of one or two Sundays, they have not once preached to the people, not even on the day of the commemoration of Christ's death, or of his resurrection, or on this day. Sometimes, too, many of the parochial clergy so recite and administer the service, that the people have no more understanding of the mysteries of Christ, than if the Latin instead of the vulgar tongue were still in use. And when complaints respecting these shocking abuses of the church are laid by godly men before the rulers of the kingdom, they say it is the business of the bishops to remedy the evil. When they are laid before the bishops, those, namely, who have long since made a profession of the gospel, their reply is that they cannot rectify them without an act of parliament for that purpose. And though the great council of the nation is assembled every year, so many secular matters are forced upon their attention, that the cause of Christ can

61

find no room for admission. Then they commit the consideration of these matters to so many individuals, and those too of such discordant sentiments, that they cannot even be got together and assembled, much less come to any right and solid decision upon affairs of such importance. In which procrastinating of the cause of Christ the bishops, to whom the idleness and luxury of Antichrist is more agreeable than the cross of Christ, are aided by the activity of many noblemen, enriched by the possessions of the church, and who themselves consider that the present desolation of the churches will be more to their interest, than the godly reformation of them.

We must observe in addition to these evils, that not a few persons, laying aside all desire after true repentance, faith, good works, the communion and discipline of the church, do nothing but dispute and contend, and often very profanely, how they may seclude Christ our Saviour from our sacraments and holy assemblies, and confine him to his place in heaven. And these chiefly follow those teachers who dare to write and assert publicly, that it is a fanatical attempt to construct any system of ecclesiastical and penitential discipline, whereby those who have openly offended should be compelled to do penance, and, when that is performed, to be absolved of such offence, and receive absolution of the church for their particular sins. Thus they allow themselves to put such interpretations upon any part of God's word, however clear it may be, which their own wisdom, or even dislike, not to say hatred of those who teach more correctly, or perhaps both of these motives, may suggest.

I have written to you, most excellent Calvin, thus freely, that you may be more earnest in your prayers for these churches, and that, when you write to the Duke of Somerset, you may most seriously admonish him respecting this desolation and betrayal of the churches, which with very few exceptions are entrusted to those who neither know, nor care to know, anything about Christ. I request, moreover, that no-one, except Farel and Viret, read this letter; for you are aware of the inexpediency of these things being made public, and especially by our means. Redouble your prayers for the most serene king, who is making wonderful progress both in piety and learning. For you may easily perceive the danger in which he is placed, humanly speaking, when the papists are everywhere so furious, and when they see and know that the king is exerting all his power for the restoration of Christ's kingdom. But they see his elder sister most pertinaciously defend and maintain popery, either because her disposition leads her to do so, or because she places so much confidence in her cousin.* But indeed the coldness of our exertions in behalf of Christ's kingdom deserves these dangers and oppositions.

Thank the Lord with me, that he has in great measure relieved me from the diseases which had a second time attacked me most severely till the middle of March. For I am again able after a manner to perform my duty, though great weakness still remains in my legs, arms and hands, which I am not yet able to use in writing. My stomach too is easily put out of order, and my bowels are in an obstinate state. Pray ye the Lord for me, that, if possible, he may either deliver me from hence, or make me in some way useful to his church; yea, that he sanctify his name in me in whatever way seemeth him best. Farewell with all your friends, the worthy Farel, Viret, and your other associates of the same stamp.

* Mary's cousin was the Emperor Charles V.

4 Calvin to Cranmer, 1552

Translation from Parker Society, 'Original Letters relative to the English Reformation', ed. H. Robinson, ii (1847) pp. 711-14: letter cccxxxvii. No surviving manuscript; first published by Beza; Latin text in vol. 14 of Calvin's 'Opera' (1875: in the 'Corpus Reformatorum'): letter 1619.

Geneva [about April 1552?]

Most illustrious lord, you truly and wisely judge that in the present disturbed state of the church no more suitable remedy can be adopted than the assembling together of godly and discreet men, well disciplined in the school of Christ, who shall openly profess their agreement in the doctrines of religion. For we see by what various devices Satan is endeavouring to abolish the light of the Gospel, which, having arisen upon us through the wonderful goodness of God, is shining forth in every quarter. The hireling dogs of the pope are barking unceasingly, that the pure word of Christ may not be heard. Impiety is everywhere boiling forth and raging with such licentiousness, that religion is little better than an open mockery. Those who are not avowedly hostile to the truth indulge themselves nevertheless in a wantonness which, unless it be checked, will occasion to us sad confusion. Nor does this disease of foolish curiosity and intemperate audacity prevail only among the common people; but what is more disgraceful, it is becoming too rife even among the order of the clergy. It is too well known by what reveries Osiander* is deceiving himself, and fascinating

* Andreas Osiander (Hosemann) 1498-1552. Lutheran theologian who quarrelled with some points of Luther's interpretation of justification by faith alone. Cranmer had married his niece at Nuremberg in 1532: she survived the Archbishop.

certain other persons. The Lord, indeed, as he has been wont
to do from the beginning of the world, is able wonderfully,
and by means unknown to us, to preserve the truth from
being rent in pieces by the dissensions of man. Nevertheless
he would by no means have those persons inactive, whom he
himself has placed on the watch; since he has appointed them
his ministers, by whose aid he may purify sound doctrine in
the church from all corruption, and transmit it entire to
posterity. For yourself, most accomplished prelate, it is
especially necessary, in proportion to your more exalted
position, to bestow all your attention upon these matters, as
you do. And I do not say this, as though I considered it
needful to spur you on afresh, who are not only outrunning
us of your own free will, but are also of your own accord
urgent in exhorting others; but that I may encourage you by
my congratulations in so happy and excellent a course of
action.

We hear indeed that the Gospel is making favourable
progress in England. But I doubt not that you find it there
also to be the case, what Paul experienced in his time, that
when a door is opened to receive pure doctrine, there forthwith arise many adversaries. But though I am aware of the
number of champions you have at hand well qualified to
confute the lies of Satan, yet such is the wickedness of those
parties whose great business it is to create confusion, that the
diligence of good men in this respect can never be deemed
either excessive or superfluous. I know too, in the next place,
that your care is not confined to England alone, but that you
are at the same time regardful of the world at large. Then not
only is to be admired the generous disposition of the most
serene king, but also his rare piety in honouring with his
favour the godly design of holding an assembly of this kind,
and in offering a place of meeting within his realm. And I
wish it could be effected, that grave and learned men from
the principal churches might meet together at a place
appointed, and, after diligent consideration of each article of
faith, hand down to posterity a definite form of doctrine
according to their united opinion. But this also is to be
reckoned among the greatest evils of our time, that the
churches are so estranged from each other, that scarcely the
common intercourse of society has place among them; much

65

less that holy communion of the members of Christ, which all persons profess with their lips, though few sincerely honour it in their practice. But if the teachers conduct themselves with more coldness than they ought to do, the chief blame rests with sovereigns themselves, who either from being entangled in secular matters disregard the welfare of the church and all godliness; or, satisfied each of them with his own individual tranquillity, are not touched by any feeling of concern for others. Thus it is that, the members being scattered, the body of the church lies torn in pieces.

As far as I am concerned, if I can be of any service, I shall not shrink from crossing ten seas, if need be, for that object. If the rendering a helping hand to the kingdom of England were the only point at issue, that of itself would be a sufficient motive to me. But now, when the object sought after is an agreement of learned men, gravely considered and well framed according to the standard of scripture, by which churches that would otherwise be far separated from each other may be made to unite; I do not consider it right for me to shrink from any labours or difficulties. But I hope my want of ability will occasion me to be excused. I shall have sufficiently performed my duty, if I follow up with my prayers what shall be undertaken by others. Master Philip [Melanchthon] is too far off for letters to go backwards and forwards in a short time. Master Bullinger has probably replied to you already. I wish my efficiency corresponded to the ardour of my inclinations. However, what I declined to do at the beginning, the very difficulty of the case, of which you are sensible, compels me to attempt; that is, not to exhort you only, but implore you to persevere, until at least something be effected, if all things do not turn out according to your wish. Farewell, most accomplished and sincerely revered prelate. May the Lord continue to guide you by his Spirit, and give his blessing to your endeavours.

5 Calvin to Edward VI, 1551

Translation from Parker Society, 'Original Letters relative to the English Reformation', ed. H. Robinson, ii (1847) pp. 707-11: letter cccxxxvi. French text in Calvin, 'Opera', vol. 14 (1875): letter 1444; also in Jules Bonnet's edition of Calvin's letters (Paris, 1854) i 325-31.

Geneva [1 January 1551?]

Sire

If I had to make excuse to your Majesty for the liberty I have taken in dedicating to you these books* which I herewith present to you, I must have found an apologist to address you on my behalf. For my letters would be so far from possessing any influence for this purpose, that they would have required a new apology for themselves. In fact, as I should never have taken upon myself to address to you the commentaries which I have published in your name, so I should not presume to write to you now, were it not for the confidence I have already entertained that both my letter and commentaries would be favourably received. For since, regarding me as of the number of those who exert themselves in advancing the kingdom of the Son of God, you have not disdained to read what I had not expressly dedicated to your Majesty; I have thought that if in serving Jesus Christ, my master, I should equally bear testimony to the especial reverence and affection that I bear you, I could not fail to meet with a favourable and courteous reception.

What is more, Sire, as I feel assured that my letters will be received by you as I desire, I shall make no difficulty in

* Commentaries on Isaiah (taken to England in February).

praying and exhorting you in the name of him to whom you
yield all authority and power, to take courage in the pursuit
of what you have so well and happily begun, as well in your
own person as in the state of your realm. It is that the whole
may be consecrated to God, and to our good Saviour, who
has so dearly bought us. For with respect to the general
reformation, it is not yet so well established, as not to make it
desirable to carry it still farther; and in fact it would be very
difficult to cleanse at once so great a sink of superstition as
we find in the papacy. Its root is too deep, and has long since
extended too far, to come to the end of it so soon. But
difficult or tedious as it may be, such is the excellence of the
work, that one is never weary of the pursuit. I doubt not,
Sire, but that Satan is placing many hinderances in the way,
to retard and cool your zeal. A great portion of your subjects
are not aware of the good you are procuring them. The great,
who are elevated in point of rank, are oftentimes too apt to
consider the world, without any regard to God. And they
daily raise up to themselves new combats which they never
before thought of. Now I have good hope, Sire, that God has
endowed you with such magnanimity and firmness, that,
notwithstanding all this, you will not be wearied or
enfeebled. But the thing is in itself of such extreme importance, that it well deserves the exertion of all human power
to accomplish it. And even when one shall have come to the
end of it, there will yet remain some work to be done.

We see that in the time of good king Josiah, who had the
especial testimony of the Holy Spirit, that he had performed
every duty of an excellent prince in faith, zeal, and all
holiness, nevertheless the prophet Zephaniah shows that there
still remained some remnants of former superstitions even in
the city of Jerusalem. Thus, Sire, though you are most
laboriously engaged with your Council, you will never be able
entirely to eradicate all the evil which so well deserves to be
corrected. But this ought to be a great motive to animate and
encourage you, and even if you cannot effect all that would
be desirable, it is a very abundant consolation, when you see
that the exertion made by this good king is a service well-
pleasing to God; in such wise that the Holy Spirit magnifies
the reformation effected by him, as if there had been nothing
left to blame in it. Only then, Sire, aim at the mark which is

68

set before you in the example of this holy king, so that it may be testified of you that you have not only destroyed impieties which were repugnant to the honour and service of God, but also that you have abolished and razed to the foundations everything that tends only to the nourishment of superstition. For when God wishes to commend to the utmost those faithful princes who have restored and re-established the purity of his service, he especially adds, that they also broke down the high places, that the memory of the idolatrous worship might be destroyed.

It is true, Sire, that there are certain things indifferent which we may lawfully bear with. But we must always observe this rule, that there must be sobriety and moderation in ceremonies, so that the light of the Gospel be not obscured, as though we were still under the shadows of the law; and then, that there be nothing inconsistent with, and unconformable to, the order established by the Son of God, and that the whole may tend and conduce to the edification of the church. For God does not allow anyone to sport with his name, mingling frivolities among his holy and sacred ordinances. Now there are manifest abuses which are not to be endured; as, for instance, prayer for the dead, placing before God in our prayers the intercession of saints, and adding their names to his in taking an oath. I doubt not, Sire, but that you have been informed of these things. I implore you in the name of God to persevere, so that everything may be restored to its proper integrity.

There is another point, Sire, which ought to be especially regarded by you, namely, that the poor flocks be not destitute of pastors. Ignorance and barbarism have pressed so heavily in this accursed papacy, that it is not easy to obtain, at the first attempt, persons fit and qualified to discharge that office. However, the thing is well worth taking pains about; and let your ministers, Sire, keep their eye upon it, that the food of life may be afforded to the people, as it ought to be. Without that, all the holy and good ordinances you can make will avail but little to reform their hearts in good earnest.

In fine, forasmuch as schools are the seedplots of future pastors, it is quite necessary to keep them pure and unmixed with any weeds. I say this, Sire, because in your universities,

69

as they tell me, there are many young persons supported by exhibitions, who, instead of affording good hopes of being of service to the church, rather show symptoms of a desire to injure and overthrow it, not concealing the fact of their being opposed to the true religion. Wherefore, Sire, I again implore you in the name of God, that you be pleased to give some order upon this subject, so that the property which ought to be as it were sacred, be not converted to a profane use, and to the nourishment of venomous beasts, whose only desire it is to poison everything for the future. For by these means the Gospel will always be driven back by the schools, which ought to be as it were the pillars of it.

Meanwhile, Sire, all right-minded persons praise God, and feel themselves greatly obliged to you, for having graciously been pleased to grant churches to your subjects who speak the French and German languages, as far as respects the use of the sacraments and spiritual discipline. I hope that the license you have been pleased to afford them will have its effect. Nevertheless, Sire, I cannot refrain from again entreating you, knowing as I do how necessary it is, not only for the peace and satisfaction of the well-disposed, who desire to serve God and to live peaceably in obedience to you, but also to keep in order vagabond and dissolute persons, if they have retired into your realm.

I am well aware, Sire, that you have at your command persons of the most accurate information, who can inform you of these things by word of mouth far better than I can by writing; and also that in your Council you have persons endowed with wisdom and zeal to advance whatever may be expedient. I doubt not but that, among others, the Duke of Somerset will exert himself in the advancement of what he has been faithfully employed upon till now. But I believe, Sire, that all this will not hinder you from receiving with kindness whatever you know to have proceeded from the same source.

In fine, Sire, while I am fearful of having already wearied you by my excessive prolixity, I pray you that in this respect as well as others, you will be pleased to excuse and pardon me of your gracious kindness, to which I most humbly supplicate to be commended, having implored our good God and Father to maintain you in his holy protection, to defend

you by his Spirit, and to cause his name to be glorified by
you more and more.

6 Calvin to Edward VI, 1552

Translation from Parker Society, 'Original Letters relative to the English Reformation', ed. H. Robinson, ii (1847) pp. 714-15: letter cccxxxviii. French original in British Museum Harleian MSS; French text in Calvin, 'Opera', vol. 14 (1875): letter 1636, and in Bonnet, i 345-7.

[Geneva, 4 July 1552]

Sire

Much as I ought to fear being troublesome to your Majesty, and for this reason abstain from writing to you more frequently, I have nevertheless taken the liberty to send you a short exposition that I have made upon the 87th Psalm, in the hope that you would be pleased with it, and that the perusal may be very profitable to you. As I was expounding it one day in a sermon, the argument appeared to me so suitable to you that I was immediately induced to write out the whole, such as you will see it when it shall please your Majesty to devote a single hour of your time to that purpose. It is true that I treat the subject in general terms, without a personal address to yourself, but I have only had reference to you in writing it; and in effect, in appropriating it, as your prudence may dictate, to your own use, you will find it to contain a lesson and a doctrine very profitable to your Majesty.

You well know, Sire, what danger there is to kings and princes, lest the height to which they are elevated should dazzle their eyes, and amuse them here below, causing them to forget the kingdom of heaven; and I doubt not but that God has warned you of this danger that he might preserve you from it, and that you will guard against it a hundred

72

times better than those who experience it without being aware of it. Now in the Psalm before us is set forth the grandeur and dignity of the church, which ought in such wise to draw over to itself both great and small, that all the riches and honours of the world cannot hold them back, nor keep them from aiming at this object, namely to be enrolled among the people of God. It is a great thing to be a king, especially of such a country; yet I have no doubt but that you esteem it incomparably better to be a Christian. It is therefore an inestimable privilege that God has made you, Sire, a Christian king, to the end that you may act as his vicegerent in maintaining the kingdom of Jesus Christ in England. You see then, that in acknowledging this especial benefit, which you have received from his infinite goodness, you ought to be very zealous in employing all your powers to his honour and service, affording an example to your subjects to do homage to this great King to whom your Majesty is not ashamed to subject yourself in all humility and reverence under the spiritual sceptre of his Gospel. If you have hitherto so acted that we have wherewith to glorify God on your behalf, this psalm will serve at all times for your encouragement and support. Meanwhile, Sire, I entreat you that this brief writing may serve me as a protestation and testimony to your Majesty of the great desire I have to employ myself in doing more, when the means shall be afforded me.

Sire, after having most humbly commended myself to your grace, I implore our good God to fill you with the gifts of his Holy Spirit, to guide you in all wisdom and virtue, and to make you flourish and prosper to the glory of his name.

PART IV

1567: The London Separatist Congregation

Thomas Lever, Master of St John's College, Cambridge, in the reign of Edward, was in Strasbourg, Zürich and Geneva in the Marian period, and returned to England in February 1559, aged 38. In August 1559 he wrote to Henry Bullinger of Zürich, about the six-month period of his new life in England (1). 'When I returned to England [I saw] masses and all the follies and abominations of popery everywhere sanctioned by the authority of the laws, and the gospel nowhere to be met with': except 'in a congregation that remained in concealment during the whole time of persecution, and then not venturing forth beyond such private houses as were open to them'. This was 'a congregation of faithful persons concealed in London during the time of Mary, among whom the gospel was always preached, with the pure administration of the sacraments'. From November 1558 the congregation, though it was still in private houses, was not concealed. Indeed for nine months, according to Lever, the authorities 'connived at their frequent assembling in private houses'; and 'large numbers flocked to them'. 'And when the Lord's supper was administered among them no strangers were admitted, except such as were kept free from popery', or such as 'sought pardon and reconciliation in presence of the whole assembly': 'I have frequently been present on such occasions, and have seen many returning with tears, and many too in like manner with tears receiving such persons into communion; so that nothing could be more delightful than the mutual tears of all parties'. He concluded with a typical passage expressing the puritan mind and hope of the 1560s, based on St Paul's theme of the 'godly remnant': 'God will at *length give the victory to the little ones of the weak flock of Christ, against the powerful tyrants of the world.'*

But in September 1560 there was a royal Proclamation (2): the Queen *'commands on pain of imprisonment that no minister or other person make any conventicles or secret congregations either to read or to preach or to minister the sacraments or to use any manner of divine service'*. Everything must be done *'in open churches according to the order of the church of England'*; and persons arranging *'secret conventicles'* were to be imprisoned without bail until the next assizes.

This was not the end of the matter. Edmund Grindal, a Marian exile in Strasbourg and Frankfurt, and Bishop of London from 1559 to 1570, wrote to Bullinger in August 1566 that *'many of the people'* had it *'in contemplation to withdraw from us, and set up private meetings'* (3). Most of them *'have now returned to a better mind'*: or so the bishop then thought. I print here the text, as it was published in 1593, of a meeting in June 1567 between the ecclesiastical commissioners and the Lord Mayor, and seven laymen (none of them Marian exiles) who had *'severed yourselves from the society of other Christians'*, *'gathered together and made assemblies, using prayers and preachings and ministering the sacraments'*. There had been a gathering of about 100 people on the previous day in the Plumbers' Hall: hired ostensibly for a wedding reception. Fifteen had been imprisoned.

Grindal, then in his late forties, seems somewhat out of his depth: the establishment liberal faced with a genuine radicalism. He was personally ill at ease: *'I have said mass: I am sorry for it'*; *'you see me wear a cope or a surplice'* in St Paul's Cathedral — *'I had rather minister without these things, but for order's sake and obedience to the prince'*. A little old-hat, perhaps, in his dwelling on the Edwardian church: *'the whole state of the church reformed in King Edward's days, which was well reformed according to the word of God, yea, and many good men have shed their blood for the same'* — *'there be good men and good martyrs that did wear these things in King Edward's days'*: Ridley and Cranmer (Grindal's appeal to *'the order of charity'* is much like Cranmer); but this meant nothing to the Plumbers' Hall men — as it was to mean nothing to Milton. The Bishop's *main intellectual point had been made by Ridley in 1550. That is, Grindal's conviction that 'that which God commandeth may not be left undone' and 'that which God forbiddeth may not be done', there being an area of 'things which God neither commandeth nor forbiddeth', things 'indifferent', 'of the middle sort' — and here it lies 'in the prince's power to command for order's sake' (a quote from Bullinger strengthens the point). The clinching episcopal reproof — 'You are not obedient to the prince' tends to slide off into personalities ('Have we not a godly prince? Answer, is she evil?'). 'I have talked with many men, and yet I never saw any behave themselves so unreverently before magistrates': 'we like not the holding of it'. The most attractive of the examiners is the Lord Mayor, gamely bluffing his way through — 'I cannot talk with you in celestial matters, but I have a mother wit' — and telling a fuddy-duddy story about the fate of an alderman who goes out without his robe.*

The most talkative of the Plumbers' Hall men were William Nixon, the baker William White, John Smith and (especially) Robert Hawkins. Nixon refers to the 1550 Ridley—Hooper debate, and says that he does not so much condemn the Edwardians as wish positively to 'go forward to perfection'. William White, however, dismisses Cranmer's Liturgy as 'pieced and patched out of the popish portas', appealed to the example of Christ casting out the buyers and sellers from the Temple, and maintained that there is 'a great company of papists' in London 'whom you do allow to be preachers and ministers, and thrust out the godly'. John Smith, an especial friend of Coverdale (who lived till 1569), thanked God 'for reformation; and that is it we desire, according to God's word': 'we remembered that there was a congregation of us in this city in Queen Mary's days; and a congregation at Geneva, which used a book and order of preaching, ministering of the sacraments and discipline, most agreeable to the word of God; which book is allowed by that godly and well learned man, Master Calvin, and the preachers there; which book and order we now hold'. Robert Hawkins, with his quotes from Melanchthon and references to Foxe's 'Book of Martyrs (the 1563 'Acts and Monuments') (4), was the most vehement of the group: 'They will not join with you. I heard one of them say that he had rather be torn in a hundred

77

pieces than to communicate with you. We hold nothing, but that which is maintained by the word of God.' A favourite puritan quotation from Paul was 2 Corinthians 6: 'Be ye not unequally yoked together with unbelievers: for what fellowship hath righteousness with unrighteousness? And what communion hath light with darkness? And what concord hath Christ with Belial?' (Colet had been fond of the passage.) Hawkins uses it here to buttress his assertion: 'It cannot be proved, that the ceremonies of Antichrist, works of darkness, and the pope's canon law, may be clean to a true Christian.' It was as simple as that. 'Churches be necessary to keep our bodies from the rain, but surplices and copes be superstitious and idolatrous': 'It had been better we had never been born than to suffer God to be dishonoured and his word defaced for prince's pleasures' — kings have their rule 'not to decline neither to right hand nor to the left from the word of God'. This was the central point of the debate.
White: *We will be tried by the word of God, which shall judge us all at the last day.*
Dean Goodman: *But who will you have to be judge of the word of God?*
Hawkins: *Why, that was the saying of the papists in Queen Mary's time. . . .*
White: *We will be tried by the best reformed churches.*

The editor of the 1593 printing of this dialogue adds that 'to prison they all went, or most part of them. Such was the great charity of the bishops.' The whole thing is a cry of pain. And Grindal's troubles were not over. There was further crisis in the winter of that year of 1567 (5): 'Some London citizens of the lowest order, together with four or five ministers, remarkable neither for their judgement nor learning, have openly separated from us: and sometimes in private houses, sometimes in the fields and occasionally even in ships, they have held their meetings and administered the sacraments. Besides this, they have ordained ministers, elders and deacons after their own way, and have even excommunicated some who had seceded from their church.' (Thomas Lever they regarded as a semi-papist, and forbade members to hear his sermons: so much for all those tears!) Grindal called the congregation factio: a 'party' (6). 'The number of this sect is about 200: But consisting of more women than men.' The minister was Richard Fitz. Seventy-two members of this congregation were imprisoned in 1568: including over thirty women (and William White, John Smith and William Nixon) (7). Twenty-seven members of the Fitz congregation signed a petition in 1571 (8); eighteen were illiterate, making a mark only — fourteen of these were women; and altogether there were sixteen female subscribers. 'We, a poor congregation whom God hath separated from the churches of England, and from the mingled and false worshipping therein used, out of the which assemblies the Lord our only saviour hath called us, and still calleth, saying, Come out from among them, and separate yourselves from them, and touch no unclean thing, then I will receive you, and I will be your God.' A touching sense here of plain folk seeking a cleft in the grey heavens (9).

But what English separatism needed was a prophet: it found one in. the 1580s, in that troubled spirit Robert Browne.

1. 'Zurich Letters', ii 29.
2. Grindal, 'Remains' (Parker Society) p. 298.
3. 'Zurich Letters', i 168-9.
4. See William Haller, 'Foxe's Book of Martyrs and the Elect Nation' (1963).
5. 'Zurich Letters', i 201-2: Grindal to Bullinger, June 1568.
6. Ibid., Latin texts, p. 119.
7. Champlin Burrage, 'The Early English Dissenters', ii (1912) pp. 9-11.
8. Ibid., pp. 15-17.
9. I am reminded, strongly and not too irrelevantly, of what has been described as the most moving final stage direction in the English language: 'They pick up their clothes and weary, bleeding, drugged and drunk, climb the rope ladder into the blazing light': Joe Orton, 'What the Butler Saw' (1969). Orton was murdered in 1967.

7 Account of the Examination of Certain Londoners before the Ecclesiastical Commissioners, 20 June 1567

'The true report of our examination and conference (as near as we can tell to remembrance) had the 20 day of June, Anno 1567, before the Lord Mayor, the Bishop of London, the Dean of Westminster, master Watts, and other Commissioners'. Reprinted 1593 by Robert Waldegrave (Edinburgh?) in: 'A Part of a Register: Containing sundry memorable matters, written by divers godly and learned in our time, which stand for and desire the reformation of our church in discipline and ceremonies according to the pure word of God and the law of our land'. This collection contained forty-one items, of which this is no. 4. Reprinted (with some errors of transcription) by William Nicholson in 1843: Grindal, 'Remains' (Parker Society) pp. 201-16.

When we were come in, we did our obeisance, and they bade us come near, and the bishop's registrar called us by name: John Smith, William Nixon, William White, James Ireland, Robert Hawkins, Thomas Boweland, and Richard Morecraft. The bishop said, Is here all? One answered, No, there are ten or eleven in the Compter.*
Bishop Grindal:- I know that well enough.
The bishop said unto the mayor: My lord, will you begin?
The mayor said unto him, I pray you begin.
Bishop Grindal:- Well then, here you have showed yourselves disorderly, not only in absenting yourselves from your parish churches, and the assemblies of other Christians in this commonwealth, which do quietly obey the Queen's proceedings, and serve God in such good order, as the Queen's grace, and the rest having authority and wisdom, have set forth and

* The Counter prison.

established by Act of Parliament; but also you have gathered together, and made assemblies, using prayers and preachings, yea, and ministering the sacraments among yourselves; and thus you gather together many times, yea, and no longer ago than yesterday, you were together to the number of an hundred; whereof there were about fourteen or fifteen of you sent to prison. And our being here is to will you to leave off, or else you shall see the Queen's letter, and the council's hand at it. (Then he opened it, and showed it us, but would not read it. The effect of it, he said, was to move us to be conformable by gentleness, or else at the first we should lose our freedom of the city, and abide that would follow.) And moreover, you have hired the Plumbers' Hall, saying, you would have it for a wedding. Where is Boweland?

Thomas Boweland:- Here I am, and if it please you.

Bishop Grindal:- Did you hire the hall?

One of us said: 'In that we said to the sheriffs, it was for a wedding, we did it to save the woman harmless, and at her request.'

Bishop Grindal:- Yea, but you must not lie; that is against the admonition of the apostle: 'Let every man speak the truth to his neighbour.' And herein you have put the poor woman to great blame, and enough to lose her office: this is against the order of charity.

Here we would have answered, but he would not suffer us, but said, You shall be heard anon.

Bishop Grindal:- But to the matter. In this severing yourselves from the society of other Christians, you condemn not only us, but also the whole state of the church reformed in King Edward's days, which was well reformed according to the word of God, yea, and many good men have shed their blood for the same, which your doings condemn.

Robert Hawkins:- We condemn them not, in that we stand to the truth of God's word.

But he would not suffer us to answer to it.

Bishop Grindal:- But have you not the gospel truly preached, and the sacraments ministered accordingly, and good order kept, although we differ from other churches in ceremonies, and in indifferent things, which lie in the prince's power to command for order's sake? How say you, Smith? You seem to be the ancientest of them; answer you.

John Smith:- Indeed, my lord, we thank God for reformation; and that is it we desire, according to God's word. (And there he stayed.)

William White:- I beseech you, let me answer.

Bishop Grindal:- Nay, William White, hold your peace, you shall be heard anon.

William Nixon:- I beseech you, let me answer a word or two.

Bishop Grindal:- Nixon, you are a busy fellow. I know your words; you are full of talk. I know from whence you came.

Robert Hawkins:- I would be glad to answer.

Bishop Grindal:- Smith shall answer. Answer you, Smith.

John Smith:- Indeed, as you said even now, for preaching and ministering the sacraments, so long as we might have the word freely preached, and the sacraments administered without the preferring of idolatrous gear above it, we never assembled together in houses. But when it came to this point, that all our preachers were displaced by your law, that would not subscribe to your apparel and your law, so that we could not hear none of them in any church by the space of seven or eight weeks, except Father Coverdale, of whom we have a good opinion; and yet (God knoweth) the man was so fearful, that he durst not be known unto us where he preached, though we sought it at his house. And then were we troubled and commanded to your courts from day to day, for not coming to our parish churches. Then we bethought us what were best to do; and we remembered that there was a congregation of us in this city in Queen Mary's days; and a congregation at Geneva, which used a book and order of preaching, ministering of the sacraments and discipline, most agreeable to the word of God; which book is allowed by that godly and well learned man, Master Calvin, and the preachers there; which book and order we now hold. And if you can reprove this book, or anything that we hold, by the word of God, we will yield to you, and do open penance at Paul's Cross; if not, we will stand to it by the grace of God.

Bishop Grindal:- This is no answer.

William White:- You may be answered, if you will give leave.

Bishop Grindal: White, you shall speak anon; let the elder speak first.

John Smith:- Would you have me go back from the better, to such churches that I had as leave go to mass as go to them,

82

they are so evil-favouredly used; as the parish church where I dwell is one. He is a very papist that is there, and yet he hath another place too.

Dean Goodman:- Lo, he counteth the service and reformation in King Edward's days as evil as the mass.

Bishop Grindal:- Lo, because he knoweth one that is evil, he findeth fault with all. But you may go to other places, as at St. Laurence.

William White:- You say we find fault with all, for one papist. If it were well tried, there should a great company of papists be found in this city, whom you do allow to be preachers and ministers, and thrust out the godly for your pleasure's sake.

... *Roper*:- I know one that in Queen Mary's time did persecute God's saints, and brought them forth to Bishop Bonner, and now he is minister allowed of you, and never made recantation.

Bishop Grindal:- Can you accuse any of them of false doctrine, and show us of it?

William Nixon:- Yea, that I can, and he is even now in this house that I can accuse of false doctrine. Let him come forth and answer his doctrine that he preached upon the 10th of John. (And so I looked back upon Bedel, and Bedel hung down his head, and the bishop looked upon the dean, and one looked upon another.)

Dean Goodman:- You would take away the authority of the prince, and liberty of a Christian man.

Bishop Grindal:- Yea, and therefore you suffer justly.

Robert Hawkins:- But it lieth not in the authority of the prince, and liberty of a Christian man, to use and to defend that appertaining to papistry and idolatry, and the pope's canon law, as we may plainly see in the 7th of Deuteronomy, and other places of the Scriptures.

Dean Goodman:- When do you hear us maintain such things in our preachings?

Robert Hawkins:- Though you do it not in your preachings, yet you do it in your deeds and by your laws.

William White:- The prophet saith, That the foolish say not with their mouths, there is no God, but in their hearts; their doings are corrupt and vain.

Robert Hawkins:- You preach Christ to be priest and prophet, but you preach him not to be king, neither will you suffer him to reign with the sceptre of his word in his church alone; but the pope's canon law and the will of the prince must have the first place, and be preferred before the word and ordinance of Christ.

Dean Goodman:- You speak unreverently here of the prince before the magistrates: you were not bidden to speak; you might hold your peace.

Robert Hawkins:- You will suffer us to make our purgation, seeing that you persecute us.

Bishop Grindal:- What is so preferred?

William Nixon:- Why, that which is upon your head and upon your back, your copes and your surplices, and your laws and ministers; because you will suffer none to preach nor minister, except he wear them, or subscribe to them.

Bishop Grindal:- No, how say you to Sampson and Lever, and other: do not they preach?

William White:- Though they preach, you have deprived them and forbidden them, and the law standeth in force against them still, howsoever you suffer them now. And for what purpose you will not suffer other, whom you cannot reprove by the word of God, I know not.

Bishop Grindal:- They will not be preachers, nor meddle with you.

William White:- Your doings is the cause.

Robert Hawkins:- They will not join with you. I heard one of them say that he had rather be torn in a hundred pieces than to communicate with you. We hold nothing, nor allow any thing but that which is maintained by the word of God; the which word, saith Esau, 'shall come forth of Sion, and give sentence among the heathen, and reform the multitude'. And Christ saith, 'The word that I have spoken, shall judge in the last day', when both the prince, and you, and we, shall stand naked before the judgement-seat of Christ. And if you can prove that we hold not the truth, show it and we will leave it.

John Smith:- And if you cannot, we pray you, let us not be thus used.

Dean Goodman:- You are not obedient to the authority of the prince.

William White:- Yes, that we are; for we resist not, but suffer that the authority layeth upon us.

Bishop Grindal:- So do thieves suffer that the law layeth

84

upon them.

William White:- What a comparison is this? They suffer for evil doing, and you punish us for seeking to serve God according to his word.

William Nixon:- Both the prince and we must be ruled by the word of God, as we read in the first book of Kings, the 12th chapter, that the king should teach only the word of God.

Bishop Grindal:- What, that the king should teach the word of God? Lie not.

William Nixon:- It is that both king and people should obey the word of God, or else they shall perish.

Bishop Grindal:- Indeed it is true in effect, that the prince should and must obey the word of God only. But I will show you this consisteth in three points. The first is, that which God commandeth may not be left undone. The second is, that which God forbideth may not be done. And the third consisteth in things which God neither commandeth nor forbideth, and they are of the middle sort, and are things indifferent. And such things princes have authority to order, or to command.

Prisoners:- Prove that, said one. Where find you that? said another.

Bishop Grindal:- I have talked with many men, and yet I never saw any behave themselves so unreverently before magistrates.

William White:- I beseech you, let me speak one word or two.

Bishop Grindal:- White, stay a little, you shall speak anon.

Robert Hawkins:- Kings have their rule and commandment in the 17th of Deuteronomy, not to decline neither to the right hand nor to the left from the word of God, howsoever you make your distinction.

John Smith:- How can you prove that indifferent, which is abominable?

Bishop Grindal:- What: you mean of our caps and tippets, which, you say, came from Rome?

James Ireland:- It belongeth to the papists; therefore throw it to them.

Canon Watts:- You would have us use nothing that the papists used; then should we use no churches, as the papists have used.

Robert Hawkins: - Churches be necessary to keep our bodies

85

from the rain, but surplices and copes be superstitious and idolatrous.

William White:- Christ did cast out the buyers and sellers in the temple and their ware, and yet the temple was not overthrown for all that.

Bishop Grindal:- Things not forbidden of God may be used for order and obedience' sake: you shall hear the mind and judgement of a well learned man, whom you like of, namely, Master Bullinger; (then he read out of a book this in effect): 'It is not yet proved that these garments had their first origin from Rome. And though we use them not here in our ministry, yet we may lawfully use them as things that have not yet been removed away.' These be Bullinger's words: therefore we desire and wish you to leave off and be conformable.

John Smith:- What if I can show you Bullinger against Bullinger in this thing?

Bishop Grindal:- I think not, Smith.

John Smith:- Yes, that I can.

Bishop Grindal:- Well, all reformed churches do differ in rites and ceremonies, and we agree with all reformed churches in substance of doctrine.

Canon Watts:- Yea, that we do.

Robert Hawkins:- Yea, but we should follow the trueth and best way. Christ saith, 'Go you forth and preach to all nations, baptizing them in the name of the Father, of the Son and of the Holy Ghost, teaching them to observe all things that I have commanded you'. But you have brought the gospel and sacraments into bondage to the ceremonies of anti-Christ, and you defend idolatry and papistry. There is no ordinance of Christ but you have mingled your own inventions withal. How say you to godfathers and godmothers in baptism?

Canon Watts:- O! a wise reason.

Bishop Grindal:- How say you to the church of Geneva? They communicate with wafer cakes, which you are so much against.

William Nixon:- Yea but they do not compel to receive so, and with none other.

Bishop Grindal:- Yes, in their parish churches.

William White:- The English congregation did minister with loaf bread there.

Bishop Grindal:- Because they were of another language.

William White:- It is good to follow the best example: but we must follow them as they follow Christ.

Dean Goodman:- All the learned men in Europe are against you.

Canon Watts:- Ye will believe no man.

John Smith:- Yes, we reverence the learned in Geneva, or in other places wheresoever they be; yet we build not on them our faith and religion.

Bishop Grindal:- Will you be judged by the learned in Geneva? They are against you.

Robert Hawkins:- We will be judged by the word of God, which shall judge us all at the last day, therefore sufficient to judge now. But how can they be against us, seeing they know not of our doings; also, holding of the same truth as they do (except they will be against the truth and against themselves)?

Bishop Grindal:- Here is the letter that came from Geneva, and they are against you and your doings and going from us, in these words. Then he turned to this place, which is: That against the prince's and bishops' wills they should exercise their office, we do so much the more tremble at, because of these reasons, which of themselves are plain enough, albeit we do not utter them. Mark how that he saith he doth 'tremble' at your cause.

Robert Hawkins:- Why, the place is against you: for they do tremble at the prince's case and yours, because that you by such extremities, should drive us against our wills to that which of itself is plain enough, albeit they would not utter them.

Then the bishop wrong himself and said: See, ye enter into judgement against us.

Robert Hawkins:- Nay we judge not; but we know the letter well enough, for we have it in our houses; it maketh nothing against us.

Bishop Grindal:- We grant it doeth not. But yet they count this apparel indifferent, and not impious and wicked in their own nature; and therefore they counsel the preachers not to give over their function or flocks for these things.

Robert Hawkins:- But it followeth in the same letter that if

87

they should be 'compelled to allow it by subscription' or silence, that they should give over their ministry.

William Nixon:- Let us answer to your first question.

Bishop Grindal:- Say on, Nixon.

William Nixon:- We do not refuse you for preaching the word of God, but because you have tied the ceremonies of Antichrist to it, and set them before it, so that no man may preach or minister the sacraments without them. For before you compelled them by law, all was quiet.

Bishop Grindal:- See how you be against indifferent things, which may be borne withal for order and obedience sake.

Mayor:- Well, good people, I would you would wisely consider these things, and be obedient to the Queen's Majesty's good laws, as I and other of the Queen's subjects are, that you may live quietly and have liberty, as my lord here and masters have said. And as for my part, I would you were at your heart's ease, and I am sorry that you are troubled; but I am an officer under my prince, and therefore blame not me. I cannot talk learnedly with you in celestial matters, but I have a mother wit, and I will persuade the best that I can. The Queen hath not established these garments and things for any holiness' sake or religion, but only for a civil order and comeliness; because she would have the ministers known from other men, as the aldermen are known by their tippets, and the judges by their red gowns, and sometimes they wear coifs; and likewise lords' servants are known by their badges. I will tell you an example. There was an alderman within this year, that went in the street, and a boisterous fellow met him and went between him and the wall and put him towards the channel, and some that were about him said to him, 'Knowest thou not what thou doest? He is an alderman.' And he said, 'I knew him not, he might have worn his tippet.' Even so, when the ministers began to be despised, the Queen's grace did ordain this priests' apparel, but the people cannot be content and like it. Now what may the papists say? Some of them goeth to the court, whispering, saying that you cannot be content that the Queen should command anything in the church, not so much a cap or a tippet, whereupon the Queen may have occasion to say: 'Will they not be content that I should rule in the Church, I will restore that my forefathers have followed.' And therefore, masters, take heed.

88

Robert Hawkins:- I beseech you to let me answer your lord-ship before all your wisdoms. Philip Melancthon, writing upon the 14th chapter to the Romans, hath these words: 'When the opinion of holiness, of merit, or necessity, is put unto things indifferent, then they darken the light of the gospel, and ought by all means to be taken away.'

Bishop Grindal:- It is not commanded of necessity in the church, or of heavenly things.

Robert Hawkins:- You have made it a matter of necessity in the church, and that many a poor man doeth feel.

William Nixon:- Even so, my lord, as you do say that the alderman is known by his gown and tippet, even so by this apparel that these men do now wear were the papist mass-priests known from other men.

Dean Goodman:- What a great matter you make of it.

Robert Hawkins:- The apostle Paul would not be like the false apostles in anything, and therefore you have the apostle against you.

Bishop Grindal:- There be good men and good martyrs that did wear these things in King Edward's days; do you condemn them?

William Nixon:- We condemn them not: we would go forward to perfection, for we have had the gospel a long time amongst us. And the best of them that did maintain it did recant for it at their death, as did Ridley, sometime bishop of London, and Doctor Taylor. Ridley did acknowledge his fault to Hooper, and when they would have put on the same apparel upon him, he said, they were abominable and too fond for a vice in a play.

Bishop Grindal:- Where find you that in the book of letters of the martyrs?

Robert Hawkins:- It may be showed in the book of the monuments of the church, that many which were burned in Queen Mary's time died for standing against popery, as we now do.

Bishop Grindal:- I have said mass: I am sorry for it.

James Ireland:- But you go like one of the mass-priests still.

Bishop Grindal:- You see me wear a cope or a surplice in Paul's. I had rather minister without these things, but for order's sake and obedience to the prince.

. . . *Roper:*- Master Crowley saith he could not be persuaded to minister in those conjuring garments of popery.

William Nixon:- Your garments are accursed as they are used.

Bishop Grindal: Where do you find them forbidden in the scriptures?

William Nixon:- Where is the mass forbidden in the scriptures?

Bishop Grindal:- The mass is forbidden in the scripture, as thus: It was thought to be meritorious, it did take away free justification, it was made an idol; and idolatry is forbidden in the scriptures.

Robert Hawkins:- By the same argument I will prove your garments forbidden in the scriptures.

Bishop Grindal:- Let us hear.

Robert Hawkins:- I do prove it out of the 138th psalm, and out of the 10th chapter of the second to the Corinthians. In the psalm the prophet saith that 'God hath exalted his word according to his great name'. The epistle saith that 'the weapons of his warfare are not carnal things, but things mighty in God, to overthrow strongholds and imaginations of men, and to bring into captivity all imagination that exalteth itself against the knowledge of God'. But you have brought the word of God into captivity to the pope's garments and his canon law: and therefore they are idols, and forbidden in the scripture. 'Whatsoever' saith Christ 'is highly esteemed before men, is abominable before God': Luke xvi. 15.

William White:- Reprove that we hold by the scripture, and prove that you would have us come to by the scripture and we will yield to you. And if you cannot, why do you persecute us?

Bishop Grindal:- You are not obedient to the prince.

Dean Goodman:- Doth not St Peter say, 'Be obedient to all manner ordinance of man?'

William White:- Yea, as they obey God.

William Nixon:- This hath always been the doings of popish bishops. When as they cannot maintain their doings by the scriptures, nor overcome them, then they make the mayor and the aldermen their servants and butchers, to punish them that they cannot overcome by scripture. But I trust that you, my lord, seeing you have heard and seen it, will take good advisement.

Mayor:- Good lord, how unreverently do you speak here before my lords and us in comparing so.

Bishop Grindal:- Have we not a godly prince? Answer, is she evil?

William White:- What a question is that, the fruits do show.

Thomas Bowland:- No: but the servants of God are persecuted under her.

Bishop Grindal:- Yea, go to; mark this, my lord. (Reader, see Luke xix. 7.)

Robert Hawkins:- Why, this question the prophet may answer in the psalm: 'How can they have understanding that work iniquity, spoiling my people, and that extol vanity?'

Dean Goodman:- Do we hold any heresy? Do we deny any article of the faith, as 'I believe in God the Father Almighty, and in Jesus Christ his Son?' Do we deny any of these articles? Do we maintain purgatory or pilgrimages? No, we hold the reformation that was in King Edward's days.

One of us said, No more did the papists in words.

William White:- You build much of King Edward's time. A very learned man as any is in the realm, (I thing you cannot reprove him,) writeth these words of King Edward's time: 'I will let pass to speak of King Henry's time, but come to King Edward's time, which was the best time of reformation: all was driven to a prescript order of service, pieced and patched out of the popish portas of matins, mass, and evensong; so that when the minister had done his service, he thought his duty done. To be short, there might no discipline be brought into the church.'

William Nixon:- Yet they never came so far as ye have done, to make a law that none should preach or minister without these garments.

Bishop Grindal:- Saint Paul saith, that 'to the clean all things are clean': that which other have evilly abused we may use well, as not receiving them for any such purpose of holiness or religion.

William Nixon:- Howsoever you received them we now see you have exalted them, and brought the word of God in subjection and slavery to them.

Robert Hawkins:- It cannot be proved, that the ceremonies of Antichrist, works of darkness, and the pope's canon law, may be clean to a true Christian; for the apostle saith, 'There is no fellowship between Christ and Belial, light and darkness.' 2 Cor. vi. 14, 15.

91

Dean Goodman:- All have learned are against you.

William White:- I delivered a book to Justice Harris, which is the Order that we hold. Reprove the same by the word of God, and we will leave it and give over.

Bishop Grindal:- We cannot reprove it. But to gather together disorderly, to trouble the common quiet of the realm against the prince's will, we like not the holding of it.

William White:- We hold nothing that is not warranted by the word of God.

Robert Hawkins:- Why, that which we do, we do it by the commandment of God: we have the example of the first and apostolic church for our warrant, as in the 16th to the Romans, v. 17. 'I beseech you, brethren, mark them that cause division, and give occasion of evil, contrary to the doctrine which ye have learned, and avoid them.'

Dean Goodman:- Yea, but the manner which you hold is unorderly, and against the authority of the prince.

Robert Hawkins:- Why, the truth of God is a truth, wheresoever it be holden, or whosoever doth hold it, except ye will make it subject to places and persons, and to the authority of the prince. It had been better we had never been born than to suffer God to be dishonoured, and his word defaced for prince's pleasures.

Bishop Grindal:- All the learned are against you, will you be tried by them?

William White:- We will be tried by the word of God, which shall judge us all at the last day.

Dean Goodman:- But who will you have to be judge of the word of God?

Robert Hawkins:- Why, that was the saying of the papists in Queen Mary's time. I have heard it, when the truth was defended by the word of God, then they would say, 'Who shall judge of the word of God? The Catholic church must be judge.'

William White:- We will be tried by the best reformed churches. The Church of Scotland hath the word truly preached, the sacraments truly ministered, and discipline according to the word of God; and these be the notes by which the true church is known.

Dean Goodman:- We have a gracious prince.

We said, 'God preserve her grace and the council.'

92

William White:- I would have answered to a thing that has been said: That which God commandeth to be done, that ought to be done; and that which God forbiddeth to be done, that ought not to be done.

Bishop Grindal:- Yea, I said so.

William White:- Now it is manifest, that that which God commandeth to be done is left undone, and that which God forbiddeth to be done, that is done by authority. As this: God saith, 'Six days thou shalt labour and do all that thou hast to do: but the seventh day is the sabbath of the Lord thy God, etc.' But the prince's law saith, Thou shalt not labour seven days but shall keep the popish holy-days. And again Christ commandeth Discipline in the 18th of Matthew, and it was put in practice of the apostles: but in the Church of England there is none but the pope's Discipline. And Christ saith in the last chapter of the Revelation: 'If any man shall add to the prophecy of this book, God shall add unto him all the plagues that are written in this book; and if any man shall diminish, God shall take his part out of this book of life, and from the holy city.' How will you avoid this?

Bishop Grindal:- Why, is it not a good work to hear a good sermon or two upon the holy-days?

William White:- We are not against that. But what shall we do when the sermons be done? If we do any work, we are commanded to your courts.

Bishop Grindal:- You may be well occupied in serving of God.

William White:- So we are all occupied, when we are at our work that God commandeth. The sabbath is appointed to rest in, and to serve God. Exodus, xx. 10.

Dean Goodman:- Why then you would have no sermons nor prayer all the week.

William White:- Who is not against that? I think him to be no Christian that does not pray and serve God every day before he begin his work.

William Nixon:- You can suffer bear-baiting and bowling and other games to be used on the sabbath day, and on your holy-days, and no trouble for it.

Dean Goodman:- Then you would have no holy sabbath days, because the papists used them.

William White:- We ought to do that God commandeth.

Dean Goodman:- Why then you must not use the Lord's prayer, because the papists used it, and many other prayers, because the priests used them; you would have nothing but the word of God. Is all the psalms you sing the word of God? They were turned into metre.

William White:- Is every word that is preached in a good sermon the word of God?

Dean Goodman:- No.

William White:- But every word and thing agreeing with the word of God, is as the word of God.

Bishop Grindal:- There has been no heretic but that he hath challenged the word to defend him.

William White:- What is that to us? If you know any heresy we hold, charge us with it.

Bishop Grindal:- Holy-days may be well used.

Robert Hawkins:- Well, master Hooper saith in his commentary upon the commandments that holy-days are the leaven of Antichrist.

[Printer's note (1593):]

Here they entered into a question of ministering the sacrament in a private house. And further is not come into my hands.

PART V

1583: Autobiography of Robert Browne

Robert Browne was born in Rutland about 1553, and went up to Corpus Christi College, Cambridge, in 1570, at the height of the turmoils arising from the case of Thomas Cartwright, the ejected Lady Margaret Professor of Divinity. He took his B.A. in 1573. He begins his autobiography at this point, and there is little to be said before allowing the reader to get on with it.

Some notes on the Cambridge men he mentions as 'forward in religion' may be in order. Richard Greenham was a sizar of Pembroke; B.A. 1564; Fellow 1567; rector of Dry Drayton (near Cambridge) 1570-1 died 1594. Greenham petitioned in favour of Cartwright in Cambridge in 1570. Thomas Robardes went up to Queens' as a sizar in 1562, became a Fellow of Corpus in 1569, petitioned in Ca.nbridge against Whitgift's new statutes in May 1572 (in which year he was bursar of Corpus) and died in 1596. Robert Harrison (1548-85) started as an undergraduate at St John's (1564), moved to Corpus in time to take his B.A. from that college in 1568, and his M.A. in 1572. He was a schoolmaster in the 1570s. William Harrison, born about 1550, went up to St John's in 1567, and became a Fellow in 1573; ordained in 1575, he was to be a vicar in Lincolnshire until his death in 1633. Philip Browne (apparently no relation of Robert) went up to Clare in 1571. And Robert Barker matriculated from Corpus in 1573. Browne himself was not ordained until 1591: upon which he held the living of Achurch, Northamptonshire, until his death in 1633. Among Browne's Cambridge enemies, a character in the autobiography, was Richard Bancroft (1544-1610), who entered Christ's in 1563, took his

95

B.A. in 1567, took his M.A. from Jesus in 1570, and was ordained in 1574.

In 1582 Browne published his eighteen-page pamphlet 'A Treatise of Reformation without tarrying for any' (1); the first of three books he was to print that year. It was a defence of the emigration of his Norwich congregation to Zeeland, a reply to those who marvelled that we 'leave our country'. 'Therefore doth Paul call that part of church government which is to separate the ungodly, the power of our Lord Jesus Christ.' The emigration was in 1581. And very moving, near the end of my extract, is the sentence: 'But last of all was this thing decided: Whether God did call them to leave their country, and to depart out of England.' This looks forward, of course, to the American experience. 'They all agreed and were fully persuaded that the Lord did call them out of England': thus William Bradford, Governor of Plymouth Plantation, when looking back on the story of the godly 'in the north parts' (between Lincoln and Sheffield) at the beginning of the reign of James I (2). 'They shook off the yoke of anti-christian bondage, and, as the Lord's free people, joined themselves (by a covenant of the Lord) into a church estate'; 'by a joint consent they resolved to go into the Low Countries' — where it seemed 'they were come into a new world'. After about a dozen years, when at Leyden (1619) 'they began to incline to this conclusion: of removal to some other place'. And 'the place they had thoughts of was some of those vast and unpeopled countries of America'. Once the thirty-five Leyden pilgrims neared America, 'if they looked behind them, there was a mighty ocean'. If in front — 'what could they see but a hideous and desolate wilderness'. (Hooker had pointed out that puritanism might work well in a wilderness.) This tying of the American to the Tudor experience was very common in the seventeenth-century historians of New England. Thomas Shepard of Emmanuel, describing how the Lord carried 'His poor despised people' to 'a wilderness', referred back to 'Queen Mary's bloody days', and the 'case of conscience frequently put and oft resolved' then, 'whether it was lawful to flee out of the land': put by, Shepard states, John Bradford, John Philpot and Peter Martyr (3). Edward Johnson (born in Canterbury, Kent) wrote in 1654 that

96

Christ 'begins with our English nation'. The crucial date was 1628: when it was obvious which was 'the place where the Lord will create a new heaven and new earth in, new churches and a new commonwealth together' (4). Cotton Mather, summing things up at the end of the seventeenth century, invoked John Foxe, John Wyclif, Cranmer and Bucer. And summarised one strand of the sixteenth-century experience: 'the first age was the golden age; to return unto that will make a man a protestant, and, I may add, a puritan' (5).

A final minor point. We know from the Elizabethan play 'Thomas More' that the Brownists had a sectarian habit of cutting their hair very short. The original roundheads. Werner Stark has drawn attention to the connection of hair length and sectarianism, in his 'Sectarian Religion' (1967) (6). Stark does not include much direct material on Tudor England — he is especially good on Russia and the United States; but his invigorating, important, and often witty book should be recommended here.

1. Printed in Peel and Carlson (eds), 'Writings of Robert Harrison and Robert Browne', pp. 152-70. The quotation I give is on p. 169.

2. Bradford, 'Of Plymouth Plantation', finished 1650: extracts in Miller and Johnson (eds), 'The Puritans' (Harper Torchbook ed.) i 91-117.

3. Shepard, 'Defence of the Answer' (London, 1648). Extracts in Miller and Johnson: quotation on p. 119.

4. Johnson, 'Wonder-Working Providence of Sion's Saviour'. Miller and Johnson: quotations pp. 144, 145.

5. Mather, 'Magnalia Christi Americana' (written in English) (London, 1702). Miller and Johnson: quotations pp. 165, 167.

6. P. 141 (being vol. ii of his 'The Sociology of Religion: a study of Christendom').

8 Extracts from Browne's 'True and short Declaration'

From 'A true and short Declaration, both of the joining together of certain persons, and also of the lamentable breach and division which fell amongst them': written 1583; copy in Lambeth Palace Library (shelf mark: 1590. 14/Z) is catalogued as published in 1590, but no date of publication is in fact given.

For a version of this text as printed, with the original spelling and punctuation, see A. Peel and L. H. Carlson (eds), 'The Writings of Robert Harrison and Robert Browne' (1953) pp. 397-429: being volume II in the series 'Elizabethan Nonconformist Texts'.

My selection gives about 40 per cent of the full work.

There were certain persons in England: of which some were brought up in schools and in the University of Cambridge, and some in families and households, as is the manner of that country.

Some of these which had lived and studied in Cambridge were there known and counted forward in religion, and others also, both there and in the country, were more careful and zealous than their froward enemies could suffer. They in Cambridge were scattered from thence, some to one trade of life and some to another: as Robert Browne, Robert Harrison, William Harrison, Philip Browne, and Robert Barker.

Some of these applied themselves to teach scholars; to which labour Robert Browne also gave himself for the space of three years. He, having a special care to teach religion with other learning, did thereby keep his scholars in such awe and good order, as all the townsmen where he taught gave him witness. Yet the world being so corrupt as it is, and the times so perilous, he greatly misliked the wants and defaults which he saw everywhere, and marked plainly that, without redress, neither the parents could long rejoice in their children, nor the children profit so much in religion as that their other studies and learning might be blessed thereby.

Hereupon he fell into great care and was sore grieved while he long considered many things amiss; and the cause of all to be the woeful and lamentable state of the church. Wherefore he laboured much to know his duty in such things, and because the church of God is his kingdom, and his name especially is thereby magnified, he wholly bent himself to search and find out the matters of the church: as how it was to be guided and ordered, and what abuses there were in the ecclesiastical government then used. These things he had long before debated in himself and with others, and suffered also some trouble about them at Cambridge; yet now, on fresh, he set his mind on these things, and night and day did consult with himself and others about them lest he should be ignorant or mistake any of those matters. Whatsoever things he found belonging to the church, and to his calling as a member of the church, he did put it in practice. For even little children are of the church and kingdom of God; yea, of such, saith Christ, does his kingdom consist; and therefore both in his school he laboured that the kingdom of God might appear, and also in those of the town with whom he kept company.

So by word and practice he tried out all things, that he might be stayed* both in judgement and counsel, and also in enterprising matters as his duty should lead him. But this his dealing got him much envy of the preacher and some others where he taught, and much trouble also where he broke his mind more plainly unto them. Presently, after this, he was discharged of his school by the grudge of his enemies.

Yet he taught still, with great goodwill and favour of the townsmen, till such time as the plague increased in the town and he was sent for away by his friends. Therefore because his scholars, though never so well plied† and profited by him, were notwithstanding either flitting away upon such occasions, or too hastily sent to the University, or because of their misguiding there, to some occupations, he thought that

* Supported.   † Employed.

99

the fruit of his labour was too much uncertain and took counsel if by some better way he might profit the church. Then he gave warning to the town and departed to come home as his father willed him. So might he have lived with his father, being a man of some countenance, and have wanted nothing, if he had been so disposed; but his care as always before, so then especially, being set on the church of God, he asked leave of his father and took his journey to Cambridge, from whence a few years before he had departed.

He there had dealing with Master Greenham of Drayton, who of all others he heard say was most forward, and thought that with him, and by him, he should have some stay of his care and hope of his purpose. Wherefore, as those which in old time were called the prophets and children of the prophets and lived together because of corruptions among others, so he came unto him. He was suffered, as others also in his house, to speak of that part of scripture which was used to be read after meals. And although he said that without leave and special word from the bishop, he was to suffer none to teach openly in his parish, yet without any such leave he suffered Robert Browne.

Notwithstanding, when Robert Browne saw that the bishop's feet were too much set in every place, and that spiritual infection too much spread even to the best reformed places, he took that occasion which the Lord did first give him for redress; and when certain in Cambridge had both moved him, and also with consent of the Mayor and Vice-chancellor called him, to preach among them, he dealt in this manner.

He first considered the state of Cambridge, how the church of God was planted therein. For he judged that the church was to call and receive him if he should be there chosen and appointed to preach. Then he did think on this, who should be chiefest or have charge before others to look to such matters. For the bishops take upon them the chiefty: but to be called and authorized by them, he thought it unlawful. And why he was of this mind, he had these and suchlike warrants: namely, they should be chiefest which partake unto us the chiefest graces and use of their callings. And that doeth Christ, as it is written: of his fullness have all we received and grace for grace (John 1.16). And to him hath

100

God made all things subject, saith Paul (Ephesians 1.22), even under his feet, and hath appointed him over all things, to be the head of the church which is his body, even the fullness of him which filleth all in all things. Now next under Christ is not the bishop of the diocese, by whom so many mischiefs are wrought, neither anyone which hath but single authority, but first they that have their authority together: as first the church, which Christ also teacheth where he saith: if he will not vouchsafe to hear them tell it unto the church, and if he refuse to bear the church also, let him be unto thee as an heathen man and a publican (Matthew 18.17). Therefore is the church called the pillar and ground of truth (1 Timothy 3.15) and the voice of the whole people, guided by the elders and forwardest, is said to be the voice of God. And that 149th Psalm doth show this great honour which is to all the saints. Therefore the meetings together of many churches, also of every whole church and of the elders therein, is above the apostle, above the prophet, the evangelist, the pastor, the teacher, and every particular elder. For the joining and partaking of many churches together, and of the authority which many have, must needs be greater and more weighty than the authority of any single person. And this also meant Paul where he saith (1 Corinthians 2.22) we are yours, and you are Christ's, and Christ is God's. So that the apostle is inferior to the church, and the church is inferior to Christ, and Christ concerning his manhood and office in the church is inferior to God.

This he judged, not only to be against the wickedness of the bishops, but also against their whole power and authority. For if the authority of the church and of the forwardest brethren or elders therein be above the bishops, how should it not follow but that the bishops may be commanded, accused and charged by the church, yea also discharged and separated as is their desert? But now, because of their popish power and canon laws they have lift up their authority more high than the church can take accounts of them, and not only by force do thrust out and trouble whom they list, but also reign as lords and dukes in their dioceses, their authority must needs be usurped. For the apostles did give accounts to the church of all their doings, as we read in the Acts 11.4, Acts 15.2,3, and Romans 15.31. But these being got above the apostles will sit in the throne of Christ and as Christ is not inferior to the church no more will they be. For Christ has chosen us, saith the scripture, and not we him (John 15.16) and therefore he is the greater than us all. And seeing the church cannot choose the bishops nor those hirelings whom the bishops thrust upon them, therefore they also will be greater than the church, and with whom then do they compare themselves in degree but with Christ, and so make themselves antichrists? Nay, they presume further than Christ, which would not thrust his apostles upon any congregation, nor suffer them to take charge of any which did not willingly receive them (Luke 10.10). But these do force upon the people everywhere and in sundry places against their wills not only ministers unknown but also such as are known to be blind buzzards, wicked fellows and idle shepherds. Likewise Christ hath all rule in his hand; as it is written that we are complete in him which is the head of all principality and power (Colossians 2). And he cannot sin nor offend the law of God, nor be accused by the same, for so the scripture testifieth, that none could reprove him of sin, though he offered himself to them to accuse him if they could (John 8). And he is that high priest, as again it is written (Hebrews 7) which is holy, harmless, undefiled, separate from sinners, and made higher than the heavens. How high then do they lift themselves which will rule alone as lords over the flock, though the word hath said it shall not be so? (Luke 22.26; 1 Peter 5.3). Which will be rabbis, doctors and reverend fathers, though we have but one doctor and father, as saith that high doctor Christ (Matthew 23); which also take upon them not as servants in the house as was Moses (Hebrews 3) but have sent after him that is son and heir in his own house saying they will not have him to reign over them (Luke 19.14). For they have refused his government and chosen their own popish discipline instead thereof.

This appeareth because they enter and take on them their offices in popish-wise and as that law prescribeth them, and also do misguide the people by that popish tyranny. For who knoweth not but that they watch for the living or bishopric when it shall fall and then sue and pay well for the same if they obtain it. So are they ravenous and wicked persons, as

102

saith the scripture (Zechariah 3). They are makeshifts and troublers, seeing they rule rather because they seek their own advantage, or glory, or mischievous purpose, than the welfare and benefit of the church. Yea, they all look to their own way, as saith the Prophet (Isaiah 56.11) every one for his advantage and for his own purpose. Who knoweth not also but that they which are not duly received and called to guide, and that by due consent and agreement, they are either antichrists in the church or tyrants in the commonwealth, because they usurp in the church or commonwealth. Such are they of whom Paul speaketh (2 Corinthians 11.20) that the Corinthians did suffer them too much. For they did suffer if a man brought them into bondage, if a man devoured, if a man took, if a man exalted himself, if a man smote them on the face. For indeed the people do suffer the bishops, though they take from them their liberty of choosing good pastors and refusing evil, yea, they suffer themselves to be robbed and beaten by those spiritual courts, they suffer the great untowardness and wickedness of the bishops to be coloured and hidden by their outward brag and countenance, as by their pomp, authority, titles, and power, and sometimes by their fair flattering sermons and pleasings. For they rule by three sorts of laws, as by the civil, the canon, the common law, which are three kingdoms unto them, or as the pope's triple crown, and by pretending* the fourth law, which is the word of God, they overrule too too much; they spare not to come upon the people with force and power, and they care not to bridle them with new and yearly injunctions, and also with the old laws and penalties of the court of Rome.

While Robert Browne thought these things in himself he moved the matter divers times unto others.

Some did gainsay, and those of the forwardest, affirming that the bishops' authority is tolerable, and he might take licence and authority of them. Others of them said they would not counsel nor meddle for another man's conscience in that matter, but they themselves judged that the bishops preached the word of God and therefore ought not lightly to be rejected. Also they said that seeing they had the word and the sacraments, they must needs have withal the church and

* Claiming.

people of God, and seeing this was under the government of the bishops, and by means of them, they could not wholly condemn the bishops, but rather judge them faulty in some part.

Then did Robert Browne again and again discuss these matters, as he had often before, as whether the bishops could be said to preach the word of God and minister the sacraments or no. For if that were true, then also might they call and place ministers, and seeing they themselves did minister so great a thing as is the word and the sacraments, they might also minister their help in other things not so great. Therefore to know whether they preached the word of God he searched and found by the scriptures what it is to preach the word: namely to do the Lord's message, as it is written in Jeremiah 23.22, in teaching the people those things whereby they might turn them from their evil ways and from the wickedness of their inventions. Therefore except they have a due message, they cannot preach the word of message. For I sent them not, saith the Lord, in that place, nor commanded them, therefore they bring no profit unto this people. Again, except they preach those things first for which first and chiefly they were sent, namely whatsoever is to reclaim the people, first from some especial wickedness wherein they sin, and so from all other defaults, they cannot be said to preach the word. Therefore seeing the bishops' calling and authority was showed before for to be unlawful, and seeing also they call not the people from the chiefest abominations, which are the cause of the rest, but rather wilfully and with cruelty do lead them in the same, as will afterward appear, they cannot preach the word of God. For to make a sermon is not to preach the word of God, no, nor yet to make a true sermon. For the servant that telleth a true tale hath not done his master's message nor the errand for which he was sent, except he tell and speak that for the which his master sent him. Therefore though the bishops teach the people, and give them laws, and make many injunctions, yea, though they be laws of Christ, yet if they abuse the obedience of the people to hold and follow with some laws of Christ their own laws especially, what are they but antichrists? And how can they then but only in name and in show preach the laws of Christ?

For example, while they pervert the law of God in this
104

they cannot be said to preach his law, namely whereas God commandeth to plant and to build his church by gathering the worthy and refusing the unworthy (Matthew 10.11; Acts 19.9; Ezra 6.21) they hook by their contrary laws both papists and careless worldlings, as crooked trees, to build the Lord's sanctuary, and force the wretched to their worshippings and service, as if dogs might be thrust upon God for sweet sacrifice. Proud forcing is meek building with them, and devotion compelled is their right religion.

Thus herein they pollute the Lord's sanctuary and wrest his law, how much more by a thousand more abominations, whereof afterward we briefly touch some. For by them do they feed themselves and the people with the bread of uncleanness instead of the pure word of God. They make it ready with the dung that cometh of man, even with their traditions, tolerations, and falsifyings.

And if the Pharisees made the word of God of none effect or authority by their traditions, as it is written (Mark 7.13), much more these. They by their corbans* or offering of gifts gave occasion to children to dishonour their parents. And these by their spiritual courts, by their fond excommunications, dispensations, absolutions etc, yea, by their taking of bribes and fees, do let so many loose to all misrule and filthiness. They taught the gold of the temple to be greater than the temple which sanctifieth the gold (Matthew 23.17). And these teach that to sin is damnable, but to pollute the Lord's spiritual temple by mingling the clean and wretched together, which is the cause of all sin, is no matter of damnation; forsooth, it is a thing tolerable, because they cannot remedy it. They taught that the offering on the altar was greater than the altar, though it sanctify the offering. And these teach that to want the sacraments, that is lamentable, but to want the kingdom of God, and the visible shew of his rule in his church, whereby the sacrament is sanctified — that they make no matter.

If then for such doctrine they were called blind guides and fools by Christ himself (Matthew 23.16,17); yea, and though they sat in Moses' seat that is at first were lawfully called to teach the people, yet the people were charged by Christ to let

* Offerings.

alone such blind guides and not be guided by them (Matthew 15.14): how much more should we let these blind guides alone which never were lawfully called, and also sit in the seat of antichrist. For what is the seat of antichrist but that popish government and lordship in the communion of such Roman offices and horrible abuses by them? And while they sit in the temple of God (2 Thessalonians 2.4) and exalt their traditions above God's, what are they but Antichrists? Do they then preach the Lord's word of message, or is not his word a fire and like an hammer that breaketh the stone (Jeremiah 23.29)? But all their preaching cannot break and bring men from any smaller or greater disorders which wicked church laws or church prelates command them.

Thus was he settled not to seek any approving or authorizing of the bishops. But because he knew the trouble that would follow if he so proceeded, he sought means of quietness so much as was lawful; and for dealing with the bishops he was of this judgement, that men may now deal with them as before they might with the pharisees: that is, so far as we neither sin against God nor give offence to men. Therefore if Christ did his father's will when he sat in the midst of the doctors, hearing them and asking them questions (Luke 2.46) and if Paul did his duty when he sat down in the synagogue, as it were offering himself and seeking leave to speak to the people (Acts 13.14), if he also did lawfully apply himself to their ceremonies (Acts 21.26), then thus far also is there meddling with the bishops, to try and prove them, or to be tried of them as we see the like did fall out in Christ, also to yield to their power, so that wherein we yield it be not against the truth, and we do not establish it, as we know Paul did to the power of the priests, of the pharisees, and of the chief of the synagogue. Therefore he thought it lawful first to be tried of the bishops, then also to suffer their power, though it were unlawful, if in anything it did not hinder the truth. But to be authorized of them, to be sworn, to subscribe, to be ordained and to receive their licensing, he utterly misliked and kept himself clear in those matters.

Howbeit, the bishop's seals were gotten him by his brother, which he both refused before the officers, and being written for him would not pay for them, and also being afterward paid for by his brother, he lost one and burnt

106

another in the fire, and another being sent him to Cambridge he kept it by him till in his trouble it was delivered to a justice of the peace, and so from him, as is supposed, to the Bishop of Norwich.*

Yet lest his dealing on this matter should encourage others to deal in worse manner, he openly preached against the calling and authorizing of preachers by bishops and spoke it often also openly in Cambridge, that he taught among them, not as caring for, or leaning upon, the bishops' authority, but only to satisfy his duty and conscience. And this his duty he said was, first to discharge his message before God, and deserve no reproof of them, and then also either to find them worthy, or else, if they refused such reformation as the Lord did now call for, to leave them, as his duty did bind him. For he did not take charge of them; as he often gave them warning, and also did often show the cause, namely for that he saw the parishes in such spiritual bondage that whosoever would take charge of them must also come into that bondage with them.

Therefore he, finding the parishes too much addicted and pliable to that lamentable state, he judged that the kingdom of God was not to be begun by whole parishes, but rather of the worthiest, were they never so few. For it is as a grain of mustard seed saith Christ, at the first (Matthew 13), and as a little leaven hid in three pecks of meal. So he, having tried about half a year both by open preaching and by daily exhortation in sundry houses, that either by bondage of the bishop in that diocese, or of the colleges, or of wicked ministers and readers of service, or by the proneness of the parishes to like of that bondage, no redress could be waited for, he knew that the Lord had appointed him there to be occupied only to try and prepare him to a further and more effectual message, and to be a witness of that woeful state of Cambridge, whereinto those wicked prelates and doctors of divinity have brought it. This he foresaw before he preached among them, and therefore, when they gathered him a stipend and would have had him take charge, he refused, and did both send back the money they would have given him, and also gave them warning of his departure. So he continued

* The Bishop of Norwich from 1575 to 1584 was Edmund Freke.

preaching a while till he fell sore sick. And in his sickness, while he ceased his labour, he was forbidden to preach by a letter shown him from the Council. For indeed he had dealt boldly in his duty, and provoked the enemies. The bishop's officer, named Bancroft, did read the letter before him; but he, nothing moved, therewith did answer that if he had taken charge in that place he would no whit less cease preaching for that; but as he was he took not on him, he said, though the letter were not, to preach there any longer.

Of Robert Browne coming to Norwich and how the company there joined together

After these things, when he was recovered of his sickness, and had gotten his strength, he took counsel still and had no rest, what he might do for the name and kingdom of God. He often complained of these evil days and with many tears sought where to find the righteous, which glorified God, with whom he might live and rejoice together that they put away abominations.

While he thus was careful, and besought the Lord to show him more comfort of his kingdom and church than he saw in Cambridge, he remembered some in Norfolk whom he heard say were very forward. Therefore he examined the matter and thought it his duty to take his voyage to them. First, because he considered that if there were not only faults but also open and abominable wickedness in any parish or company, and they would not or could not redress them, but were held in bondage by antichristian power, as were those parishes in Cambridge by the bishops; then every true Christian was to leave such parishes, and to seek the church of God wheresoever. For where open wickedness is incurable and popish prelates do reign upholding the same, there is not the church and kingdom of God: as it is written (2 Chronicles 15.4), for a long season Israel hath been without the true God, and without priest to teach, and without law. So that though there be a name of priests, and of preaching, and of God amongst any, yet if there be set over them idle shepherds, popish prelates, and hireling preachers worse than they, that uphold antichristian abominations, there God does not reign in his kingdom, neither are they his church, neither is there his word of message. For no man can serve two

108

contrary masters, saith Christ (Matthew 6), neither can they be the Lord's people without his staff of beauty and bands (Zechariah 11.7): that is, without the Lord's government. For his covenant is disannulled, as it followeth in the 10th verse. Now his government and sceptre cannot be there, where much open wickedness is incurable. For if open wickedness must needs be suffered, it is suffered in those who are without; as Paul saith, what have I to do to judge those which are without? (1 Corinthians 5.12.)

And again he saith even of these latter times, that men shall be lovers of themselves, covetous, boasters, proud, cursed speakers, disobedient to parents, unthankful, unholy, without natural affection, truce breakers, false accusers, intemperate, fierce, despisers of them which are good, traitors, heady, high minded, lovers of pleasure more than lovers of God, having a show of godliness but having denied the power thereof. From such we must turn away as Paul warneth (2 Timothy 3.5); that is, we must count them none of the church, and leave them, whether in all these or some of them they be openly so faulty as that they be incurable.

Also if any be forced by laws, penalties and persecution, as in those parishes, to join with any such persons, either in the sacraments or in the service and worship of God, they ought utterly to forsake them, and avoid such wickedness. For the abomination is set up. Antichrist is got into his throne, and who ought to abide it. Yet who ought not to seek from sea to sea and from land to land, as it is written (Amos 8.12), to have the word and the sacraments better ministered and his service and worship in better manner.

So while he thought on these things, and was purposed to try also in Norfolk the forwardness of the people, it fell out that Robert Harrison, one whom he partly was acquainted with before, came to Cambridge. What was his purpose in coming and how he thought to have entered the ministry and did use some means to that end it is needless to rehearse. Only this I show, that he seemed to be very careful in that matter and though he leaned too much upon men for that matter, as upon Master Greenham, Master Robardes and others and was careful amiss for the bishop's authorizing yet his mind and purpose might be judged to be good, and no otherwise but well did Robert Browne judge of him. When he

109

had talked with Robert Browne, and showed him the matter whereabout he went, he received this answer at his hands, that it was unlawful to use either Master Greenham's help or any man's else for the bishops' authorizing. So he showed him how before he had dealt concerning the bishop, and was now so far from seeking licence, ordaining or authorizing at his hands, that though he never had them, yet for that he knew of them, he abhorred such trash and pollutions as the marks and poison of antichrist. Notwithstanding he said that if his conscience led him to deal as before he had dealt, he would do for him what he might, for he had before requested his help.

But Robert Harrison, either changing his mind or disappointed of his purpose, returned to Norwich, whither also a short time after Robert Browne took his journey. He came to Robert Harrison's house, who then was master in the hospital at Norwich. He there finding room enough, and Robert Harrison willing enough that he should abide with him, agreed for his board and kept in his house. They often had talk together, of the lamentable abuses, disorders and sins which now reign everywhere. At the first they agreed well together, but yet so as that in some things Robert Harrison doubted; notwithstanding he came on more and more, and at last wholly yielded to the truth, when he saw it began to prevail and prosper.

The order agreed on for the guiding and establishing of the company in all godliness and suchlike

This doctrine before being showed to the company, and openly preached among them, many did agree thereto; and though much trouble and persecution did follow, yet some did cleave fast to the truth; but some fell away from, when trial by pursuits, losses, and imprisonments came, and further increased; then Robert Barker, Nicholas Woedowes, Tatsel, Bond and some others forsook us also, and held back and were afraid at the first.

There was a day appointed and an order taken for redress of the former abuses, and for cleaving to the Lord in greater obedience: so a covenant was made and their mutual consent was given to hold together. There were certain chief points proved unto them by the scriptures, all which being parti-

110

cularly rehearsed unto them with exhortation, they agreed
upon them and pronounced their agreement to each thing
particularly, saying, to this we give our consent. First therefore they gave their consent to join themselves to the Lord in
one covenant and fellowship together, and to keep and seek
agreement under his laws and government, and therefore did
utterly flee and avoid suchlike disorders and wickedness as
was mentioned before. Further they agreed of those which
should teach them and watch for the salvation of their
souls, whom they allowed and did choose as able and meet
for that charge. For they had sufficient trial and testimony
thereof by that which they heard and saw by them, and had
received of others. So they prayed for their watchfulness and
diligence, and promised their obedience.

Likewise an order was agreed on for their meetings
together, for their exercises therein, as for prayer, thanksgiving, reading of the scriptures, for exhortation and edifying,
either by all men which had the gift, or by those which had a
special charge before others. And for the lawfulness of
putting forth questions to learn the truth, as if anything
seemed doubtful and hard, to require some to show it more
plainly or for any to show it himself and to cause the rest to
understand it. Further for noting out any special matter of
edifying at the meeting, or for talking severally thereon with
some particulars, if none did require public audience, or if no
weightier and more necessary matter were handled of others.
Again it was agreed that any might protest, appeal, complain,
exhort, dispute, reprove, etc, as he had occasion, but yet in
due order, which was then also declared. Also that all should
further the kingdom of God in themselves, and especially in
their charge and household, if they had any, or in their
friends and companions and whosoever was worthy. Furthermore they particularly agreed of the manner how to watch to
disorders, and reform abuses; and for assembling the
company; for teaching privately, and for warning and
rebuking both privately and openly; for appointing public
humbling in more rare judgements, and public thanksgiving in
stranger blessings; for gathering and testifying voices in
debating matters and propounding them in the name of the
rest that agree; for an order of choosing teachers, guides and
relievers, when they want, for separating clean from unclean,

111

for receiving any into the fellowship, for presenting the daily success of the church, and the wants thereof, for seeking to other churches to have their help, being better reformed, or to bring them to reformation; for taking an order that none contend openly, nor persecute, nor trouble disorderly, nor bring false doctrine nor evil cause after once or twice warning or rebuke.

Thus all things were handled, set in order, and agreed on to the comfort of all, and so the matter wrought and prospered by the good hand of God. But last of all was this thing determined: Whether God did call them to leave their country, and to depart out of England.

Some had decreed it to be gone into Scotland, and by writing, sending, and riding to and fro did labour in the matter and seemed to be jealous lest their counsel should not take place. But Robert Browne, being then held as prisoner at London, did send down his answer by writing to the contrary. For he judged that it was against duty (and so wrote unto them) if they first should agree to go into Scotland when as yet they had not sifted whether they were to leave England. Also he sent unto them that they were to do that good in England which possibly they might do before their departure, and that they ought not to remove before they had yet further testified the truth, and the Lord had with strong hand delivered them from thence. And rather indeed would he have it to be a deliverance by the Lord, than a cowardly fleeing of their own devising. Further he gave them his reasons why Scotland could not be meet for them, seeing it framed itself in those matters to please England too much. We knew also that we could not there be suffered, either because some corruption should come upon us from their parishes, which we ought to avoid, or because we there should have great trouble wrought us from England, as if we kept still in England. So when some were better advised they changed their minds for going into Scotland. Notwithstanding again they would be gone into Jersey or Guernsey and had the consent as they said of divers others that thought it meet they should learn the state of those countries. Robert Browne said he was not against their going to that purpose. But yet he told them there was no such haste to be gone out of England and that further delay and deliberation should be

112

had in that matter.

But at last, when divers of them were again imprisoned, and the rest in great trouble and bondage out of prison, they all agreed and were fully persuaded that the Lord did call them out of England.

PART VI

1572: John Field

Dr Patrick Collinson, a former research pupil of Sir John Neale, has drawn attention to John Field: in his massively comprehensive 1957 London Ph.D. thesis, 'The Puritan Classical Movement in the Reign of Elizabeth I'; his lively 1961 article on 'John Field and Elizabethan Puritanism' (1); and his 1967 'The Elizabethan Puritan Movement' (based on the unpublished thesis). What I have biographically to say can be no more than a summary of Collinson.

Field, born about 1545, was a Londoner, who went to Christ Church, Oxford, in the early 1560s: 'the puritanism of Elizabethan Oxford has been persistently underestimated'. He was ordained by Grindal at Lambeth Palace in 1566; and became a preacher at the church of Holy Trinity, in the Minories, without Aldgate. The Minories church was a royal peculiar, exempt from the Bishop's jurisdiction, the ministers and preachers thereof being appointed and supported by the parishioners. Thomas Wilcox, curate of All Hallows, Honey Lane, also preached at the Minories. So, until his death in 1569, did Miles Coverdale, who was born one year after Cranmer, and may be considered the senior of English protestant thinkers — another link between Elizabethan puritanism and the early Reformation. Field then became curate of the nearby parish of St Giles, Cripplegate. Collinson emphasises the role of the 'godly laity' in London in the late 1560s, and the importance of the regularly paid puritan parish clergy: within a year after Elizabeth's accession some of these clergy were meeting in 'exercises' or 'conferences'; by 1566 they met every morning. The earliest puritan manifesto, Robert Crowley's 'Brief Discourse against the

115

outward Apparel and ministering Garments of the popish Church' (1566), was based on material collected from the London ministers (2).

Then came the 1571 subscription crisis, described by Field at the beginning of 'View of popish Abuses'. Parliament ended on 29 May 1571. 'Immediately after', says Field, 'Ministers of God's holy word and sacraments were called before' the ecclesiastical commissioners. This was in fact a special examination of certain marked men: including Thomas Lever and John Field. They were asked to subscribe to three articles: concerning the Prayer Book, that 'all and every the contents therein be such as are not repugnant to the word of God'; that the vestments and attire prescribed by law for the clergy were 'not wicked or against the word of God but tolerable, and being commended for order and obedience sake are to be used'; and that the Thirty-nine Articles, or at least those of them concerning 'the true christian faith and the doctrine of the sacraments', contain 'true and godly doctrine'. Those who refused, says Field, 'were unbrotherly and uncharitably intreated, and from their office and places removed'. Field had proposed a qualified acceptance to Edwin Sandys, now Bishop of London; the godly would not wear the surplice, but would not condemn those who did (a curiously Cranmerian idea). This was refused, and early in 1572 Field was suspended, and reduced, like the layman Robert Browne, to schoolteaching. 'I sigh and sob daily unto God that I may have a lawful entrance to teach the flock of Christ. . . . And I await when the Lord will give me a place, a flock, a people to teach. I study for it and employ my whole travail unto it; and nothing is more grievous unto me than that, through the over-much tyrrany of those that should be encouragers, I am compelled instead to teach children, so that I cannot employ myself wholly unto that which I am bent most earnestly' (2).

In March 1572, Field and Wilcox began work on their 'joint manifesto', and later in the year the two works were published together, under the editorship of Field: the 'Admonition to Parliament' and the 'View of Popish Abuses': 'Two treatises ye have here ensuing without partiality or blind affection'.

Wilcox's 'Admonition (4)' is confident in its cliquishness:

116

God 'hath, by us, revealed unto you at this present the sincerity and simplicity of his gospel'. However, 'they' 'slanderously charge poor men (whom they have made poor) with grievous faults, calling them puritans, worse than the donatists'. The imperative is clear: 'if God's word were precisely followed'; 'that nothing be done in this or any other thing, but that which you have the express warrant of God's word for'. It was a basic conviction of the puritan mind that 'it is not enough to take pains in taking away evil, but also to be occupied in placing good in the stead thereof'. Thus the debate is not merely about the 'abandoning all popish remnants both in ceremonies and regiment' but also about the 'placing in God's church those things only which the Lord himself in his word commandeth'. 'Either must we have a right ministry of God, and a right government of His church, according to the scriptures set up (both of which we lack) or else there can be no true religion.' So Wilcox sets out 'a true platform of a church reformed': the reader is to look at it, and consider 'the great unlikeness betwixt it and this our English church'. 'The outward marks whereby a true christian church is known are: preaching of the word purely, ministering of the sacraments sincerely, and ecclesiastical discipline, which consisteth in admonition and correction of faults severely.' We must have in mind the 'primitive church' — 'in the old church', 'in the old time'. Then, 'every pastor had his flock, and every flock his shepherd'; there were preachers, not 'bare readers'; and the clergy were elected 'by the common consent of the whole church'. Look at 'the best reformed churches throughout Christendom': 'Is a reformation good for France? and can it be evil for England? Is discipline meet for Scotland? And is it unprofitable for this realm? Surely God hath set these examples before your eyes to encourage you to go forward to a thorough and speedy reformation. You may not do as heretofore you have done, patch or piece, nay rather go backward, and never labour or contend to perfection. But altogether remove whole anti-Christ, both head, body and branch, and perfectly plant that purity of the word, that simplicity of the sacraments, and severity of discipline, which Christ hath commanded and commended to His church.' Thus, in England, 'the whole regiment of the church' should be committed to 'ministers,

117

seniors and deacons'; there must be 'equality of ministers'; and 'in every congregation a lawful and godly seignory'. The clerics in the Church of England are not 'proved, elected, called or ordained' according to God's word. The church still contains too many 'popish mass-mongers, men for all seasons' (5). The 'Admonition' develops into an attack on archbishops, bishops and the whole hierarchy of ecclesiastical dignitaries: 'that proud generation whose kingdom must down, hold they never so hard, because their tyrannous lordship cannot stand with Christ's kingdom', their authority being 'forbidden by Christ'. All this put into effect, Christ will be 'more sincerely and purely, according to his revealed will, served than heretofore he hath been, or yet at this present is'. 'Christ being restored into his kingdom to rule in the same by the sceptre of his word.'

Field's 'View of Popish Abuses' repeats many of Wilcox's points. Vestments 'can no authority by the word of God, with any pretence of order and obedience, command them, nor make them in any wise tolerable; but, by circumstances, they are wicked and against the word of God'. (Exactly the same as John Hooper in 1550.) Prayer in the Church of England was a matter of formality, 'not of any prick of conscience, or piercing of the heart'. Prayer should 'touch the heart'; in the primitive church 'ministers were not tied to any form of prayers invented by man, but as the spirit moved them, so they poured forth hearty supplications to the Lord'. (We remember that Calvin's ultimate defence of his exposition of election and reprobation was that he felt it in his heart to be true.)

The short section on the Thirty-nine Articles is often ignored. Field objected to praying 'that all men may be saved', and said that the Articles need 'a godly interpretation in a point or two, which are either too sparely or too darkly set down'. Cartwright's 'Second Admonition', later in 1572, complained of the phrase in Article XVI, 'after we have received the Holy Ghost, we may depart from grace given'. This seemed to go against the Calvinist interpretation of Christian 'securitas': it 'speaketh very dangerously of falling from grace, which is to be reformed, because it too much inclineth to their error' — the error of Augustine's British adversary Pelagius, by whose ideas, according to Cartwright,

118

many bishops had been seduced (they were also unsound on Eucharistic theology) (6). At about this time, Field and Wilcox were drawing up a 'Confession of Faith', which runs to eighteen pages as printed in 1593 (7). Election and reprobation come in on page four, and not, as in the Thirty-nine Articles, halfway through (in fact the Articles never specifically mention reprobation).

Field begins his 'View' with an attack on the imperfections of the Prayer Book. There are fourteen points here. Then (points 15-17) he condemns the prelates and their jurisdiction, and the covetousness which dominates ecclesiastical patronage (shades of Colet's 1512 sermon in St Paul's). He makes short of the Archbishop's Court of Faculties, and other church courts. And launches into a stinging section on clerical apparel: while being aware, as Wilcox was, that the debate did not end there — 'Neither is the controversy between 'them' and 'us' as they would bear the world in hand — as for a cap, a tippet, or a surplice — but for great matters concerning a true ministry and regiment of the church according to the word.' What is different from the rather sober Wilcox is the style. Field places himself here in a tradition of earthy English invective which dates back to Tyndale and looks forward to the exhilarating part iv of Hobbes's Leviathan, 'Of the Kingdom of Darkness'. Field was not Marprelate, for he died in March 1588: the first Marprelate Tract appeared in October. But a comparison of Field and Marprelate, in the works I print in this book, will surely convince the reader of a continuity in the techniques of abuse. The puritan old guard disliked Field's work; as they were to disapprove of Marprelate.

Shortly after their joint volume appeared, Field and Wilcox were sentenced to a year in prison by the Lord Mayor and aldermen of London. When released, Bishop Sandys recommended that they be banned from the City: where the people 'resort unto them as in popery they were wont to run on pilgrimage' (8). But they stayed: and in 1581 Field became lecturer at St Mary Aldermary, until he was suspended in 1585. By that time Field had become the most effective organiser of the 'presbyterian advance', the 'effectual practising of the ecclesiastical discipline', which became a deliberate design, at any rate in London, by 1584.

Field was also collecting material relevant for the puritan propagandists of the 1580s: he had earlier been one of John Foxe's assistants in the collection and printing of documentary material. He also was an expert at influencing parliamentary elections, and attempting to enlarge the number of 'godly gentry' in the House of Commons. Though he was depressed by 1587: 'seeing we cannot compass these things by suit nor dispute, it is the multitude and people that must bring the discipline to pass which we desire' (9). (The thing which Hooker feared in the chapter I print later.)

John Field was really the great puritan impresario. It was therefore perhaps not entirely inappropriate that one of his seven children, Nat, born in 1587, was to be kidnapped and become a boy player in the Burbage company, and later a playwright. John, of course, was a great enemy of the theatre, as he reveals in the 'View'. The story gives the historian the same satisfaction he finds in the career of John Knox's sons, Eleazor and Nathaniel, who became strongly anglican Fellows of St John's College, Cambridge.

1. In 'Elizabethan Government and Society: essays presented to Neale', ed. S. T. Bindoff, J. Hurstfield, C. H. Williams (1961).

2. A copy of this book was displayed in the exhibition on 'Elizabethan Puritanism' held at Lambeth Palace Library in 1967. Dr Collinson wrote the notes to this exhibition.

3. Quoted by Collinson, Neale essays, p. 133.

4. Printed in Frere and Douglas (eds), 'Puritan Manifestoes', pp. 8-19.

5. P. 9. As we would say, vicars of Bray. Robert Bolt, in finding a title for his Thomas More play, picked the phrase *omnium horarum homo*, which Erasmus borrowed from antiquity and applied to More in the preface to 'The Praise of Folly'. Bolt was presumably unaware of Elizabethan usage of the phrase.

6. Frere and Douglas (eds), 'Puritan Manifestoes', p. 118.

7. About 8000 words: 'The Part of a Register' (Edinburgh, 1593) pp. 528-46.

8. Quoted Collinson, 'The Elizabethan Puritan Movement', p. 150.

9. Ibid., p. 292.

9 Field, 'A View of Popish Abuses'

'A View of popish Abuses yet remaining in the English Church, for which the godly Ministers have refused to subscribe', from the second edition of the volume 'An Admonition to Parliament' in the Cambridge University Library: Syn. 8. 57. 75; with the signature 'Jo: Feilde' on the flyleaf, and this manuscript verse:

> Let love still last
> That knitteth fast
> All Christians' hearts
> Hold it as best
> Let go the rest
> As is our parts

All marginal biblical references omitted. W. H. Frere and C. E. Douglas, 'Puritan Manifestoes' (1907, 1954), printed the first edition, from a British Museum copy.

The book was quickly issued three times: first edition, second edition and reprint of the second edition. Reprint also in 1578.

Abide patiently the Lord's leisure. Cast thy care upon the Lord, and he will bring it to pass, he will do it.

The jeopardous time is at hand, that the wrath of God shall be declared from heaven upon all ungodliness of those seducers that withold the truth in unrighteousness, and set his commandments at naught, for their own traditions.

Whereas immediately after the last Parliament, holden at Westminster, begun in anno 1570 and ended in anno 1571, the ministers of God's holy word and sacraments were called before her Majesty's high commissioners and enforced to subscribe to the articles, if they would keep their places and

122

livings, and some for refusing to subscribe were unbrotherly and uncharitably intreated, and from their offices and places removed: May it please therefore this honourable and high court of Parliament, in consideration of the premises, to take a view of such causes as then did withold, and now doth, the foresaid ministers from subscribing and consenting unto those foresaid articles, by way of purgation to discharge themselves of all disobedience towards the church of God and their sovereign, and by way of most humble entreaty for the removing away and utter abolishing of all such corruptions and abuses as witheld them, through which this long time brethren have been at unnatural war and strife among themselves, to the hindrance of the gospel, to the joy of the wicked, and to the grief and dismay of all those that profess Christ's religion and labour to attain Christian reformation.

THE FIRST ARTICLE

'First, that the book commonly called the book of common prayers for the Church of England, authorised by Parliament, and all and every the contents therein, be such as are not repugnant to the word of God.'

Albeit, right honourable and dearly beloved, we have at all times borne with that which we could not amend in this book, and have used the same in our ministry so far forth as we might, reverencing those times and those persons in which and by whom it was first authorized, being studious of peace and of the building up of Christ's church, yet now being compelled by subscription to allow the same, and to confess it not to be against the word of God in any point but tolerable: We must needs say as followeth, that this book is an unperfect book, culled and picked out of that popish dunghill, the portas* and mass book, full of all abominations. For some, and many, of the contents therein be such as are against the word of God, as by his grace shall be proved unto you. And by the way, we cannot but much marvel at the crafty wiliness of those men whose parts had been first to have proved each and every content therein to be agreeable

* Portable breviary (containing the divine office for each day).

to the word of God, seeing that they enforce men by subscription to consent unto it, or else send them packing from their callings.

1. They should first prove by the word that a reading service going before, and with, the administration of the sacraments is according to the word of God; that private communion, private baptism, baptism ministered by women; holy-days ascribed to saints, prescript services for them; kneeling at communion, wafer cakes for their bread when they minister it, surplice and cope to do it in; churching of women, coming in veils, — which is not commanded by law, but yet the abuse is great by reason that superstition is grown thereby in the hearts of many, and others are judged that use it not, abusing the psalm to her: 'I have lifted up mine eyes unto the hills', etc.; and such other foolish things; are agreeable to the written word of the Almighty. But their craft is plain. Wherein they deceive themselves, standing so much upon this word *repugnant* as though nothing were repugnant or against the word of God but that which is expressly forbidden by plain commandment. They know well enough, and would confess, if either they were not blinded or else their hearts hardened, that in the circumstances each content wherewith we justly find fault (and they too contentiously for the love of their livings maintain, smelling of their old popish priesthood) is against the word of God. For besides that this prescript form of service, as they call it, is full of corruptions, it maintaineth an unlawful ministry, unable to execute that office.

By the word of God, it is an office of preaching. They make it an office of reading. Christ said, go preach; they in mockery give them the Bible, and authority to preach, and yet suffer them not, except that they have new licences. So that they make the chiefest part, which is preaching, but an accessory, that is, a thing without which their office may and does consist. In the scriptures there is attributed to the ministers of God the knowledge of the heavenly mysteries, and therefore as the greatest token of their love they are enjoined to feed God's lambs, and yet, with these, such are admitted and accepted as only are bare readers, that are able to say service and minister a sacrament according to *their* appointment. And that this is not the feeding that Christ
124

spake of, the scriptures are plain. For bare reading of the word, and single service saying, is bare feeding; yea it is as evil as playing upon a stage, and worse too, for players yet learn their parts without book, and these, a many of them can scarcely read within book. These are empty feeders, dark eyes, ill workmen to hasten in the Lord's harvest, messengers that cannot call, prophets that cannot declare the will of the Lord, unsavoury salt, blind guides, sleepy watchmen, untrusty dispensers of God's secrets, evil dividers of the word, weak to withstand the adversary, not able to confute. And to conclude, so far from making the man of God perfect to all good works, that rather the quite contrary may be confirmed.

By this book, bare reading is good tilling, and single service saying is excellent building, and he is shepherd good enough, that can as popish priests could, out of their portas say fairly their divine service. Nay, some in the fulness of their blasphemy have said that much preaching bringeth the word of God into contempt, and that four preachers were enough for all London; so far are they from thinking it necessary, and seeking that every congregation should have a faithful pastor. Paul was not so wise as these politique men when he said 'we cannot believe except we hear, and we cannot hear without a preacher', etc.: seeing we may hear by reading, and so believe without a preacher. Foolishly he spake when he said he must be apt to teach, since every man of the basest sort of the people is admitted to this function, of such as Jeroboam did sometimes make his priests. We will say no more in this matter, but desire you to consider with us what small profit and edification this silly reading has brought to us these thirteen years past, (except perhaps by some circum-cellion* or new apostle, we have had now and then a fleeing sermon). Surely our sins are grown ripe, our ignorance is equal with the ignorance of our leaders, we are lost, they cannot find us, we are sick, they cannot heal us, we are hungry, they cannot feed us, except they lead us by other men's lights, and heal us by saying a prescript form of service, or else feed us with homilies that are too homely to be set in the place of God's scriptures. Are not the people well modified think you,

* Vagabond monk.

when the homily of sweeping the church is read unto them? But drunken they are, and show their own shame, that strive so eagerly to defend their doings that they will only not acknowledge their imperfections, but will enforce other men to allow them.

2. In this book also, it is appointed that after the Creed, if there be no sermon, a homily must follow, either already set out, or hereafter to be set out. This is scarce plain dealing, that they would have us consent unto that which we never saw, and which is to be set out hereafter — we having had such cause already to distrust them by that which is already set out, being corrupt and strange, to maintain an unlearned and reading ministry — and since it is plain that men's works ought to be kept in, and nothing else but the voice of God and holy Scriptures (in which only are contained all fulness and sufficiency to decide controversies must sound in his church, for the very name Apocrypha testifieth that they were read in secret and not openly.

3. In this book, days are ascribed unto Saints and kept holy with fasts on their evens, and prescript service appointed for them, which beside that they are, of many, superstitiously kept and observed, are also contrary to the commandment of God. Six days shalt thou labour, and therefore we, for the superstition that is put in them, dare not subscribe to allow them.

4. In this book we are enjoined to receive the communion kneeling, which beside that it has in it a show of popish idolatry doth not so well express a supper, neither agreeth it so well with the institution of Christ, as sitting doth. Not that we make sitting a thing of necessity belonging unto the sacrament, neither affirm we that it may not be received otherwise, but that it is more near the institution, and also a mean to avoid the danger of idolatry, which was in times past too common, and yet is in the hearts of many who have not forgotten their bread God, so slenderly have they been instructed. Against which we may set the commandment: thou shalt not bow down to it, nor worship it.

5. As for the half Communion, which is yet appointed like to the commemoration of the Mass, we say little of it, saving that we may note how near the translator bound himself to the Mass book, that would not omit it. We speak not of the

126

name of *priest* wherewith he defaceth the minister of Christ (because the priest that translated it would perhaps fain have the ministers of Christ to be joined with him) seeing the office of priesthood is ended, Christ being the last priest that ever was. To call us therefore priests as touching our office is either to call back again the old priesthood of the law, which is to deny Christ to be come, or else to keep a memory of the popish priesthood of abomination still amongst us. As for the first, it is by Christ abolished, and for the second it is of Antichrist, and therefore we have nothing to do with it. Such ought to have no place in our church, neither are they ministers of Christ, sent to preach his gospel, but priests of the pope to sacrifice for the quick and the dead, that is to tread under their feet the blood of Christ. Such ought not to have place amongst us, as the scriptures manifestly teach. Besides that, we never read in the New Testament that this word priest, as touching office, is used in the good part; except it speak of the Levitical priesthood, or of the priesthood of Christ.

6. Sixthly, in this book three or four are allowed for a fit number to receive the communion, and the priest alone together with one more, or with the sick man alone may in time of necessity (that is, when there is any common plague or in time of other visitation) minister it to the sick man, and if he require it, it may not be denied. This is not I am sure like in effect to a private mass: that scripture, 'drink ye all of this', maketh not against this, and private communion is not against the scriptures!

7. And as for private baptism, that will abide the touchstone. Go ye, saith Christ and teach, baptising them, etc. Now teaching is divorced from communions and sacraments. They may go alone without doctrine. Women that may not speak in a congregation, may yet in time of necessity minister the sacrament of baptism, and that in a private house. And yet this is not to tie necessity of salvation to the sacraments, nor to noose men up in that opinion. This is agreeable with the scriptures, and therefore when they bring the baptised child, they are received with this special commendation: I certify you, that you have done well, and according unto due order, etc. But now we speak in good earnest, when they answer this. Let them tell us how this gear agreeth with the

127

scriptures, and whether it be not repugnant or against the word of God. But some will say that the baptism of women is not commanded by law. If it be not, why do you suffer it, and wherefore are the children so baptised accordingly? Common experience teacheth that it is used almost in all places, and few speak against it. And this I am sure of, that when it was put in the book that was the meaning of the most part that were then present, and so it was to be understood, as common practice without controlment doth plainly declare.

8. The public baptism, that also is full of childish and superstitious toys. First, in their prayer they say that God by the baptism of his son Jesus Christ did sanctify the flood Jordan, and all other waters, to the mystical washing away of sin; attributing that to the *sign* which is proper to the work of God in the blood of Christ; as though virtue were in water to wash away sins! Secondly, they require a promise of the godfathers and godmothers (as they term them) which is not in their powers to perform. Thirdly, they profane holy baptism in toying foolishly, for that they ask questions of an infant, which cannot answer, and speak unto them as was wont to be spoken unto men, and unto such as being converted answered for themselves, and were baptised. Which is but a mockery of God, and therefore against the holy scriptures. Fourthly, they do superstitiously and wickedly institute a new sacrament, which is proper to Christ only: marking the child in the forehead with a cross in token that hereafter he shall not be ashamed to confess the faith of Christ. We have made mention before of that wicked divorce of the word and sacraments. We say nothing of those that are admitted to be witnesses — what ill choice there is made of them; how convenient it were, seeing the children of the faithful only are to be baptised, that the father should, and might, if conveniently, offer and present his child to be baptised, making an open confession of that faith wherein he would have his child baptised: as is used in well reformed churches.

9. As for matrimony, that also has corruptions too many. It was wont to be counted a sacrament; and therefore they use yet a sacramental sign, to which they attribute the virtue of wedlock. I mean the wedding ring, which they foully

128

abuse and dally withal, in taking it up and laying it down. In putting it on they abuse the name of the Trinity, they make the new married man, according to the popish form, to make an idol of his wife, saying: 'with this ring I thee wed, with my body I thee worship', etc. And because in popery no holy action might be done without a mass, they enjoin the married persons to receive the communion (as they do their bishops and priests when they are made, etc.) Other petty things out of the book we speak not of: as that women, contrary to the rule of the apostle, come, and are suffered to come, bareheaded, with bag-pipes and fiddlers before them to disturb the congregation; and that they must come in at the great door of the church or else all is marred; with divers other heathenish toys in sundry countries, as carrying of wheatsheaves on their heads, and casting of corn, with a number of suchlike, whereby they make rather a May game of marriage than a holy institution of God.

10. As for confirmation, which the papists and our men say was in times past apostolical, grounding their opinion perhaps upon some dream of Jerome, yet as they use it, by the bishop alone, to them that lack both discretion and faith, it is superstitious and not agreeable to the word of God, but popish and peevish. As though baptism were not already perfect, but needed confirmation, or as though the bishop could give the Holy Ghost!

11. They appoint a prescript kind of service to bury the dead; and that which is the duty of every Christian they tie alone to the minister, whereby prayer for the dead is maintained, and partly gathered out of some of the prayers — where they pray that we with this our brother and all other departed in the true faith of thy holy name, may have our perfect consummation and bliss, both in body and soul. We say nothing of the threefold peal, because that it is rather licensed by injunction than commanded in their book; nor of their strange mourning by changing their garments, which if it be not hypocritical yet it is superstitious and heathenish because it is used only of custom; nor of burial sermons which are put in place of trentals,* whereout spring many abuses, and therefore in the best reformed churches are

---

* A series of thirty requiem masses.

129

removed. As for the superstitions used both in country and city for the place of burial — which way they must lie; how they must be fetched to church; the minister meeting them at church-stile with surplice, with a company of greedy clerks; that a cross, white or black, must be set upon the dead corpse; that bread must be given to the poor, and offerings in burial time used, and cakes sent abroad to friends — because these are rather used of custom and superstition than by the authority of the book, small commandment will serve for the accomplishing of such things. But great charge will hardly bring the least good thing to pass, and therefore all is let alone, and the people as blind and ignorant as ever they were. God be merciful unto us, and open our eyes that we may see what that good and acceptable will of God is, and be more earnest to provoke his glory.

12. Churching of women after childbirth smelleth of Jewish purification. Their other rites and customs in their lying in, and coming to church, is foolish and superstitious, as it is used. She must lie in with a white sheet upon her bed, and come covered with a veil, as ashamed of some folly. She must offer; but these are matters of custom and not in the book. But this Psalm (as is noted before) is childishly abused: 'I have lift up mine eyes unto the hills, from whence comes my help. The sun shall not burn thee by day, nor the moon by night.'

13. In all their order of service there is no edification, according to the rule of the Apostle, but confusion. They toss the Psalms in most places like tennis balls. They pray that all men may be saved; and that they may be delivered from thundering and tempest when no danger is nigh. That they sing Benedictus, Nunc Dimittus and Magnificat, we know not to what purpose, except some of them were ready to die, or except they would celebrate the memory of the virgin and John the Baptist, etc. Thus they profane the holy scriptures. The people, some standing, some walking, some talking, some reading, some praying by themselves, attend not to the minister. He again posteth it over as fast as he can gallop. For either he hath two places to serve, or else there are some games of Sodom to be played in the afternoon: as lying for the whetstone, heathenish dancing for the ring, a bear or a bull to be baited, or else jackanapes to ride on

130

horseback; or an interlude to be played, and if no place else can be gotten this interlude must be played in the church, etc. Now the people sit, and now they stand up. When the Old Testament is read, or the lessons, they make no reverence, but when the gospel cometh, then they all stand up. For why, they think that to be of greatest authority, and are ignorant that the scriptures came from one spirit. When Jesus is named, then off goeth the cap, and down goeth the knees, with such a scraping on the ground that they cannot hear a good while after, so that the word is hindered; but when any other names of God are mentioned they make no courtesy at all, as though the names of God were not equal, or as though all reverence ought to be given to the syllables. We speak not of ringing, when Matins is done, and other abuses incident. Because we shall be answered that by the book they are not maintained: only we desire to have a book to *reform* it. As for organs and curious singing, though they be proper to popish dens (I mean to cathedral churches) yet some others also must have them. The Queen's chapel, and these churches (which should be spectacles of Christian reformation), are rather patterns and precedents to the people of all superstitions.

14. Their Pontifical (which is annexed to the book of common prayer, and whereunto, subscribing to the articles, we must subscribe also) whereby they consecrate bishops, make ministers and deacons, is nothing else but a thing word for word drawn out of the pope's Pontifical, wherein he shows himself to be Antichrist most lively. And as the names of Archbishops, Archdeacons, Lord Bishops, Chancellors, etc, are drawn out of the pope's shop together with their offices, so the government which they use, by the life of the pope, which is the canon law, is antichristian and devilish, and contrary to the scriptures. And as safely may we, by the warrant of God's word, subscribe to allow the dominion of the pope universally to reign over the church of God, as of an Archbishop over an whole province, or a Lord Bishop over a diocese, which containeth many shires and parishes. For the dominion that they exercise, the Archbishop above them, and they above the rest of their brethren, is unlawful and expressly forbidden by the word of God.

15. Again, in that they are honoured with the titles of great rulers, as Lord, Lord's grace, Metropolitan, primate of

all England, honour, etc, it is against the word of God.

Moreover, in that they have civil offices joined to the ecclesiastical, it is against the word of God. As for an Archbishop to be a Lord President; a Lord Bishop to be a county Palatine, a prelate of the garter who hath much to do at St. George's feast, when the Bible is carried before the procession in the cross's place, a justice of peace, or justice of quorum, a high Commissioner, etc; and therefore they have their prisons, as clinks, gatehouses, coalhouses, towers and castles, which is also against the scriptures. This is not to have keys but swords, and plain tokens they are that they exercise that which they would so fain seem to want: I mean, dominion over their brethren. And which of them have not preached against the pope's two swords: now whether they use them not themselves?

16. In that the Lord Bishops, their suffragans, archdeacons, chancellors, officials, proctors, doctors, summoners, and such ravening rabblers take upon them, which is most horrible, the rule of God's church — spoiling the pastor of his lawful jurisdiction over his own flock given by the word, thrusting away most sacrilegiously that order which Christ hath left to his church, and which the primitive church hath used — they show they hold the doctrine with us but in unrighteousness: with an outward show of godliness, but having denied the power thereof, entering not in by Christ, but by a popish and unlawful vocation. We speak not how they make ministers by themselves alone, and of their sole authority (and that in secret places), of their election and probation — that it is of him to whom by no right it belongeth. And that when they have made them, either they may tarry in their college and lead the lives of loitering losels* as long as they live, or else gad abroad with the Bishops' bulls like to circumcellions, to preach in other men's charges where they list, or else get benefices by friendship or money or flattery where they can catch them; or to conclude, if all these fail, that they may go up and down like beggars and fall to many follies; or else, as many have done, set up bills at Paul's or at the Royal Exchange, and in such

* Rakes.

132

public places, to see if they can hear of some good masters to entertain them into service. Surely, by the canon law, by which the bishops reign and rule, they ought to keep those ministers which they make, as long as they have no livings and places. We know three or four bishops in this realm would have kept such houses as never none did in this land if this rule had been observed. They clapped them out so fast by hundreds, and they make them pay well for their orders, and surely to speak the truth they were worthy: for the bishops (what odds soever there were of their gifts) yet in their letters gave them *all* a like commendation. They put on their surplices, or else subscribed, like honest men! Fie upon these stinking abominations.

17. We should be too long to tell your honours of cathedral churches: the dens aforesaid of all loitering lubbers, where master Dean, master Vicedean, master Canons or Prebendaries the greater, master petty Canons or Canons the lesser, master Chancellor of the church, master Treasurer (otherwise called Judas the pursebearer), the chief chanter, singing men (special favours of religion), squeaking choristers, organ players, gospellers, pistlers, pensioners, readers, vergers, etc., live in great idleness, and have their abiding. If you would know whence all these came, we can easily answer you: that they came from the pope, as out of the Trojan horse's belly, to the destruction of God's kingdom. The church of God never knew them; neither doth any reformed church in the world know them.

18. And birds of the same feather are covetous patrons of benefices, parsons, vicars, readers, parish priests, stipendaries, and riding chaplains, that under the authority of their masters spoil their flocks of the food of their souls. Such seek not the Lord Jesus, but their own bellies; clouds they are without rain, trees without fruit, painted sepulchres full of dead bones, fatted in all abundance of iniquity, and lean locusts in all feeling, knowledge and sincerity.

[Marginal note to point 19:] To prove that the regiment of the church should be spiritual, read Calvin in his commentaries upon these places: Ephesians 11, 23; I Thessalonians 5, 13; I Timothy 5, 2; Hebrews 10, 30.

19. What should we speak of the Archbishop's court, since all men know it, and your wisdoms cannot but see what it is.

As all other courts are subject to this by the pope's prerogative, yea, and by statute of this realm yet unrepealed, so it is the filthy quagmire and poisoned plash of all the abominations that do infect the whole realm. We speak not of licences granted out of this court to marry in forbidden times, as in Lent, in Advent, in the gang week when the priest in his surplice, singing gospels and making crosses, rangeth about in many places, upon the ember days, and to forbidden persons, and in exempt places. We make no mention of licences to eat white meat and flesh in Lent, and that with a safe conscience for rich men that can buy them with money; nor we say nothing how dearly men pay for them. As for dispensations with beneficed boys, tolerations for non-residents, bulls to have two benefices, to have three, to have more and as many as they list or can get, these are so common that all godly and good men are compelled with grief of heart to cry out upon such abominations. We omit excommunication for money, absolution for the same, and that by absolving one man for another, which how contrary it is to the scriptures the complaints of many learned men by propositions in open schools proposed, by writings in printed books set out, and by preaching in open pulpits, have been sufficiently witnessed. To conclude, this filthy court has full power, together with the authority of this petty pope, metropolitan and primate of all England, to dispense in all causes wherein the pope was wont to dispense: under which are contained more causes and cases than we are able to reckon. As for my Lord's grace, the Archbishop of York, we deal not with him. We refer him to that learned epistle which Beza wrote to him about these matters.*

20. And as for the commissary's court, that is but a petty little stinking ditch that floweth out of that former great puddle, robbing Christ's church of lawful pastors, of watchful seniors and elders, and careful deacons. In this court as in the other, one alone does excommunicate, one alone sitteth in judgement, and, when he will, can draw back the judgement which he hath pronounced, having called upon the name of God, and that for money, which is called the changing of penance. In this court, for non-payment of twopence a man

* Beza's letter to Grindal, Geneva, July 1566, was printed in the 'Admonition' volume. Grindal went to York in 1570.

shall be excommunicated if he appear not when he is sent for; if he do not as his ordinary would, from whom he had his popish induction and institution, and to whom he has sworn Canonicam obedientiam, canonical obedience; if he learn not his catechism like a good boy without book, when it were more meet he should be able to teach others. To conclude, if he be not obedient to all these Lord Bishops' officers, by and by he must be cut off by excommunication. And, as it is lightly granted and given forth, so if the money be paid and the court discharged, it is as quickly called in again. This court polleth parishes, scourgeth the poor hedge-priests, loadeth churchwardens with manifest perjuries, punisheth whoredoms and adulteries with toyish censures, remitteth without satisfying the congregation, and that in secret places, giveth out dispensations for unlawful marriages, and committeth a thousand suchlike abonimations. God deliver all Christians out of this antichristian tyranny, where the judge's advocates and proctors for the most part are papists; and as for the scribes and notaries, as greedy as cormorants; and if they all should perhaps see this writing, they would be as angry as wasps and sting like hornets. Three of them would be enough to sting a man to death, for why, they are high commissioners. All this we say springeth out of this Pontifical, which we must allow by subscription, setting down our hands that it is not repugnant or against the word of God — we mean this antichristian hierarchy and popish ordering of ministers: strange from the word of God, and the use of all well reformed churches in the world.

21. We have almost let pass one thing worth the remembrance, which is that they take upon them blasphemously, having neither promise nor commandment, to say to their new creatures: 'receive the Holy Ghost' — as though the Holy Ghost were in their power to give without warrant, at their own pleasure.

And thus much be spoken as touching this book, against which to stand is a wonder to two sorts of men, the one ignorant, the other obstinate. The Lord give those that be his, understanding in all things, that they may have judgement. As for the other, whom the God of this world hath blinded (lest they should see and confess the truth and so be saved) and that do in the full growth of wickedness maliciously

135

resist the truth, God confound them, that peace may be upon Israel and his saving health upon this nation. Amen.

THE SECOND ARTICLE

'That the manner and order appointed by public authority about the administration of the sacraments and common prayers, and that the apparel by sufficient authority appointed for the ministers within the Church of England, be not wicked, nor against the word of God, but tolerable, and, being commanded for order and obedience sake, are to be used.'

For the order of administration of sacraments and common prayer enough is said before: all the service and administration is tied to a surplice; in Cathedral churches they must have a cope; they receive the communion kneeling; they use not for the most part common bread according to the word of God and the statute, but starch bread according to the Injunction. They commonly minister the Sacraments without preaching the word.

And as for the apparel, though we have been long borne in hand, and yet are, that it is for order and decency commanded, yet we know and have proved that there is neither order nor comeliness nor obedience in using it. There is no order in it, but confusion; no comeliness, but deformity; no obedience, but disobedience, both against God and the Prince. We marvel that they could espy in their last Synod that a grey amice, which is but a garment of dignity, should be a garment (as they say) defiled with superstition; and yet that copes, caps, surplices, tippets, and suchlike baggage, the preaching signs of popish priesthood, the pope's creatures, kept in the same form to this end, to bring dignity and reverence to the ministers and sacraments, should be retained still and not abolished. But they are as the garments of the Idol, to which we should say, avaunt and get thee hence. They are as the garments of Balaamites, of popish priests, enemies to God and all Christians. They serve not to edification; they have the show of evil (seeing the popish priesthood is evil); they work discord; they hinder the preaching of the Gospel; they keep the memory of Egypt still amongst us, and

136

put us in mind of that abomination whereunto they in times past have served; they bring the ministry into contempt; they offend the weak, they encourage the obstinate. Therefore can no authority by the word of God, with any pretence of order and obedience command them, nor make them in any wise tolerable; but, by circumstances, they are wicked and against the word of God.

If this be not plain enough by that which is already set forth, we mind by God's grace to make it plainer, and should do it better, if it were as lawful for us (as for our adversaries) to publish our minds in print. Neither is the controversy between them and us as they would bear the world in hand — as for a cap, a tippet, or a surplice — but for great matters concerning a true ministry and regiment of the church according to the word. Which things once established, the other melt away of themselves. And yet consider I pray you, whether their own argument doth not choke themselves, for even the very name of trifles doth plainly declare that they ought not to be maintained in Christ's church. And what shall our bishops gain by it? Forsooth, that they be maintainers of trifles and trifling bishops, consuming the greatest part of their time in those trifles, whereas they should be better occupied. We strive for true religion and government of the church, and show you the right way to throw out Antichrist both head and tail; and that we will not so much as communicate with the tail of the beast. But they, after they have thrust Antichrist out by the head, go about to pull him in again by the tail, cunningly colouring it lest any man should espy his footsteps, as Cacus did when he stole the oxen. For if it might please her Majesty, by the advice of you, Right Honourable, in this high Court of Parliament, to hear us by writing or otherwise, to defend ourselves, then (such is the equity of our cause) that we would trust to find favour in her Majesty's sight. Then should appear what slender stuff they bring to defend themselves that are so impudent by open writing to defend it. Then those patched pamphlets made by sudden upstarts and new converts should appear in their colours, and truth have the victory and God the glory. If this cannot be obtained, we will by God's grace address ourselves to defend his truth by suffering, and willingly lay our heads to the block, and this shall be our

137

peace, to have quiet consciences with our God, whom we will abide for with all patience until he work our full deliverance.

THE THIRD ARTICLE

'That the articles of religion which only concern the true Christian faith, and the doctrine of the Sacraments, comprised in a book imprinted 'Articles, whereupon it was agreed by both Archbishops, etc.' and every of them, contain true and godly Christian doctrine.'

For the Articles: concerning that substance of doctrine, (using a godly interpretation in a point or two, which are either too sparely or else too darkly set down) we were and are ready according to duty to subscribe unto them. We would to God that as they hold the substance together with us, and we with them, so they would not deny the effect and virtue thereof. Then should not our words and works be divorced, but Christ should be suffered to reign, a true ministry according to the word instituted, discipline exercised, sacraments purely and sincerely ministered. This is that we strive for, and about which we have suffered, not as evil doers, but for resisting popery, and refusing to be strong with the tail of antichristian infection, ready to render a reason of our faith, to the stopping of all our enemies' mouths. We therefore for the church of God's sake, which ought to be most dear unto you, beseech you for our Sovereign's sake, upon whom we pray that all God's blessings may be poured abundantly, we pray you to consider of these abuses, to reform God's church according to your duties and callings, that as with one mouth we confess one Christ, so with one consent this reign of Antichrist may be turned out headlong from amongst us, and Christ our Lord may reign by his word over us. So your seats shall be established and settled in great assurance, you shall not need to fear your enemies for God will turn away his threatened plagues from us. Which he in mercy do, for his Christ's sake. Amen.

138

PART VII

1571-1572 The Puritans and Parliament

The 'Supplication' which I print first in this section, with its hope that the Parliament of 1571 will make provision for reformation, is at its most attractive in the passages reflecting a sense of pastoral responsibility. 'The people ... remain in great peril ... daily to fall into the ditch'; 'the lamentable estate of so many thousands of your Majesty's subjects, daily in danger to be lost for want of the food of the word and true discipline'. The same concern is reflected in the third document, a projected preface (not in fact printed) to one of the two 'Admonitions to Parliament' of 1572. There is also an attempt in this preface to give a summing up of the trend of events in England since 1558. 'It hath been thought good to bear with the weakness of certain for a time', the 'certain' being those 'too much addicted to ceremonies'. We have seen Cranmer writing in 1549 about those who 'think it a great matter of conscience to depart from a piece of the least of their ceremonies (they be so addicted to their old customs)'. In 1558/9, the preface author implies, it was necessary to make some concessions to such persons, after the Marian interlude. But now we see (he argues) that since 1558 things have in fact got worse: the ceremony-men, 'from their weakness ... are grown to malicious wilfulness'. What is needed in England now is reformation according to the 'primitive church', following 'Geneva, France, Scotland, and all other churches rightly reformed' (A point expanded by Cartwright in the 'Second Admonition to Parliament'). 'A thorough reformation both of doctrine, ceremonies and regiment'. John Jewel had written in 1562 to Peter Martyr of Zürich (sometime Professor at Oxford) making a similar

139

historical point. Compromise was understandable at the very beginning of the reign, 'by reason of the times'; but now, over three years later, 'the full light of the gospel has shone forth', and we must remove rubbish (the surplice, for instance) (1). The Rites and Ceremonies Bill of 1572 (my central extract here) repeats the argument. By the 1559 Act of Uniformity and Book of Common Prayer 'divers orders of rites, ceremonies and observations' were 'permitted', because 'the people' then were 'blinded with superstition'. Hope was thwarted, and things did not get better in the 1560s.

Not in general, that is. But in the 1560s 'many congregations' grew to 'desire of attaining to some further form' (of liturgy); 'a great number of learned pastors and zealous ministers' have 'omitted the precise rule and strait observation' of the law, have established 'godly exercises for the better instruction and edifying of their congregations' (on the lines presumably of the Zurich 'Prophetzei' of the 1520s); and in general 'have conformed themselves more nearly to the imitation of the ancient apostolical church and the best reformed churches in Europe'. But the 'godly exercises' have been restrained; and reformation hindered by the laws of ecclesiastical polity in the 1560s — acts, injunctions, advertisements and decrees.

In January 1559, at the coronation of Elizabeth, mass was said in Latin, the gospel and the epistle, however, being read in English. The Prayer Book in use from June — the result of parliamentary pressure — was however the Cranmer Liturgy of 1552, slightly modified. The 1559 Act of Uniformity (2) said that a cleric refusing to use the book would be put in prison (after conviction by jury): six months for a first offence, life for a third. And the 'ornaments of the church and of the ministers thereof' were to be as in 1549 — that is, a surplice for ordinary services, and for the communion a white alb with a chasuble or cope. Were to be so 'until other order shall be therein taken' by Elizabeth and the ecclesiastical commissioners, the Queen having the right in future to 'publish such further ceremonies or rites as may be most for the advancement of God's glory, the edifying of his church, and the due reverence of Christ's holy mysteries and sacraments'. The possible nature of that 'further order' has been a subject for dispute: it has recently been persuasively argued

140

that Elizabeth was thinking of something more 'ceremonial' even than the first Cranmer Liturgy: the 1548 Communion Order (3). It is certain that the Royal Injunctions of June 1559 were more in the spirit of 1549 than of 1552. And in 1560 a Latin version of the Prayer Book was printed for use in college chapels, and for private devotion.

The controversy about 'massing ornaments' bedevils the 1560s. Does Elizabeth favour 'our cause'? wrote John Jewel, back from Zürich in 1559. Can we hope for 'better things'? (4) The answer increasingly appeared to be no. In 1565 Elizabeth wrote to Archbishop Parker denouncing 'diversity, variety, contention and vain love of singularity', and insisting, as absolutely necessary to 'unity, quietness and concord', that there must remain in England 'one rule, form and manner of order' (5). The result of this prod was Parker's regulations ('The Book of Advertisements') of 1566, and the consequent suspension of some clergy — those 'expressly refusing conformity' (6). The 'Advertisements' insisted on the surplice: but we know that by 1561 the use of the surplice had been abandoned in some areas of England. Parker discussed 'these precise folk' with the Queen in March 1566; she 'willed me to imprison them' (7). (Elizabeth was a curious combination of the impetuous and the inscrutable.) The theme of to quit or not to quit obsessed many clerics in the 1560s. The working of their consciences is best seen in the letters they wrote to Switzerland (8). By 1567 Beza wrote from Geneva to Bullinger in Zürich that England had become another Babylon. (Beza had succeeded Calvin, who died in 1564.)

When Parliament met in May 1572 the Queen had been on the throne for over thirteen years. In those years Parliament had met for about ten months: six weeks in 1559, thirteen weeks in 1563, sixteen weeks in 1566/7, and eight weeks in 1571. The membership of the House of Commons had increased from 404 to 438. In a waspish speech delivered in person, Elizabeth condemned the 1566/7 session as mischievous, especially because of certain 'broachers and workers' (10). The Speaker said that the Queen 'ought to make laws whereby God may be truly worshipped', to 'extinguish and put away all hurtful and unprofitable ceremonies in any case contrary to God's word' (and then

141

maintained that Elizabeth had already done this!) (11). In April 1571 an M.P. attacked the provision for kneeling at communion, saying that in such matters every man should be set 'at liberty in this behalf to do according to his conscience' (12). The 1571 session is associated particularly with the name of William Strickland. The Liturgy, he said, has 'errors', all 'which might well be changed'; there are 'some things inserted more superstitious, than in so high matters be tolerable'. We must have 'all things brought to the purity of the primitive church' (13). There were 'divers long arguments' against Strickland's bill about the Liturgy. Some Establishment men spoke 'commending the zeal; but that the time and the place were not fit. And since we acknowledge her to be supreme head, we are not in these petty matters to run before the ball' (14). Strickland was imprisoned for a period. And at the end of the session Nicholas Bacon, Keeper of the Great Seal, complained that certain M.P.s had been 'audacious, arrogant and presumptious, calling her Majesty's grants and prerogatives in question'. The Queen (too politic now to appear in person) asked Bacon to condemn them 'for their audacious, arrogant and presumptuous folly, thus by superfluous speech spending much time meddling with matters neither pertaining to them, nor within the capacity of their understanding' (15). Furthermore, Bacon said, religious bills 'should first have been debated in the convocation and by the bishops, and not by them' (16).

In 1572 Parliament met for four weeks. The Rites and Ceremonies Bill was read a first and second time on 17 and 19 May, and then sent to committee for a modification. It asked that the Act of Uniformity should be enforced only against adherents of 'any manner of papistical service'. The godly, in using the litargy, should be allowed to 'omit and leave' out at their discretion; or, better, use any part of the printed service book used by the French and Dutch Reformed Churches in England based on the Genevan Service Book (17). 'Godly exercises' should, also, be allowed to continue, for the instruction of the congregation. On 22 May the royal edict came: that 'from henceforth no Bills concerning Religion shall be preferred or received into this House, unless the same should be first considered and liked by the clergy' (18).

142

This edict was made more official by a Proclamation of 11 June 1573 (19). The Queen's policy is to provide 'uniform, godly and quiet order within her realm, to avoid all controversies, schisms, and dissensions that may arise'. The 1559 Prayer Book is to be used, 'and none other contrary or repugnant'. It is acknowledged that some clerics 'use of their own devising other rites and ceremonies than are by the laws of the realm received and used'. There are those whose dominating aim is to 'make division and dissension in the opinions of men, and to breed talks and disputes against the common order': 'some persons of their natures unquietly disposed, desirous to change, and therefore ready to find fault with all well established orders'. Such people have printed certain books 'under the title of 'An Admonition to the Parliament''.

1. 'Zurich Letters', i 100.
2. G. R. Elton, 'The Tudor Constitution' (1960) prints the text (pp. 401-4): as does Claire Cross, 'The Royal Supremacy in the Elizabethan Church' (1969).
3. By an American Episcopalian priest, William P. Haugaard: 'Elizabeth and the English Reformation'.
4. 5 November 1559, 'Zurich Letters' i 52-4.
5. Parker, 'Correspondence', pp. 223-7. Also in Cross, 'Royal Supremacy in the Elizabethan Church'.
6. Parker to Grindal, 'Correspondence', p. 274.
7. Ibid., p. 278.
8. 'Zurich Letters' (2 vols in Parker Society).
9. 'Zurich Letters', ii 153.
10. D'Ewes, 'Journals', p. 117.
11. Ibid., p. 114.
12. Ibid., p. 167.
13. Ibid., p. 157.
14. Ibid., p. 166.
15. Ibid., p. 151.
16. Neale, 'Elizabeth I and her Parliaments', i 238.
17. See Horton Davies, 'The Worship of the English Puritans' (1948). And Dr Collinson's chapter on worship in 'The Elizabethan Puritan Movement', pp. 356-71.

18. D'Ewes, 'Journals', p. 213.
19. Frere and Douglas (eds), 'Puritan Manifestoes', pp. 153-4.

10 'Supplication to her Majesty in Parliament'

Dr Williams's Library, Morrice MSS 'B': 'The Seconde Parte of a Register', i, ff. 160-1. Partial transcript in A. Peel (ed.), 'The Seconde Parte of a Register' (1915) i 75-7.

In most humble wise beseechen your Highness, your Majesty's most loving, faithful and obedient subjects, the Commons in this present Parliament assembled.

That whereas by the lack of the true discipline of the church, among other abuses, great numbers of men are admitted to occupy the place of ministers in the Church of England, who are not only altogether unfurnished of such gifts as are by the Word of God necessarily and inseparably required to be incident to their calling, but also are infamous in their lives and conversations; and also divers of the ministry whom God has endowed with ability to teach are by mean of non-residencies, pluralities, and suchlike dispensations, so withdrawn from their flocks that their gifts are almost altogether become unprofitable; whereby an infinite number of your Majesty's subjects, for want of the preaching of the word (the only ordinary mean of salvation of souls, and the only good mean to teach your Majesty's subjects to know their true obedience to your Majesty, and to the magistrates under you, and without which the Lord God hath pronounced that the people must needs perish) have already run headlong into destruction, and many thousands of the residue yet remain in great peril (if speedy remedy be not provided) daily to fall into the ditch, and to die in their sins, to the great danger and charge of those to whom the Lord God hath committed the care and provision for them in this behalf.

And by means whereof, the common blaspheming of the Lord's name, the most wicked licentiousness of life, the abuse of excommunication, the commutation of penance, the great multitude of atheists, schismatics, heretics, daily springing up, and, to conclude, the continual hardening and increasing of obstinate papists, which ever since your Majesty's sworn enemy the Pope did by his bulls pronounce his definitive sentence against your Highness' person and proceedings,* have given evident testimony of their corrupt affection toward him, and of their wilful disobedience to your Majesty, in that they forbear to participate with your Majesty's faithful subjects in prayer and administration of sacraments, wherein they most manifestly declare that they carry very unsound and very undutiful hearts to your Majesty.

In consideration therefore of the premises, having regard first and principally to the advancement of the glory of God, next to the long and most blessed continuance of your Majesty's reign and safety, which we most instantly beseech almighty God long to preserve, then to the discharge of our most bounden obedience, which in all duty and reverence we bear unto your Majesty; besides, being moved to pitiful consideration of the lamentable estate of so many thousands of your Majesty's subjects, daily in danger to be lost for want of the food of the word and true discipline; and lastly, respecting the peace of our own consciences and the salvation of our souls; being at this present assembled by your Majesty's authority to open the griefs and to seek the salving of the sores of our country, and these before remembered beyond measure exceeding in greatness all the residue which can be disclosed in your Majesty's Commonwealth:- we are most humbly to beseech your Majesty, seeing the same is of so great importance, if the Parliament at this time may not be so long continued, as that by good and godly laws established in the same, provision may be made for supply and reformation of these great wants and grievous abuses, that yet by such other good means as to your Majesty's most godly wisdom shall seem best, a perfect redress of the same may be had.

Which doing, your Highness shall do such acceptable

* The papal bull *Regnans in Excelsis*, excommunicating and deposing Elizabeth, was signed by Pius V in 1570. Text and translation in G. R. Elton, 'The Tudor Constitution' (1960) no. 197.

service to the Lord God as shall procure at his hands the sure establishing of your seat and sceptre; and the number of your Majesty's faithful subjects (the bond of conscience being of all other the straightest by mean of preaching and discipline) shall be so multiplied, and the great swarms of malefactors, schismatics, atheists, anabaptists and papists (your most dangerous enemies) so weakened and diminished that by the help and assistance of almighty God, if all popish treasons and traitorous practices should conspire together in one against your Majesty, they should never be able to shake your estate, and we your Majesty's most loving obedient subjects, together with the remembrance of those inestimable and innumerable benefits which by your Majesty's means the Lord God has already blessed us withal, far beyond any of our neighbours round about us, shall not only more and more be stirred up to dutiful thankfulness to your Majesty, and to continual and earnest prayer to almighty God (which we will nevertheless) for the long and prosperous continuance of your Majesty's reign, but also both we and the residue of your Majesty's most faithful subjects, and our posterities, shall be bound to continue in the obedient duty which we owe to your most royal Majesty; and to conclude, your Majesty shall be recommended to all posterities for such a pattern to be followed that nothing may seem to be added to the perfection of your renown.

11 1572 Bill 'Concerning Rites and Ceremonies'

Critical edition of text in W. H. Frere and C. E. Douglas, 'Puritan Manifestoes' (1907, 1954) pp. 149-51.

Where in the first year of your Majesty's most happy reign and government over us, your Highness' most humble and obedient subjects, which we beseech the eternal God in continual blessed success long to preserve and continue, a certain book of order of uniformity of common prayer and ministration of the sacrament (for the renewing of the building of the house of God, the Church of Christ) through his grace and unspeakable mercy, and your Grace's godly zeal toward the advancement of his glory was by authority of Parliament established, prescribed, and ordained, to be by all your Grace's subjects fully and directly obeyed, observed, and performed, to all purposes, constructions, and intents, under the pains and penalties therein comprised, in which, though there be a soundness in substantial points of doctrine, yet by reason of the late backsliding of the people from true religion to superstition, divers orders of rites, ceremonies and observations were therein permitted in respect of the great weakness of the people then blinded with superstition. Sith it has now pleased the almighty God, through this long continuance of the exercise of preaching of the Gospel under your Highness' authority, to direct the cause thereof to such a prosperous end as many congregations within this your Highness' realm are grown to desire of attaining to some further form than in that book is prescribed, and considering that God in his manifold blessing toward us hath raised up a great number of learned pastors and zealous ministers within this your Majesty's dominions, who, in discharge of their consciences have therefore eftsones according to that talent and measure of knowledge which God hath given them,

148

endeavoured and enterprised with all humility and quiet manner (with favourable permission of some godly bishops and ordinaries) to further the spreading of his spiritual building by putting in some godly exercises for the better instruction and edifying of their congregations, and therefore have omitted the precise rule and strait observation of the form and order prescribed in that book, with some part of rites and ceremonies therein appointed, and have conformed themselves more nearly to the imitation of the ancient apostolical church and the best reformed churches in Europe, as well in the form of common prayer, ministration of the sacraments, examination of the communicants, catechizing of the youth and instruction of the older, with divers other profitable exercises, to the great increase of true knowledge, furtherance of God's glory, and extinguishing of superstition and the advancing of true religion, and forasmuch as there be a number of malicious adversaries of the truth which do seek by all means to hinder and disturb these godly proceedings, and for that purpose do cover their malice under pretence of conformity and obedience to the same prescribed form in the said book expressed, and do rigourously require the precise observing of every part and parcel thereof, so that if a godly minister do vary from it, and use any order more sincere, and such as by the judgement of all godly learned is more profitable to edify than that prescribed in the book, or do but upon any just occasion either omit anything to be said, or but read one chapter for another, these men are ready to accuse, and have accused and presented before your Highness' justices of assizes in their circuits, and some others of them before certain other your Highness' justices, and some others indited in general sessions as wilful disobedient persons and contempners of your Highness' laws and ordinances, by means whereof great disquietness is bred among your Highness' subjects, the course of the gospel is greatly hindered, many godly preachers restrained from their godly exercises, to the great dishonour of God, grief of the godly and triumph of the enemy, and though divers godly minded prelates would be right willing to favour and maintain the use of the same godly exercises, saying that they tend very much to edification, yet for reverence of the said law, and for fear of the rigour of the same, they be disuaded, or rather restrained, from so well

149

doing: for the removing of which foresaid impediments, and for the further advancing of the true religion of Christ, whereby his name in us may be the more fully glorified and we through those godly exercises the better instructed:-

May it therefore please your most excellent Majesty of your gracious accustomed godly zeal towards the furtherance of the Gospel, that it may be enacted by the assent of your Lords spiritual and temporal, and the commons in this present Parliament assembled, that the same statute made in the said first year of your Highness' most happy reign, and every branch, clause and article therein contained concerning the prescribing of the form of common prayer and ministration of the sacraments, with the penalties therein expressed for the violating and infringing of the same, may remain and be in force against such persons only as do or shall use any manner of papistical service, rites or ceremonies by the same Act abolished, or do or shall use the same form so prescribed more superstitiously than the same Act doth authorize and allow. And furthermore that it may be enacted that it shall and may be lawful to and for all and every parson, vicar and minister, being a preacher allowed, and having the charge of any congregation, with the consent of the most part of bishops of this realm, to omit and leave any part of the same prescribed form appointed by and in the same book of common prayer, in such sort, and at times as to such parson, vicar, or minister shall be thought most necessary and expedient to preach the word of God, or to use any other godly exercise for the instruction of his congregation. And further that it may be lawful by like consent for all and every such parson, vicar, and minister to use any time or times hereafter any part of the prayers, rites, or ceremonies prescribed and appointed by and in the same book of common prayer, or otherwise with like consent to use such form of prayer and ministration of the word and sacraments, and other godly exercises of religion, as the right godly reformed churches now do use in the French and Dutch congregation, within the city of London or elsewhere in the Queen's Majesty's dominions, and is extant in print, any act or acts, injunction, advertisement, or decree heretofore had or made to the contrary notwithstanding.

150

12 1572: Possible Preface for an 'Admonition to Parliament

Dr Williams's Library, Morrice MSS 'B' 'The Seconde Parte of a Register', pt i, f. 599.

Forasmuch as heretofore it hath been thought good to bear with the weakness of certain for a time, who were too much addicted to ceremonies, thinking thereby to win them to doctrine; which sort of people for the most part have so little profited thereby this twelve or thirteen years that from their weakness they are grown to malicious wilfulness, not only craving, contending and urging ceremonies, never caring for doctrine, but by conspiracy, rebellion and open violence have practised not only utterly to displace doctrine but to overthrow the whole state, to bring in ceremonies and all other abominations; for such as so entirely love a part, do not hate the whole.

For reformation whereof, if our bishops now with other in authority will be as diligent to urge doctrine and provide that every parish have a preaching pastor, as heretofore they were in urging ceremonies and appointing that every minister should wear a surplice, with other pelf, ye shall within short time see our God more glorified, his people better edified, our prince more dutifully obeyed, sin less frequented, godliness more exercised, and these wilful weaklings, or rather rebels, better restrained and nearer sifted.

Which thing we most humbly crave with a thorough reformation both of doctrine, ceremonies and regiment, according to the admonition by the word of the Lord hereunto annexed. Wherein by a brief comparison you may see how the state of our Church is, and how it ought to be, both by the word of God, and example of the primitive Church, as also of Geneva, France, Scotland, and all other churches rightly reformed.

After which commandment and examples we desire to have our Church reformed: both for the advancement of God's glory, the edifying of his Church, and the safety of our prince, the preservation of our country, and the salvation both of our bodies and our souls; all which, reformation being neglected, are in great danger.

PART VIII

1576: Peter Wentworth in the House of Commons

Peter Wentworth, a man of 'fervent extravagances' (1), died in the Tower at the age of 73 in 1597. He first was elected an M.P. in 1571, when he was 47. The oration I print here, lasting about an hour, was delivered on the morning of Wednesday, 8 February 1576, when Wentworth was in his early fifties. I point out these age dates to emphasise that Wentworth was not at all a 'youthful radical': he must have been one of the older Members in the House, and in the speech he called, in this increasingly club-like body, upon a folk memory dating back (or distorting back) to the 1530s: 'I have heard of old Parliament men that the banishment of the pope and popery, and the restoring of true religion, had their beginning from this House and not from the bishops.' Across which tavern tables had this interpretation of 'the Tudor Revolution in Government' been propounded? At Westminster? Or in Cornwall — Wentworth was M.P. for Tregoney? Wentworth was a member of a Buckinghamshire gentry family. His second wife was a sister of Francis Walsingham — thus, like Sir Walter Mildmay, he was a brother-in-law of Walsingham. His maiden speech, on 20 April 1571, had been an attack on Humphrey Gilbert. Gilbert, a week before, had spoken of the 'prerogative imperial', and said that the Queen might legitimately follow the French, Danish and Portuguese example, and use 'absolute power' (2). (What Gilbert really meant was that he himself should exercise such 'absolute' powers in North America.) Wentworth argued that Gilbert's speech was 'an injury to the House'; and he 'requested care for the credit of the House, and for the maintenance of free speech' and 'to

153

preserve the liberties of the House' (3). The 1576 speech was read from a carefully prepared manuscript, 'written with my hand two or three years ago.' Simonds D'Ewes, in the 1620s, transcribed it 'out of a copy I had by me' (4): the preface to D'Ewes's 'Journals' of the Elizabethan Parliaments was dated 1632 (5), although the volume was not printed until 1682. In other words, the speech was prepared during the first session of Elizabeth's fourth Parliament, May-June 1572. The second session began on 8 February 1576, the date of the delivery of the speech. 'I saw certain things happen in the last session of the last Parliament. . . .'

What had happened? For one thing, order had come from on high in May 1572 that 'her Highness' pleasure is, that from henceforth no Bills concerning Religion shall be preferred or received into this House, unless the same should be first considered and liked by the clergy' (6). There had been attempts in that session to force a modification of the Book of Common Prayer. Wentworth describes some of these events in the 1576 speech. The 'liberty of free speech' had been then 'so much and so many ways infringed' — as it had been in the third Parliament, of 1571. 'Rumours' of the anger of the Queen and the Council had been hurtful from 1571 (7). The edict of May 1572 was a 'doleful message'; 'as much as to say: Sirs, ye shall not deal in God's causes . . . ye shall in no wise seek to advance his glory'. Does the Holy Spirit descend exclusively upon the bishops?

Wentworth had been one of six M.P.s summoned by Parker in 1572, with reference to the 1571 discussions in the House of Commons about the Thirty-nine Articles of Religion. The Articles (a revision of Cranmer's Forty-two) had been agreed by the 1563 Convocation, and printed in Latin in 1564. A Commons bill to give statutory confirmation — a provision of the Tudor constitution which we have seen annoyed Bucer — was blocked by the royal veto in 1566. The Articles were further revised, and an English version issued, in 1571. A bill of 1571 gave statutory confirmation to most, but not all, of the Articles; and limited the number to which the clergy had to subscribe. This bill passed the Commons, but was vetoed after a first reading in the Lords in April 1571. The Commons were told 'that the Queen's Majesty, having been made privy to the said Articles, liketh very well of them,

154

and mindeth to publish them and have then executed by the bishops, by direction of her Majesty's regal authority of supremacy of the Church of England' (8). In fact the final statute of 1571 limited clerical subscription 'to all the Articles of Religion which only concern the confession of the true Christian faith and the doctrine of the sacraments' (9). In his interview with Parker, Wentworth said that it was the duty of an M.P. to consider how the Articles 'agreed with the word of God'; and not to make Parker and the bishops 'popes'. (In 1570 Parker had been described as 'Pope of Lambeth and of Benet College'; that is, Corpus Christi College, Cambridge, of which Parker had been Master — and whose Fellows had now coined the description.) (10)

It is important to remember that the Tudor constitution, as developed in the 1530s, had implied, in its contradictions and tensions, future dilemma. Elizabeth was 'supreme governor in this realm as well in all spiritual or ecclesiastical things as temporal' — phrasing dating, in essence, from 1534. On the other hand this was done in 1559, as in 1534, 'by authority of Parliament'; and further in 1559 (not in 1534), 'by virtue of this act'. Matters even of doctrine had been resolved in the 1530s 'by consent of the Commons' (11). Wentworth's 'old Parliament men' remembered this (and also perhaps the fact, brilliantly and indefatigably investigated by Dr Elton in his best Sherlock Holmes manner, that the 1532 'Supplication against the Ordinaries' had been based on 1529 material submitted by the House of Commons) (12). In 1559 pressure from the Commons had obliged Elizabeth to bring in a Prayer more quickly than she intended, and less 'catholic' (much less, it seems) (13) than she intended. In the Act of Supremacy of 1559 what was heresy was to be determined by 'the express and plain words of the scriptures', the first four General Councils, 'or such as hereafter shall be ordered, judged or determined to be heresy by the High Court of Parliament of this realm with the assent of the clergy in their Convocation' (14). Richard Hooker was to quote these words. Such things were a balance of ambiguities. Richard Hooker, in the 1590s, could write a sustained and thoughtful exposition of the traditions of the balance of prerogative and consent in Elizabethan England. A work of the scholar's study, conjuring order out of chaos, which resolves the

155

ambiguities into a harmony; for the moment, and for the scholar. The gist of this was in book 8 of 'The Laws of Ecclesiastical Polity', which was not published until 1648: by then it must have had a nostalgic quality! 'Where the king doth guide the state, and the law the king, the common-wealth is like a harp or melodious instrument, the strings whereof are tuned and handled all by one, following as laws the rules and canons of musical science' (15).

Elizabeth thought that church matters were for herself and the clergy. In this she was supported by 'prerogative' par-liamentarians such as Nicholas Bacon and Humphrey Gilbert — and, later, Francis Bacon and Robert Cecil. A royalist speaker in 1571 mentioned the fact that the first Christian king of England, one Lucius, in the third century, was 'Vicar of Christ over the people of Britain' (16). But Beza, in 1567, had advised the English puritans to look to the Parliament. After all, the Lollards had petitioned in English in 1395: 'we poor men, treasurers of Christ and His Apostles, to the Lords and Commons of Parliament' (17). 1572 saw the two Admonitions to Parliament; the first printed in June (the parliamentary session ended on 13 June) and the second later in the year. They were 'not presented to Parliament' but were 'intended to influence opinion in the House of Commons' (18). And the puritan protest linked with the emphasis in the Elizabethan House of Commons on 'frank and free liberties to speak their minds without any controlment, blame, grudge, menaces or displeasure, according to the old ancient order' (19). Some, taking up the parliamentary theme, seemed exclusively preoccupied with the 'liberty and privileges of this House' (Paul Wentworth, 1576 — Peter's elder brother). The issue, in relation to the prerogative, was first fully debated in the 1571 Gilbert—Wentworth clash. Christopher Yelverton thought 'it was fit for princes to have their prerogatives; but yet the same to be straightned within reasonable limits' (20). Here are the First Whigs. And they had puritan accents. Tristram Pistor said in 1571 that the cause of immediate reform was God's cause: 'seek ye first the kingdom of God' (21). In 1571 also William Strickland argued for England's being brought to the 'purity of the primitive church' (22). Wentworth knew in 1576 that he was in a certain tradition — 'I have heard learned men in this

156

place sundry times affirm'. And Wentworth, who was to be elected an M.P. again from 1586 to 1593, was to see that tradition flower, especially in the Parliament of 1586/7, particularly stormy times. Sir Walter Mildmay, recent founder of Emmanuel College, agreed then that there was 'cause to complain'; but thought it dangerous 'to cancel and cut off at one blow so many laws' (23). Anthony Cope (a nicely ironical name) brought the Geneva Prayer Book into the House in 1587 and wished that it 'and none other might be received into the church to be used' (24). And with it a petition 'that it might be enacted, that all laws now in force touching ecclesiastical government should be void'. (Did Hooker know of that?) The Speaker advised the House not to proceed; but 'notwithstanding the House desired the reading of it', and the clerk was asked to read it. (In fact some debate, covering all shades of opinion, took up the time, and the petition was not in fact read.) Cope went to the Tower in 1587. And in the same year Wentworth wrote 'A Pithy Exhortation to her Majesty for establishing her Succession to the Crown'; pithy, comments Sir John Neale, 'in content, not in length' (25).

The Wentworth speech of 1576 has a fine Miltonic ring about it. 'Sweet is the name of liberty'. A feeling for England, for the 'safe-keeping . . . of this noble realm of England', and for the 'people': 'God's people', for God's spirit speaks to all. 'Let us show ourselves a people endowed with faith; I mean with a lively faith, that bringeth forth good works, and not as dead.' The safe keeping of the realm is the responsibility of the House of Commons. It is the duty of an M.P. to 'offer' anything 'commodious, profitable, or any way beneficial for the prince or state'. 'The writ, Mr. Speaker, that we are called up by, is chiefly to deal in God's cause': 'we are incorporated into this place to serve God and all England'. Thus in 'all matters that concern God's honour', the House must insist on 'free speech and conscience': 'all matters that concern God's honour through free speech shall be propagated here and set forward, and all things that do hinder it removed'. There is an apostolic ring to the proceedings, Peter playing Paul – 'with St. Paul I do advise you all here'. And a sort of divine right of M.P.s: 'we are chosen of the whole realm, of a special trust'. In the 1572 session God

157

was 'shut out of doors'. For Christ is a sort of honorary Elizabethan back-bencher: 'God saith: 'Where two or three are gathered together in his name, there am I in the midst among them'.'

So an M.P. must discuss the 'thought', 'heart' and 'conscience' of the Queen. 'Her Majesty hath committed great fault'. She opposes herself to the 'nobility and people'. 'No state can stand where the Prince will not be governed by advice': it is 'perilous always to follow the Prince's mind'. Here Wentworth brings in Bracton, the thirteenth-century English justice and legal thinker. Elizabeth is made Queen 'by the law'; she should be 'under God and under the law', ruling not by 'will' but by 'law' — law made by the House of Commons 'for her own preservation'. An in loco parentis touch. Plus the thesis that the real evil-doers are the bishops — a 'prelatical plot' theory which owes much to Barnes, to Tyndale's 1530 'The Practice of Prelates', and revives the spirit of the House of Commons in the debates of 1529. Here the 'old Parliament men', through Wentworth, can speak again. (In 1585 a speaker making the same point was to invoke Magna Carta (26); and Speaker Edward Coke was in 1593 to draw attention to the fact that the House of Commons was a flourishing institution in Saxon England) (27). There was a future for the theme of the 'restraining of the prelates' (as an M.P. aged eighty, Sir Francis Knollys, was to put it in 1593) (28). By the late 1580s, at the time of the Marprelate Tracts, it was to become dominant.

Wentworth did not complete his prepared speech. The house 'out of a reverend regard of her Majesty's honour, stopped his further proceeding before he had fully finished' (29). He was put into custody, and, in the afternoon, examined by a committee of Privy Council M.P.s. The government thought he should be put in the Tower; and so, by judgement of the Speaker, he was. He remained there for thirty-one days, and then 'was by the Queen's special favour restored again to his liberty and place in the House'.

1. Neale, 'Elizabeth I and her Parliaments', ii 435. Neale's work is of course central in any consideration of Tudor puritanism.

2. D'Ewes, 'Journals', p. 168.

3. Ibid., p. 175.

4. Ibid., p. 236. Wentworth later said that he had 'revolved' the speech 'when I walked in my grounds' (ibid., p. 243).

5. 3 February 1631: i.e. 1632.

6. D'Ewes, 'Journals', p. 213.

7. Neale, 'Elizabeth I and her Parliaments', i 221.

8. Ibid., i, p. 206.

9. Ibid.

10. Parker, 'Correspondence', p. 429.

11. 1539 'Six Articles': Elton, 'Tudor Constitution', p. 390.

12. G. R. Elton, 'The Commons' Supplication against the Ordinaries', 'English Historical Review', lxvi (1951).

13. Haugaard, 'Elizabeth and the English Reformation'.

14. Elton, 'Tudor Constitution', p. 368. In February 1629 the House of Commons was to claim to be the judge of orthodox doctrine in England (J. P. Kenyon, 'The Stuart Constitution', no. 44).

15. Hooker (Keble ed.) iii 352.

16. D'Ewes 'Journals', p. 141.

17. Probably by John Purvey. Printed in 'English Historical Review' (April 1907).

18. Neale, 'Elizabeth I and her Parliaments', i 297.

19. D'Ewes, 'Journals', p. 66: 1563 speech of Speaker.

20. Ibid., p. 176.

21. Ibid., p. 166.

22. Ibid., p. 157.

23. Neale, 'Elizabeth I and her Parliaments', ii 161.

24. The Cope affair is in D'Ewes, 'Journals', pp. 410-11. The 'petition' is in Peel (ed.), 'Seconde Parte of a Register', ii 212-15: 'all former laws, customs, statutes, ordinances and constitutions as limit, establish or set forth to be used any service, administration of sacraments, common prayer, rites, ceremonies, orders, or government of the church within this realm, or any other of your Majesty's dominions and countries, be from henceforth utterly void and of none

effect' (p. 215).

25. Neale, 'Elizabeth I and her Parliaments', ii 252.

26. Ibid., ii 66.

27. D'Ewes, 'Journals', p. 515.

28. Ibid., p. 474. Knollys mentioned the possibility of 'praemunire' proceedings against the bishops.

29. Ibid., pp. 241-4, for an account of all this.

13 Speech of Wentworth, February 1576

Simonds D'Ewes, 'A Complete Journal of all the Votes, Speeches and Debates, both in the House of Lords and the House of Commons, throughout the whole reign of Queen Elizabeth' (1693 ed.) pp. 236-41.

Mr. Speaker, I find written in a little volume these words, in effect: 'Sweet is the name of liberty, but the thing itself a value beyond all inestimable treasure.' So much the more it behoveth us to take care lest we, contenting ourselves with the sweetness of the name, lose and forego the thing: being of the greatest value that can come unto this noble realm. The 'inestimable treasure' is the use of it in this House. And therefore I do think it needful to put you in remembrance that this honourable assembly are assembled and come together in this place for three special causes of most weighty and great importance.

The first and principal is to make and abrogate such laws as may be most for the preservation of our noble sovereign.

The second. . . .

The third is to make or abrogate such laws as may be to the chiefest surety, safe-keeping and enrichment of this noble realm of England. So that I do think that the part of a faithful-hearted subject is to do his endeavour to remove all stumbling-blocks out of the way that may impair, or any manner of way hinder, these good and godly causes of this our coming together. I was never of Parliament but the last, and the last session, at both which times I saw the liberty of free speech, the which is the only salve to heal all the sores of this commonwealth, so much and so many ways infringed, and so many abuses offered to this honourable council, as have much grieved me; even of very conscience and love for my prince and state. Wherefore, to avoid the like, I do think it

161

expedient to open the commodities that grow to the prince and whole state by free speech used in this place; at the least so much as my simple wit can gather of it, the which is very little in respect of that that wise heads can say therein — and so it is of the more force.

First, all matters that concern God's honour through free speech shall be propagated here and set forward, and all things that do hinder it removed, repulsed and taken away.

Next, there is nothing commodious, profitable, or any way beneficial for the prince or state, but faithful and loving subjects will offer it in this place.

Thirdly, all things discommodious, perilous, or hurtful to the prince or state shall be prevented, even so much as seemeth good to our merciful God to put into our minds, the which no doubt shall be sufficient if we do earnestly call upon him and fear him; for Solomon saith, 'The fear of God is the beginning of wisdom: wisdom,' saith he, 'breatheth life into her children, receiveth them that seek her, and will go beside them in the way of righteousness'; so that our minds shall be directed to all good, needful and necessary things, if we call upon God with faithful hearts.

Fourthly, if the envious do offer anything hurtful or perilous to the prince or state in this place, what incommodity doth grow thereby? Verily, I think none. Nay, will you have me to say my simple opinion therein: much good cometh thereof. How forsooth? For by the darkness of the night the brightness of the sun showeth more excellent and clear; and how can truth appear and conquer until falsehood and all subtleties that would shadow and darken it be found out? For there is offered in this place a piece of fine needlework to them that are most skilful at it, for there cannot be a false stitch (God aiding us) but will be found out.

Fifthly, this good cometh thereof; a wicked purpose may the easier be prevented when it is known.

Sixthly, an evil man can do the less harm when it is known.

Seventhly, sometime it happeneth that a good man will in this place (for argument sake) prefer an evil cause, both for that he would have a doubtful truth to be opened and manifested, and also the evil prevented. So that to this point I conclude, that in this House which is termed a place of free

162

speech there is nothing so necessary for the preservation of the prince and state as free speech; and without, it is a scorn and mockery to call it a Parliament House, for in truth it is none, but a very school of flattery and dissimulation, and so a fit place to serve the Devil and his angels in, and not to glorify God and benefit the commonwealth.

Now to the impediments thereof, which by God's grace and my little experience I will utter plainly and faithfully. I will use the words of Elcha, 'Behold, I am as the new wine which hath no vent and bursteth the new vessels in sunder; therefore I will speak that I may have a vent, I will open my lips and make answer, I will regard no manner of person, no man will I spare, for if I should go about to please men I know not how soon my maker will take me away.' My text is vehement: the which by God's sufferance I mean to observe, hoping therewith to offend none; for that of very justice none ought to be offended for seeking to do good and saying of the truth.

Amongst other, Mr. Speaker, two things do great hurt in this place, of the which I do mean to speak.

The one is a rumour which runneth about the House and this it is. Take heed what you do, the Queen's Majesty liketh not such a matter, whosoever prefereth it, she will be offended with him: on the contrary, her Majesty liketh of such a matter, whosoever speaketh against it, she will be much offended with him.

The other: sometimes a message is brought into the House either of commanding or inhibiting, very injurious to the freedom of speech and consultation.

I would to God, Mr. Speaker, that these two were buried in Hell, I mean rumours and messages, for wicked undoubtedly they are. The reason is, the Devil was the first author of them, from whom proceedeth nothing but wickedness. Now I will set down reasons to prove them wicked.

First, if we be in hand with anything for the advancement of God's glory, were it not wicked to say the Queen liketh not of it or commandeth that we shall not deal in it? Greatly were these speeches to her Majesty's dishonour, and a hard opinion were it, Mr. Speaker, that these things should enter into her Majesty's thought. Much more wicked and unnatural were it that her Majesty should like or command anything against God, or hurtful to herself and the state. The Lord grant this thing may be far from her Majesty's heart. Here this may be objected, that if the Queen's Majesty should have intelligence of anything perilous or beneficial to her Majesty's person or the state, would you not have her Majesty give knowledge thereof in this House, whereby her peril may be prevented, and her benefit provided for? God forbid, then were her Majesty in worse case than any of her subjects. And in the beginning of our speech I showed it to be a special cause of our assembly, but my intent is that nothing should be done to God's dishonour, to her Majesty's peril, or the peril of the state. And therefore I will show the inconveniences that grow of these two.

First, if we follow not the prince's mind. Solomon saith, 'the king's displeasure is a messenger of death'. This is a terrible thing to weak nature, for who is able to abide the fierce countenance of his prince; but if we will discharge our consciences, and be true to God and prince and state, we must have due consideration of the place and the occasion of our coming together, and especially have regard to the matter wherein we both shall serve God and our prince and state faithfully, and not dissembling as eye-pleasers, and so justly avoid all displeasures both to God and our prince. For Solomon saith, 'in the way of the righteous there is life'; as for any other way, it is the path to death. So that to avoid everlasting death and condemnation with the high and mighty God, we ought to proceed in every cause according to the matter, and not according to the prince's mind. And now I will show you a reason to prove it perilous always to follow the prince's mind. Many times it falleth out that a prince may favour a cause perilous to himself and the whole state. What are we then if we follow the prince's mind? Are we not unfaithful to God, our prince and state? Yes, truly, we are chosen of the whole realm, of a special trust and confidence by them reposed in us, to foresee all such inconveniences. Then I will set down my opinion herein. That is, he that dissembleth, to her Majesty's peril, is to be counted as an hateful enemy, for that he giveth to her Majesty a detestable Judas his kiss; and he that contrarieth her mind to her preservation, yea, even though her Majesty would be much offended with him, is to be adjudged an approved lover: for

164

'faithful are the wounds of a lover', saith Solomon, 'but the kisses of an enemy are deceitful'. And it is better, saith Antisthenes, to fall among ravens than among flatterers, for ravens do but devour the dead corpse, but flatterers the living. And it is both traitorous and hellish through flattery to seek to devour our natural prince, and that do flatterers; therefore let them leave it, with shame enough.

Now to another great matter that riseth of this grievous rumour. What is it forsooth? Whatsoever thou art that pronouncest it, thou dost pronounce thy own discredit. Why so? For that thou dost what lieth in thee to pronounce the prince to be perjured; the which we neither may nor will believe, for we ought not without too too manifest proof to credit any dishonour to our anointed. No, we ought not without it to think any evil of her Majesty; but rather to hold him a liar, whatsoever credit he be of. For the Queen's Majesty is the head of the law, and must of necessity maintain the law, for by the law her Majesty is made justly our queen, and by it she is most chiefly maintained.

Hereto agreeth the most excellent words of Bracton, who saith the king hath no peer nor equal in his kingdom. He hath no equal, for otherwise he might lose his authority of commanding, since that an equal hath no rule of commandment over his equal. The king ought not to be under man, but under God and under the law; because the law maketh him a king. Let the king therefore attribute that to the law which the law attributeth unto him, that is, dominion and power, for he is not a king in whom will and not the law doth rule, and therefore he ought to be under the law.

I pray you mark the reason why my authority saith the king ought to be under the law. For, saith he, he is God's vicegerent here upon earth, that is, his lieutenant to execute and do his will, the which is law or justice; and thereunto was her Majesty sworn at her coronation, as I have heard learned men in this place sundry times affirm. Unto the which I doubt not but her Majesty will for her honour and conscience sake have special regard; for free speech and conscience in this place are granted by a special law, as that without the which the prince and state cannot be preserved or maintained. So that I would wish every man that feareth God, regardeth the prince's honour, or esteemeth his own credit, to fear at all times hereafter to pronounce any such horrible speeches so much to the prince's dishonour; for in so doing he showeth himself an open enemy to her Majesty, and so worthy to be condemned of all faithful hearts.

Yet there is another inconvenience that riseth of this wicked rumour. The utterers thereof seem to put into our heads that the Queen's Majesty hath conceived an evil opinion, diffidence, and mistrust in us her faithful and loving subjects. For if she had not, her Majesty would then wish that all the things dangerous to herself should be laid open before us, assuring herself that loving subjects, as we are, would, without schooling and direction, with careful minds to our powers, prevent and withstand all perils that might happen to her Majesty. And this opinion I doubt not but that her Majesty hath conceived of us; for undoubtedly there was never prince that had faithfuller hearts than her Majesty hath here, and surely there were never subjects had more cause heartily to love their prince for her quiet government than we have. So that he that raiseth this rumour still increaseth but discredit, in seeking to sow sedition, as much as lieth in him, between our merciful Queen and us her most loving and faithful subjects, the which by God's grace shall never lie in his power, let him spit out all his venom and there withal show out his malicious heart. Yet I have collected sundry reasons to prove this a hateful and detestable rumour, and the utterer thereof to be a very Judas to our noble Queen. Therefore let any hereafter take heed how he publish it, for as a very Judas to our Majesty and enemy to the whole state we ought to accept him.

Now the other* was a message, Mr. Speaker, brought the last sessions into the House, that we should not deal in any matters of religion, but first to receive from the bishops. Surely this was a doleful message. For it was as much as to say: Sirs, ye shall not deal in God's causes; no, ye shall in no wise seek to advance his glory; and in recompence of your unkindness God in his wrath will look upon your doings, that the chief cause that ye were called together for, the which is the preservation of their prince, shall have no good success. If

* That is, of the 'two things' that 'do great hurt' in the Commons (p. 163). Wentworth has been thus far discussing the first thing: the 'rumour' of Elizabeth's partiality.

someone of this House had presently made this interpretation of this said message, had he not seemed to have the spirit of prophecy? Yet truly I assure you, Mr. Speaker, there were divers of this House that said with grievous hearts, immediately upon the message, that God of his justice could not prosper the session. And let it be holden for a principle, Mr. Speaker: that council that cometh not together in God's name cannot prosper. For God saith: 'Where two or three are gathered together in his name, there am I in the midst among them.' Well, God, even the great and mighty God, whose name is the Lord of Hosts, great in counsel and infinite in thought, and who is the only good director of all hearts, was the last session shut out of doors. But what fell out of it, forsooth? His great indignation was therefore poured upon this House; for he did put into the Queen's Majesty's heart to refuse good and wholesome laws for her own preservation, the which caused many faithful hearts for grief to burst out with sorrowful tears, and moved all papist traitors to God and her Majesty, who envy good Christian government, in their sleeves to laugh all the whole Parliament House to scorn. And shall I pass over this weighty matter so lightly? No, I will discharge my conscience and duties to God, my prince, and country. So certain it is, Mr. Speaker, that none is without fault, no not our noble Queen, since then her Majesty hath committed great fault, yea, dangerous faults to herself.

Love, even perfect love devoid of dissimulation, will not suffer me to hide them to her Majesty's peril, but to utter them to her Majesty's safety. And these they are: it is a dangerous thing in a prince unkindly to abuse his or her nobility and people, and it is a dangerous thing in a prince to oppose or bend herself against her nobility and people, yea, against most loving and faithful nobility and people. And how could any prince more unkindly intreat, abuse, oppose herself against her nobility and people than her Majesty did the last Parliament? Did she not call it of purpose to prevent traitorous perils to her person, and for no other cause? Did not her Majesty send to us two bills, willing us to make choice of that we liked best for her safety, and thereof to make a law, promising her Majesty's royal consent thereunto? And did we not first choose the one and her Majesty refused

167

it, yielding no reason; nay yielding great reasons why she ought to have yielded to it? Yet did we nevertheless receive the other; and agreeing to make a law thereof did not her Majesty in the end refuse all our travails? And did not we, her Majesty's faithful nobility and subjects, plainly and openly decypher ourselves unto her Majesty and our hateful enemies, and hath not her Majesty left us all to the open revenge? Is this a just recompence in our Christian Queen for our faithful dealings? The heathen do requite good for good; then how much more is it to be expected in a Christian prince? And will not this her Majesty's handling, think you, Mr. Speaker, make cold dealing in any of her Majesty's subjects toward her again? I fear it will. And hath it not caused many already, think you, Mr. Speaker, to seek a salve for the head that they have broken? I fear it hath, and many more will do the like if it be not prevented in time. And hath it not marvellously rejoiced and encouraged the hollow hearts of her Majesty's hateful enemies and traitorous subjects? No doubt but it hath. And I beseech God that her Majesty may do all things that may grieve the hearts of her enemies, and may joy the hearts that unfeigningly love her Majesty. And I beseech the same God to endow her Majesty with his wisdom, whereby she may discern faithful advice from traitorous sugared speeches, and to send her Majesty a melting, yielding heart unto sound counsel, that Will may not stand for a Reason. And then her Majesty will stand when her enemies are fallen, for no state can stand where the prince will not be governed by advice. And I doubt not but that some of her Majesty's council have dealt plainly and faithfully herein. If any have, let it be a sure token to her Majesty to know them for approved subjects. And whatsoever they be that did persuade her Majesty so unkindly to intreat, abuse and to oppose herself against her nobility and people, or commend her Majesty for so doing, let it be a sure token to her Majesty to know them for sure traitors and underminers of her Majesty's life, and remove them out of her Majesty's presence and favour. For the more cunning they are, the more dangerous are they unto her Majesty.

But was this all? No, for God would not vouchsafe that his Holy Spirit should all that session descend upon our bishops; so that, that session, nothing was done to the advancement of

168

his glory. I have heard of old Parliament men that the banishment of the pope and popery, and the restoring of true religion, had their beginning from this House, and not from the bishops. And I have heard that few laws for religion had their foundation from them. And I do surely think — before God I speak it — that the bishops were the cause of that doleful message; and I will show you what moveth me so to think.

I was, amongst others, the last Parliament sent to the Bishop of Canterbury for the articles of religion that then passed this House. He asked us why we did put out of the book the articles for the homilies, consecrating of bishops, and suchlike. 'Surely Sir,' said I, 'because we were so occupied in other matters that we had no time to examine them, how they agreed with the word of God.' 'What,' said he, 'surely you mistook the matter: you will refer yourselves wholly to us therein.' 'No, by the faith I bear to God,' said I, 'we will pass nothing before we understand what it is; for that were but to make you popes. Make you popes who list,' said I, 'for we will make you none.'

And sure, Mr. Speaker, the speech seemed to me to be a pope-like speech; and I fear lest our bishops do attribute this of the pope's canons unto themselves, *papa non potest errare*. For surely if they did not they would reform things amiss, and not to spurn against God's people for writing therein as they do. But I can tell them news; they do but kick against the prick, for undoubtedly they both have and do err, and God will reveal his truth maugre the hearts of them and all his enemies; for great is the truth, and it will prevail. And to say the truth, it is an error to think that God's spirit is tied only to them; for the heavenly spirit saith, 'first seek the kingdom of God, and the righteousness thereof, and all these things' (meaning temporal) 'shall be given you'. These words were not spoken to the bishops only, but to all. And the writ, Mr. Speaker, that we are called up by, is chiefly to deal in God's cause, so that our commission both from God and our prince is to deal in God's causes. Therefore the accepting of such messages, and taking them in good part, do highly offend God, and is the acceptation of the breach of the liberties of this honourable council. For is it not all one thing to say, Sirs, you shall deal in such matters only, as to say,

169

you shall not deal in such matters? And so as good to have fools and flatterers in the House as men of wisdom, grave judgement, faithful hearts, and sincere consciences, for they, being taught what they shall do, can give their consents as well as the others. Well, 'he that hath an office', saith St. Paul, 'let him wait on his office', or give diligent attendance upon his office. It is a great and special part of our duty and office, Mr. Speaker, to maintain the freedom of consultation and speech, for, by this, good laws that do set forth God's glory, and for the preservation of our prince and state, are made. St. Paul in the same place saith, 'hate that which is evil, cleave unto that which is good'. Then, with St. Paul I do advise you all here present, yea and heartily and earnestly desire you from the bottom of your hearts, to hate all messengers, tale-carriers, or any other thing, whatsoever it be, that in any manner of way infringes the liberties of this honourable council. Yea, hate it or them as venomous and poison unto our commonwealth, for they are venomous beasts that do use it. Therefore I say again and again, hate that which is evil and cleave unto that which is good; and this, being loving and faithful-hearted, I do wish to be conceived in fear of God, and of love to our prince and state. For we are incorporated into this place to serve God and all England, and not to be time-servers, as humour-feeders, as cancers that would pierce the bone, or as flatterers that would fain beguile all the world, and so worthy to be condemned both of God and man. But let us show ourselves a people endowed with faith; I mean with a lively faith, that bringeth forth good works, and not as dead. And these good works I wish to break forth in this sort, not only in hating the enemies before spoken against, but also in open reproving them as enemies to God, our prince and state that do use them; for they are so. Therefore I would have none spared or forborn that from henceforth offend herein, of what calling soever he be; for the higher place he hath, the more harm he may do; therefore if he will not eschew offences, the higher I wish him hanged. I speak this in charity, Mr. Speaker, for it is better that one should be hanged than that this noble state should be subverted.

Well I pray God with all my heart to turn the hearts of all the enemies of our prince and state, and to forgive them that

170

wherein they have offended, yea, and to give them grace to offend therein no more. Even so I do heartily beseech God to forgive us for holding our peaces when we have heard any injury offered to this honourable council. For surely it is no small offence, Mr. Speaker; for we offend therein against God, our prince and state and abuse the confidence by them reposed in us. Wherefore God, for his great mercy's sake, grant that we may from henceforth show ourselves neither bastards nor dastards therein, but that as rightly begotten children we may sharply and boldly reprove God's enemies, our prince's and state's. And so shall every one of us discharge our duties in this our high office wherein he hath placed us, and show ourselves haters of evil and cleavers to that that is good, to the setting forth of God's glory and honour, and to the preservation of our noble Queen and Commonwealth. For these are the marks that we ought only in this place to shoot at. I am thus earnest, I take God to witness, for conscience sake, love — love unto my prince and Commonwealth — and for the advancement of justice. For justice, saith an ancient father, is the prince of all virtues, yea, the safe and faithful guard of man's life, for by it empires, kingdoms, people and cities be governed; the which, if it be taken away, the society of man cannot long endure. And a king, saith Solomon, that sitteth in the throne of judgement and looketh well about him chaseth away all evil. In the which state and throne, God, for his great mercy's sake, grant that our noble Queen may be heartily vigilant and watchful. For surely there was a great fault committed both in the last Parliament and since also. That was: as faithful hearts as any were unto the prince and state received most displeasure. The which is but an hard point in policy, to encourage the enemy, to discourage the faithful-hearted — who, of fervent love, cannot dissemble, but follow the rule of St. Paul, who saith, 'let love be without dissimulation'.

Now to another great fault I found the last Parliament committed by some of this House also, the which I would desire of them all might be left. I have from right good men in other causes, although I did dislike them in that doing, sit in an evil matter against which they had most earnestly spoken. I mused at it, and asked what it meant, for I do think it a shameful thing to serve God, their prince or country,

171

with the tongue only and not with the heart and body. I was answered that it was a common policy in this House to mark the best sort of the same, and either to sit or arise with them. That same common policy I would gladly have banished this House and have grafted in the stead thereof either to rise or sit as the matter giveth cause. 'For the eyes of the Lord behold all the earth, to strengthen all the hearts of them that are whole with him.' These be God's own words, mark them well I heartily beseech you all. For God will not receive half part, he will have the whole. And again, he disliketh those two-faced gentlemen, and here be many eyes that will, to their great shame, behold their double dealing that use it.

Thus I have holden you long with my rude speech: the which, since it tendeth wholly, with pure conscience, to seek the advancement of God's glory, our honourable sovereign's safety, and to the sure defence of this noble isle of England — and all by maintaining of the liberties of this honourable council, the fountain from whence all these do spring — my humble and hearty suit unto you all is, to accept my good-will, and that this that I have here spoken out of conscience and great zeal unto my prince and state, may not be buried in the pit of oblivion and so no good come thereof.

PART IX

The Puritans and Education

In the early 1570s Thomas Cartwright, lamenting the 'ruins and desolations of the church', had especially commented upon the lack of 'godly, wise, learned, grave ministers': 'able and sufficient ministers, which preach and feed diligently and carefully the flock of Christ'. England had less than 2000 such said Cartwright (there were nearly 10,000 parishes): things were better in the Reformed Church of France. Cartwright wanted Oxford and Cambridge, the Inns of Court and the gentry to give priority to the need: 'if the ministry were reformed . . .'. Whitgift, rather defensively, calculated that Cambridge graduated about thirty 'preachers' each year, 'at the least'; though some of these (almost a quarter perhaps) remained in Cambridge as Fellows (1). Not until the invention of theological colleges in the nineteenth century was this nettle of clerical incompetence (or, at any rate, lack of academic standing) to be grasped. Most Elizabethan clergy were non-academic types, ordained after some (often slight) examination by the local bishop. Shakespeare's parson in 'Love's Labour's Lost' springs to mind: 'a marvellous good neighbour, faith, and a very good bowler'.

Even Hooker was on weak ground (and no doubt felt himself to be so) when attempting some defence of the established system of clerical training — especially of the parsons who lingered at Oxbridge. The puritan aim — 'rendering as many persons as possible fit for the sacred ministry of the word and the sacraments', to quote from the statutes of Emmanuel College — was not of course necessarily subversive of the Elizabethan Church; but it involved a criticism of that church, and especially of Oxbridge.

173

The first extract, dating from the late 1580s, takes its calculations for 'preachers' direct from Cartwright; and the suggestions of the writer go beyond mere university reform. By that time Emmanuel College had been founded in Cambridge. I have printed here selections from the 1585 statutes. True it is that they owe much to the earlier sixteenth-century statutes of Trinity and Christ's (based in turn on earlier statutes) and Emmanuel was of course part of Cambridge, not a sectarian seminary in an alien field. But at the same time something new was seen to be afoot. There were, for instance, no fellowships in law or medicine; not until 1650 was Emmanuel admitted to the 'cycle' of colleges for the nomination of proctors; and the members of the college were said by 1603 to follow 'a private course of public prayer, after their own fashion', receiving the sacrament, it seems, on benches around the communion table, the bread and wine being passed along (2). (The first communion in Emmanuel was in 1588: communion was held only twice yearly.) Sam Ward, Fellow of Emmanuel, noted in his diary that 18 January 1605 was the sad day when 'the surplice was first urged by the Archbishop to be brought into Emmanuel' — the new Archbishop, that is: Richard Bancroft (3). Richard Corbett's famous verses on the visit of James I to Cambridge in 1615 indicate the popular reputation of Emmanuel (4):

> Their colleges were new bepainted
> Their founders eke, were new besainted;
> Nothing escap't; nor post, nor door,
> Nor gate, nor rail, nor bawd, nor whore.
>   You could not know, oh strange mishap!
>   Whether you saw the Town, or Map.
> But the pure house of Emmanuel
> Would not be like proud Jezebel,
> Nor shew herself before the King
> An hypocrite, or painted thing:
>   But, that the ways might all prove fair,
>   Conceiv'd a tedious mile of Prayer.

The charter of Emmanuel was granted in 1584. In the previous year, the site and buildings of the old Dominican Friary in Cambridge had been bought by Laurence Chaderton

174

of Christ's and his brother-in-law, and the estate conveyed to Sir Walter Mildmay, public servant and philanthropist, the founder of the college. (The former chapel became the hall; another building, the chapel; the name of the street flanking the extensive property — Preachers' Street — seemed newly appropriate). Mildmay, a Christ's man (and benefactor), born about 1520, had become an M.P. and begun his government career in the exchequer in 1545, and had been knighted in 1547 at Edward VI's first investiture (5). The first undergraduates (twenty-six of them) were admitted to Emmanuel in November 1584. The new buildings (supervised by Ralph Symons) were ready by 1589. Chaderton became the first master of the college (May 1584) and remained at Emmanuel until 1622, when he was succeeded by John Preston. He died in 1640, at the age of 103. In 1639 it had been decided in Massachusetts that the new college at Cambridge should be called Harvard; John Harvard (born 1607) had gone up to Emmanuel in 1627, and died in New England in 1638, leaving his library and half his estate to the college on the Charles River. Of the hundred or so Cambridge men who emigrated to New England between 1629 and 1640, thirty-three were Emmanuel bred (6). Especially to be noted are the names of Nathaniel Ward (1578-1652), who went up to Emmanuel in 1596; John Cotton (1584-1652), a Trinity man by origin, but Fellow of Emmanuel; Thomas Hooker (1586-1647), who went to Emmanuel in 1604, and remained as Fellow; and Thomas Shepard (1605-49), who entered the college in 1620 (7).

Thomas Fuller, writing in the 1630s, made available for posterity a conversation between Mildmay and the Queen. 'Sir Walter, I hear you have erected a puritan foundation.' 'No madam, far be it from me to countenance any thing contrary to your established laws, but I have set an acorn, which when it becomes an oak, God alone knows what will be the fruit thereof' (8). In 1624 there were seventy-four freshmen — the highest number in the university.

I have included in the Emmanuel section a 1588 addition to the statutes, 'Of the continuance in the college of the Fellows', stating that Fellowships are to terminate within a year after the Fellow proceeds to the doctorate of theology. This was a provision against the college becoming a

175

'permanent home' for the not-so-worthy. It was to be incorporated into the statutes of Sidney Sussex College in 1598 — but repealed under John Preston (against Chaderton's wishes). William Harrison (no puritan) in the 1570s had attacked those who 'live like drone bees on the fat of colleges'; and cited a saying of Richard Foxe, an early Tudor Master of Pembroke, that 'long continuance in those places is either a sign of lack of friends or of learning or of good and upright life' (9). The commonwealth, as Mildmay saw, should not be deprived.

My third extract in this section is ascribed in the manuscript to 'Mr Chaderton of Cambridge': this could be William Chaderton of Pembroke, Fellow of Christ's, President of Queens', and now Bishop of Chester; but one would prefer it to be (for the purpose of this book) Laurence Chaderton (they were both Lancashire men, at any rate). The directive is for 'mutual conference' of those who have 'purposed the study of divinity': parsons, and, apparently, potential parsons, to discuss the understanding of the scriptures, with two 'leaders' at some sessions. The document is quite in line with the academic training stressed in the Emmanuel statutes. Unfortunately, disputations in the nation (away from the university) were not to the liking of Authority. Such things had happened, and sometimes the laity had been admitted to the sessions — they had happened at Zürich in the 1520s, and in Geneva, following the (presumed) advice of St Paul: 'Ye may all prophesy one by one that all may learn and all may be comforted' (10) — the Zürich 'Prophetzei'. They had happened in England in the second part of the reign of Edward VI. But in March 1574 Archbishop Parker wrote that the Queen had 'willed me to suppress those vain prophesyings' (11). About half the bishops in fact seemed to approve of them — 'those godly exercises which are the universities of the poor ministers' — and Archbishop Grindal had strongly defended them (too strongly: though he never intended the laity to take part). In 1577 Elizabeth wrote to all the bishops forbidding the exercises — 'unlawful assemblies of a great number of our people out of their ordinary parishes . . . to be hearers of their disputations, and new devised opinions, upon points of divinity' (12) — and in July 1577 Grindal was confined to his house (he lived for another six years, blind and

176

sad). But such meetings as outlined in the Chaderton directive did continue; in the north, especially, until the 1630s (13). It all illustrates the thin line in the Tudor state between learned discussion and popular dissent: between education and subversion. The confusion was often one of words. Cartwright had used the word 'conference' in the 'Second Admonition to Parliament' of 1572 to mean a meeting at the neighbourhood level of 'some certain ministers, and other brethren' (as in Corinth) 'to confer and exercise themselves in prophesying, or in interpreting the scriptures' (14) — what was by the late 1580s to be called a 'conference', 'assembly', 'exercise': or 'classical conference', 'classis' — like the Presbyteries becoming established in the Church in Scotland. All meetings, even of the Chaderton type, could be condemned as 'presbyteries' (in the prose of such anglican apologists as Richard Bancroft the term was not precise): all seemed to Authority illegal. So if Chaderton's 'mutual conference' was ever put into operation, the hand of the Ecclesiastical Commission or the Star Chamber would never have been far away. The so-called Classis Movement of the 1580s seemed a revolutionary danger to some at the time; and Patrick Collinson, in his magisterial 'The Elizabethan Puritan Movement' (1967) has argued for the extent and gravity of the movement. However that may be, it seems absurd that the Chaderton ideal should ever have been clouded.

Finally in this section, to give some perspective, I have included a section from John Knox's 'Book of Discipline', drafted in the spring of 1560 (15). The educational concise-ness and severity is apparent — note the place given to medicine. It is necessary to know only that the three universities in Scotland were fifteenth-century foundations: St Andrews dating from 1413, Glasgow from 1450 and Aberdeen from 1494 (16). For purposes of comparison, one would recommend the study 'The Scholastic Curriculum at Early Seventeenth Century Cambridge' by William T. Costello — an American Jesuit who was for a time a member of the Emmanuel High Table (what would Mildmay have made of this?). And also, looking ahead, Milton's short pamphlet 'On Education', published in 1644, and dedicated to Samuel Hartlib from Polish Prussia (17).

G   P.T.E.   177

More generally, one of the great appealing points of the puritans was their campaign, in a dark and irrational world, to rescue men from folly, and from the theory that the fault lies in our stars; to urge, in justice and conscience, that both pastors and common people should understand the meaning of words, and apply these inwardly to their hearts and outwardly to their lives and conversations. Here Mildmay (and Perkins) were at one with Erasmus (and Cranmer): and the educational theories and facts of Tudor England give the century some unity (18).

1. Whitgift, 'Works', i 311-13.
2. J. B. Millinger, 'The University of Cambridge', ii: 1535-1625 (1884) pp. 310-19, is an exuberantly written account of the founding of Emmanuel. See also E. S. Shuckburgh, 'Emmanuel College' (1904); J. C. Dickinson's essay on the college in 'The City and University of Cambridge', ed. J. P. C. Roach (1959): being vol. iii of the Victoria County History of the County of Cambridge; Nikolaus Pevsner's section in 'The Buildings of England, Cambridgeshire' (1954); and M. H. Curtis, 'Oxford and Cambridge in Transition 1558-1642' (1959). The present definitive account (1964) is in Lehmberg (see n. 5 below).
3. M. M. Knappen (ed.), 'Two Puritan Diaries', p. 130.
4. 'The Poems of Richard Corbett', ed. J. A. W. Bennett and H. R. Trevor-Roper (1955) pp. 12-13. I have modernised the spelling.
5. Stanford E. Lehmberg, 'Sir Walter Mildmay and Tudor Government' (1964). Lehmberg has a chapter of fourteen pages on Emmanuel: and reproduces two portraits of Mildmay now at Emmanuel (1574, 1584). Note especially Mildmay's donations to the College Library (p. 230). By 1610, the library had more than 500 books.
6. S. E. Morrison, 'The Founding of Harvard College' (1935) app. B: 'English University Men who migrated to New England'. I have discussed some of this material in my 'Reformation and Reaction in Tudor Cambridge' (1958).

7. All four have extracts from their works in Miller and Johnson (eds), 'The Puritans': condensed version, 'The American Puritans', ed. Miller (Doubleday, Anchor Original, 1956).

8. T. Fuller, 'The History of the University of Cambridge', first printed 1655, ed. M. Prickett and T. Wright (1840) pp. 278-9.

9. William Harrison, 'Description of England', ed. G. Edelen (1968) p. 74.

10. 1 Corinthians 14:31.

11. Parker, 'Correspondence', p. 456.

12. Grindal, 'Remains', p. 467.

13. See Marchant, 'The Puritans and the Church Courts in the Diocese of York'.

14. Frere and Douglas (eds), 'Puritan Manifestoes', pp. 107-8.

15. From W. C. Dickinson (ed.), 'John Knox's History of the Reformation in Scotland, 2 vols (1949).

16. See chapter xi, 'The Universities of Scotland', in vol. ii of H. Rashdall, 'The Universities of Europe in the Middle Ages', ed. F. M. Powicke and A. B. Emden (1936): this chapter was rewritten by R. K. Hannay, in collaboration with J. H. Baxter and R. Rait.

17. See H. R. Trevor-Roper, 'Three Foreigners: the Philosophers of the Puritan Revolution', reprinted in 'Religion, Reformation and Social Change' (1967).

18. See Mrs Joan Simon's 'Education and Society in Tudor England' (1966): especially pp. 392-403, 'humanism and puritanism'.

14 'Means for the Establishing of a Learned Ministry'

From MS. in Dr Williams's Library, Morrice MSS 'B': 'The Seconde Parte of a Register', pt i, f. 545. Also printed in A. Peel (ed.), 'The Seconde Parte of a Register' (1915) ii 198-9.

The Church of England having the benefit of two famous universities, and many good schools of cathedral churches, and suchlike means, with this discipline it hath, in twenty-eight years hath not been otherwise provided for than that for 10,000 parishes there should be but 2,000 preachers. The churches of reformed discipline, wanting all these means, and having them all against them, yet by means of Discipline furnish a great number of congregations. Amend therefore that wherein we are wanting of them, and the Church shall be served.

The multitude of parishes is to be holpen by uniting. The fewness of preachers by taking away the causes of it, which are: first, want of a due calling to the ministry, and being in, of free liberty to execute it; for the sole power of the bishop in making ministers, in giving and calling in licences to preach, with other molestations; in troubling them at their courts, and with the high commission; in citing, suspending, sequestering, depriving and imprisoning them for not sub-scribing — these are the causes why there are so few. And therefore a due order is to be set down of calling to the ministry, and exercising of it, such as is used in the reformed Churches. Then unworthy ones to be thrust out, that meet men may be placed in their rooms out of the universities, or elsewhere. Oxford will be able presently to yield 194; and if it were reformed, non-residents being removed, bad Heads displaced, and the young fruit cherished, it would yield great plenty in short time. So would Cambridge yield the like, wherein by computation 140 and above fit men are un-provided for; where, the like reformation being had, the like fruit were to be looked for.

Lastly, some help would be brought for the supply of this want if sufficient maintenance were provided for such as want, which might be brought to pass by redeeming im-propriation by the bishops' temporalities, and employment of cathedral churches, and other suchlike as do no good at all.

And if all these do not suffice for the present time, till more preachers may be provided, the shire and market towns and other chief places would be furnished with preachers, and the less have exercises of prayer and reading of the holy scriptures, but for to resort upon the Sabbath days, and for administration of the sacraments, unto the next places whereas the word is preached.

15 1585: Extracts from the
Statutes of Emmanuel College, Cambridge

Latin text in 'Documents relating to the University and Colleges of Cambridge', iii (1852) pp. 483-523. New translation by Dr F. H. Stubbings, F.S.A., Fellow and Librarian of Emmanuel. Latin copies of the statutes are in the College Library, and in the British Museum, Sloane MS. 1739.

Preface

It is an ancient institution in the Church, and a tradition from the earliest times, that schools and colleges be founded for the education of young men in all piety and good learning and especially in Holy Writ and theology, that being thus instructed they may thereafter teach true and pure religion, refute all errors and heresies and by the shining example of a blameless life excite all men to virtue. For thus we read in the sacred history that the sons of the prophets at Naioth, Gilgal, Bethel and Jericho were brought up by those great and famous prophets Samuel, Elijah and Elisha to preach the name of God and instruct the people in true religion. And it is recorded in the Acts of the Apostles that at Jerusalem there were many synagogues, belonging nigh one to every nation, to which there flowed together men from almost every part of the world as to some mart of religion and learning and virtue, among whom Saul of Tarsus (that was afterward called Paul), a most chosen instrument of the Lord and the teacher of the Gentiles, is said to have sat at the feet of the reverend Gamaliel. For men that were inspired by the divine prompting of the spirit did understand that the light of the Gospel could not be spread abroad to all posterity to the glory of God and to the salvation of men but there were created and decked out in his church, as it were in the garden of paradise, some seed-plots of those most noble plants of

182

theology and right good learning, from the which such as had grown to maturity might be transplanted to all parts of the Church, that she, being watered by their labours and increased by the gift of God, might come at last to a most flourishing and blessed estate. For in like manner as the Levites were made guardians of the fire sent down from heaven (which it was only lawful to use for the burning of sacrifice upon the altar), to cherish and preserve it; so also must the true knowledge of God (like fire descended from heaven) be preserved and cherished lest we bring other fire (belike Popery and those other heresies that come of the earth and of the imaginings of men) to kindle our incense before the Lord. And as those other streams flowed out of the fountains of the garden of Eden to water the earth; so ought schools to be opened like fountains that, arising out of the paradise of God, they may, as with a river of gold, water all regions of our land, yea of the whole earth, with a faith of purest doctrine and with a life of most holy discipline. Wherefore many men of heroic virtue among our forefathers, following the divine and ancient institution of God's prophets, have dedicated to God and to the Church colleges and σοφῶν ψυχῶν φροντιστήρια, academies of philosophic souls; whose magnificance and princely outlay I leave unto others that may more nearly approach to the dignity of so great munificence to equal them, thinking it enough for myself to copy but the virtues of them that have set us a praiseworthy example in this as in so many other things, and so far as in me lies to propagate purity of life and religion unto our posterity. But since there be no societies so small that they may either be orderly governed or long endure without some system and discipline of laws be established for their government and continuance, therefore shall we draw up certain edicts and statutes, divided under their separate heads, to define all the duties of our whole college and those particular to each; and it is our desire that all our members be subject and obedient thereunto.

Of the qualifications of the new Master to be elected
[Chapter IX]
It is proper that the head be suitable to the rest of the members, and provide for the same and diligently assist them.

We desire therefore and decree that he who is to be elected Master of the aforesaid College be by birth an Englishman, one of whom the Fellows believe, being persuaded by certain evidence or by long experience, that he will prudently administer the domestic affairs of the College with all faithfulness, industry, zeal and integrity, that he will keep up our statutes, and to the best of his ability defend the goods, lands, possessions, liberties, privileges, and every single right of the College. We also desire that no one be elected Master except he has for eight full years publicly professed the study of sacred theology, and is commonly known for such profession, has publicly preached the word of the Lord, and frequently fulfilled the office of lecturer, has been accepted into the orders of the ministry, and sincerely abhors and detests popery, heresy, and all superstitions and errors; in short who, in his own affairs, and in those that have at any time been entrusted to him by others, shall have shown himself a man of diligence, worth, and honesty, and whose reputation among good men has not been impaired or called in question, and who has reached the thirtieth year of his age, and has for sixteen years been diligently engaged in the study of letters in the University of Cambridge. If any such be found among the Fellows of the College, we enjoin in the Lord's name that the same be elected. But if not, let such a one be sought amongst them that have some time been Fellows of the same College. But if neither among these can a fit person of such kind be found then it shall be permitted to choose one from Christ's College (which we desire to be given first preference), or failing that, from the whole University of Cambridge, provided that he be distinguished in endowment with the above requisite qualities and gifts.

The Oath of the Master-Elect [from Chapter XI]

And the Master-elect shall take this oath which follows: 'I, A. B., swear by God that I will sincerely embrace the true Christian religion, contrary to popery and all other heresies; that I will set the authority of scripture before the judgement of even the best of men; that other matters, which may in no wise be proved from the word of God, I will hold as of men; but I will regard the King's authority as supreme over all men under his rule, and in no wise subject to the jurisdiction of

184

foreign bishops, princes, and powers; that I will refute all opinions that be contrary to the word of God, and that I will in the cause of religion always set what is true before what is customary, what is written before what is not written. Secondly, I swear by the same God in Christ Jesus, and I faithfully promise that I will govern this College, of which I am now elected Master, with all care and diligence, and will preserve intact all its goods, lands, tenements, possessions, revenues, liberties, rights, privileges, and all things whether movable or immovable; that I will so far as in me lies keep inviolate all statutes and ordinances of this College which I know to tend to the glory of God and to the honour and profit of the College, and will take care that they are observed by others; and that, putting aside all exception of persons, I will not make any dispensation contrary to the same statutes or any part thereof, nor cause it to be made by others, nor, if such be made, in any way acquiesce therein. All these things I promise to take upon myself (so far as they be not contrary to the Statutes of the realm that have been issued or are to be issued), so help me God through Jesus Christ.'

Of the worship of God [Chapter XX]

There are three things which above all we desire all the Fellows of this College to attend to, to wit the worship of God, the increase of the faith, and probity of morals. As regards the worship of God, we first decree that each day, and especially on Sundays, all the Fellows, Scholars, Pensioners and other residents shall attend public prayers at suitable times to be appointed by the Master or his deputy; at which we desire the Master himself to be present, if he be not lawfully hindered. And he shall at least at the beginning of each term in person deliver a sermon to the Fellows and Scholars of the same College publicly assembled in the Chapel, and shall also at the same time administer the Holy Eucharist; but we exhort him in the name of the Lord that he do both more frequently.

Of the exercises, studies, and orders of the Fellows [Chapter XXI]

As touching the increase of the faith (to which we have allotted the second place), we would admonish all those who

185

are to be admitted to this College, be they Fellows or Scholars or Pensioners, that in establishing this College we have set before us this one aim, of rendering as many persons as possible fit for the sacred ministry of the word and the sacraments; so that from this seminary the Church of England might have men whom it may call forth to instruct the people and undertake the duty of pastors (a matter of all things most necessary). Be it known therefore to any Fellows or Scholars who intrude themselves into the College of any other purpose than to devote themselves to sacred Theology and in due time to labour in preaching the word, that they render our hope vain, and hold the place of Fellow or Scholar contrary to our institution; and we solemnly admonish them diligently to look to this matter, as they must know that they shall one day give account to God of the deceit they have committed. And lest we should charge the whole burden of this duty upon their own unaided consciences, although we desire them to be learned in philosophy and the other arts, and wish the custom of the University to be retained in this, both in the hearing of lectures and in other exercises, as also in proceeding to those degrees which are proper in the arts, yet we decree that the Fellows of the aforesaid College shall every week hold one disputation in Theology, in which each in his turn shall be respondent; and there shall be two opponents, which place shall be filled by each Fellow in turn according to the custom usual in other colleges. And since we find nothing generally prescribed concerning this whole kind of scholastic exercise in theology which will fully satisfy our intentions, or will not run into some difficulty, therefore we give the Master of the aforesaid College full power, with the consent of a majority of the Fellows, to prescribe from time to time such more fruitful manner of exercises as they shall decide to be most convenient for the promotion of the study of theology and for the training of ministers of the word. And what is so prescribed we desire to be observed by all the Fellows, under such penalty as has been appointed in respect of other exercises. And of the whole number of Fellows of the said College we desire that at least the four most senior be ministers of the word and the sacraments, and that they be admitted to that order within one year of the date of publication of our statutes in the College aforesaid. And when any of these ministers shall depart from the College, we desire the next of the Fellows in order of his seniority within six months of the retirement of the said minister from the College to be promoted to the order of minister of the word and sacraments, so that there shall always be in the aforesaid College not fewer than four ministers. And anyone who shall not become a minister of the word and sacraments in accordance with this regulation shall for ever lose the rights of his fellowship. And those who shall be called to this order of the sacred ministry are to know that we have placed the fullest confidence in their wisdom and diligence, more than in the others, that the rest may be imbued and trained in Christ with the best possible instruction; and we pray them in the Lord that they will make it their duty to be diligently watchful as over a flock that is entrusted to them. At table at every meal all shall diligently and attentively hear the Bible before and after dinner and supper, until the Master or his deputy shall tell the Bibler to end. Concerning the retention of Latin speech in private and familiar intercourse, we leave it to the judgement of the Master to prescribe what he think fit in that matter, provided that they all make use thereof in such manner as the Master shall judge will be useful to them.

Of vicious manners forbidden to every Fellow [Chapter XXII]

But since it is of little profit that men be learned unless they be good also, we therefore desire and decree that none of the same Fellows shall frequent public taverns, houses of ill fame, or any improper place. None shall engage in drinking parties and carousals or the bearing of arms; none shall hold secret converse with a woman anywhere, especially in any of the rooms of the said College, which we desire no woman ever to enter, if she be alone, nor to remain in the same, except in time of sickness, being a person known and approved of the Master or his deputy. Moreover let none be a walker by night, nor sleep abroad at night outside the said College at any place within three miles of the same College, nor venture at all outside the precincts of the College after nine o'clock on any night from Michaelmas to Easter, or ten o'clock from Easter to Michaelmas, except for some necessary cause to be approved by the Master or his deputy.

187

Also none shall keep dogs or birds of prey, nor play at knucklebones, dice, or cards, even for recreation. Finally none shall show disrespect to his senior but shall give precedence to him both at home and abroad, in chapel and at table, in the schools and in the streets, unless perchance he be above him by reason of some academic degree; for, except his degree prevent it, we desire that the senior shall always go before the junior in all places.

Of the visitation of student's rooms, so that idle gatherings be not held therein [Chapter XXVIII]

Among the many undesirable things that hinder the progress of them that be studious of good learning, no little harm is done by the frequent converse of the young upon idle matters; for besides the waste of time (which is to be accounted not among the least of the damages) there is engendered in youthful minds an evil habit by which they are most easily diverted from serious things to frivolities and foolishness. We therefore decree and ordain that neither pensioners nor scholars nor sizars nor subsizars (unless they be Masters of Arts) shall presume to hold any meeting in their chambers either for play, for feasting, for conversation, or under any other pretext whatsoever. And whosoever shall act contrary to this rule, if he be of age, shall be fined twelve-pence for each occasion by the Master or, in his absence, his deputy; or if he be not yet out of the age of boyhood, he shall be punished by the Dean by beating. And that this may be more strictly observed we decree and ordain that the Fellows, one or two at a time, at the discretion of the Master, shall each in their turn inspect and visit the chambers of such pensioners, scholars, sizars, and subsizars, at night, at least twice each week; and they shall diligently discover what is going on in each, and shall commend the diligent and reprove the negligent; and whosoever they find violating this statute, they shall the next day report their names so that they may be fined as above ordained. And the fines in money from offenders of this sort shall be devoted towards the Fellows' victuals.

188

Of the qualification and election of the Scholars [Chapter XXXII]

Lest this seminary be unfit and unruly, and incapable of gentle and seemly governance, we desire and decree that the scholars shall be chosen from among such young men as are distinguished by poverty, honesty, and outstanding ability, persons of good character, talents, and promise, not Bachelors of Arts nor yet admitted to the sacred ministry, but who intend to take up theology and the sacred ministry; and they shall be at least moderately instructed and skilled in Greek, rhetoric and logic. Those that are poor shall be preferred, provided that they be equal in other qualifications. Wherefore we especially desire to give preference to those born in the counties of Essex or of Northampton; from which we desire that there shall always be two scholars in the same College; provided that there shall not at any one time be more than three scholars from either of these counties, nor from any other county in all England.

Of presentations to vacant livings [Chapter XXXVIII]

A great burden of responsibility is laid upon us by those who, relying in the good faith and judgement of the Master and Fellows, have entrusted, or intend to entrust to this our College, those churches of which they are themselves patrons, so that they may be committed to the best pastors that may be. Wherefore, in order that their pious desires and opinions may be satisfied, and in the interest of those who are assured that the well-being of souls depends to no small extent upon the pious ordering of those churches, we exhort the Master and Fellows in the Lord, that, in appointing pastors to these churches, and to those of which hereafter the care may in the same manner be given up to them by the patrons thereof, they act in sincerity, and neither regard any man's favour in that matter, nor be moved by gifts, but cast their votes for that man whom, their own conscience guiding them, they shall esteem to be best endowed with those gifts which the Holy Spirit bestows upon the true pastor, being resolved that, if any sin be therein knowingly committed by them, they must hereafter render account before the Supreme Judge, as for the betrayal of a brother's blood. And that this whole business of electing pastors may be the more carefully administered, we desire and decree, that within the space of three months from the time when they shall know that a pastor is wanting in some one of the said churches (whether this shall have come about by the death of him who last held that office, or by deprivation or by resignation, or in any other manner) they shall elect one of their own number whom they shall resolve to be most fit, and who shall hold no other ecclesiastical benefice having the cure of souls or the requirement of residence or frequent attendance annexed thereto whether by the laws, statutes or customs of this realm, or under the foundation of the benefice itself, or by local statute; and that they shall effectively present him to the bishop of the diocese in which the living shall be vacant, or to whatever other person shall have the power of instituting the pastor or rector, to be admitted and instituted as pastor or rector of the church aforesaid. But we entirely forbid that persons be chosen for presentation as pastors or rectors of the churches from elsewhere than the College itself, since we have no doubt that it will suffice to supply men fitted for that office.

Moreover we desire and decree that no one be presented to undertake the cure of a vacant church except he have first given suitable surety to the Master and Fellows of the aforesaid College that, so long as he retains the position of pastor or rector of that church to which he is presented, he will diligently reside in the aforesaid church according to the requirement of the common law; neither will he obtain or accept any dispensation which will free him from the requirement of residence; and that so long as he is pastor or rector of that church he will neither accept nor retain any ecclesiastical benifice, dignity, or office, having the cure of souls annexed thereto, or which shall tie him to residence or frequent attendance away from the said church, whether by requirement of the laws or customs of this realm or of the foundation or of local law or custom. Finally, that all base practice may be removed from this business, and all be done piously and religiously as the gravity of the matter itself requires, we desire and decree that, if the Master or any of the Fellows of the aforesaid College shall be convicted by having accepted money or any kind of gift for casting his vote in the presentation of a pastor to any of the aforesaid churches, or

190

for transferring his vote to anyone, he shall for ever lose that position which he holds in the aforesaid College. We wholly withdraw from the Master and Fellows all power of delegating advowsons to any person, as also the power of consenting to impropriations.

Of the interpretation of ambiguities and obscurities [Chapter XLI]

But if any obscurity shall appear in these our statutes which shall require interpretation of necessity, we reserve the interpretation to ourselves (so long as we shall live), and we desire that the Master, Fellows and Scholars aforesaid be content therewith, and hold and observe it for ever as a Statute of the College. And after God in his mercy shall have called us out of this life, then if any ambiguity or obscurity shall appear thereafter, we desire the Master and those Fellows who are present in the College to discuss it, and to have and to hold as true and legitimate that interpretation which the majority of them shall make. But if there shall not be agreement among those just aforesaid, or if any one of the fellows or scholars shall complain that this interpretation is unfair, then within ten days from the time of the aforesaid discussion we desire that an approach be made to the Master of Christ's College and the two senior Doctors of Divinity of the University aforesaid, and whatever opinion of the disputed statute shall be decided upon by two of the same, we desire that the aforesaid dispute be terminated thereby, and that all acquiesce therein.

Of the common estate of all who shall be in the College [Chapter XLII]

Although we willingly concede to marriage that honour which is accorded to it by the Holy Spirit in Holy Writ, and reject the opinion of those who have held that matrimony ought to be forbidden to a certain order of men, yet there are many and grave causes why we should suffer no one of those who shall be numbered among the members of our College to be married. We therefore desire and decree that if anyone hereafter who has a wife shall be elected in the College aforesaid, his election shall be held void, as of one unable to have any rights in the College aforesaid; and if he shall take a wife

191

after his election he shall forever lose all rights he may have obtained by such election.

These statutes we have published for the government of our College, and we enjoin that they be diligently and without violation observed by all members thereof; but so that we reserve to ourselves so long as we shall remain in this life, authority to add to, to take away from, to change, and to interpret them, as often as we shall see just cause arising. In faith and testimony of all which I, the above named Walter Mildmay, have affixed my seal to these presents.

Given on the first day of October, in the year of our Lord one thousand five hundred and eighty-five, and the twenty-seventh year of our most illustrious Lady Elizabeth, of England, France, and Ireland, Queen etc.

Wa. Mildmay

[1588:] Of the continuance in the College of the Fellows, and of their proceeding to the degree of Doctor of Divinity

Seeing that we have founded our College to the intent that it might be by the grace of God a seminary of learned men, from which there may be supplied to the Church as great a number as may possibly be produced therefrom to instruct the people in the Christian religion, we desire that none of the Fellows suppose that we have given him a permanent home in that College; and we are the more persuaded that this must be guarded against for that we have heard many wise and grave men complain, supporting their opinion by many examples both from their own memory and of the present time, that the overlong residence of Fellows in other Colleges has done no little hurt both to the affairs of the Commonwealth and to the interests of the Church. For not only are they themselves almost useless, but they also deprive the Commonwealth of that profit which should accrue through the example of praiseworthy industry. To the end, therefore, that in the production of learned men, which we desire to be as plentiful as may be, we may be seen to have aimed at a rich harvest, and with a view also to the dignity and reputation of our College, we desire and decree that both the Master and all the Fellows, present and future, see to it

192

that they proceed, as soon as by the public statutes of the University they can and may, to the degree of Doctor of Divinity. And if any of them, whether the Master or any one of the Fellows, shall not have obtained the degree of Doctor of Divinity within that space of time which is by statute appointed for that degree, then from the next day of admission to degrees on which he might otherwise have received his Doctorate, he shall for ever forfeit all present and future tenure of his place in the College. But after taking the aforesaid degree we desire that the Master hold office permanently; but we desire that no Fellow should hold a fellowship for more than one year from the day of admission on which he has been duly made a Doctor or on which his Doctorate becomes effective by special grace. But we desire that in reckoning that year no account be taken of any time during which it shall fall to any one of them to hold the office of Vice-Chancellor or to perform the duties of the Regius Professorship of Divinity or of that Professorship founded by the illustrious Lady Margaret, Countess of Richmond and Derby, provided that these duties be performed in their own name and right. But as soon as they shall have laid down their office or ceased to hold the post of these Professorships which we have specified, then after the expiry of such number of days as were required, not counting the time of their office or professorship, for the completion of a year, they shall permanently cease to be Fellows. But that those who retire in this manner from our College may not think themselves utterly cast off by us, we desire and decree that, whensoever any benefice under the patronage of our College happens to fall vacant after the retirement of any one of them, it shall be permitted to the Master and Fellows of the said College to present the same to the said benefice (if they think fit) just as if he still held the rights of a Fellow: provided that he do not at that time obtain any other ecclesiastical benefice having the cure of souls attached thereto, or that he effectually relinquish any which he may hold, and that he shall not already have accepted any benefices on the presentation of the College. And even so we do not desire any regard to be had for him unless, in the same manner as has been before ordained by us concerning the presentation of Fellows to benefices, he give surety that he

193

will not accept any other benefice with cure, or requiring personal residence, unless after resigning completely that which he shall obtain on the presentation of the College, and that he will reside in the benefice as required by the common law so long as he shall hold it. And lest we should be thought to have been concerned only about the Doctorate of Divinity, and to have neglected other degrees, we desire and decree that if any Fellow of our College aforesaid shall not become a Master of Arts or Bachelor of Divinity within that space of time which is laid down therefore by the Statutes of the University, then after the next congregation at which these degrees are conferred upon candidates, he shall be entirely removed from the College to the permanent exclusion of all expectation of re-election to a Fellowship in the said College; and we desire that his state be the same as that of any Master or Fellow whose removal for whatsoever reason is laid down under our other statutes.

Given on the last day of February, A.D. 1587, in the thirtieth year of the most illustrious Lady Elizabeth, of England, France, and Ireland, Queen, etc.

Wa. Mildmay

16 'Order for the Training of Divinity Students'

'An Order to be used for the training up and exercising of students in Divinity, whereby they may be made fit and meet to discharge the duties belonging to that profession': Dr Williams's Library, Morrice MSS 'A' ('Puritan Controversy'), f. 191. Partial transcript printed in A. Peel (ed.), 'The Seconde Parte of a Register' (1915) i 133-4.

The manuscript ascribed this text to 'Mr Chaderton of Cambridge'. Stephen K. Jones, formerly Librarian of Dr Williams's Library, noted that this was probably William Chaderton, Bishop of Chester, and the orders meant for use in his diocese. But it could well have been Laurence Chaderton of Emmanuel.

Because it is necessary that every minister should be able to teach sound doctrine by the true interpretation of the Word, and to confute all contrary errors, by unanswerable arguments and reasons, these two means following may seem to be very requisite for the attaining unto the aforesaid principal gifts of the ministry.

The first is mutual conference of such as being very studious, and of good towardness in learning, have purposed only the study of divinity. The order whereof is this:

All that come to this conference are to begin the Bible, and to proceed unto the end thereof; confessing of so much at one time, as shall conveniently serve for the finishing of the whole once in two years or thereabouts.

In performance thereof they must diligently search out by themselves the true sense and meaning of the text appointed: using the help of all these gifts following, or as many of them as they have received; the which God hath promised and given to his Church for that purpose.

The first hereof is the knowledge of the tongues, especially of the Hebrew and Greek; wherein God hath revealed and written his will and testament by his prophets and apostles, and thereafter hath given this gift to his church, for the

195

better understanding of the etymology, true construction, proper signification, phrase and use of all those words wherein his will is expressed.

The second is the art of Rhetoric, which teacheth truly to discern proper speeches from those that are tropical and figurative, etc.

The third is the art of reasoning, called Logic: which teacheth to find out the matter, and the whole sense that is expressed in the words, and to frame and gather necessary arguments and conclusions, as well for the proof of true, as for the disproof of false, doctrines, and that by the diligent searching and judging every argument by itself, and the right dispositions thereof in propositions, in syllogisms, in method and due order, which serveth not only for the directing of judgement, and clearing of the understanding touching the interpretation of the Word, but also for the helping and preserving of memory.

The fourth is a wise comparing together of the same or like places of the scripture which agree in words, propriety of speech, circumstance, or matter.

The fifth is the reading of the learned commentaries of the old and new writers, and of the ancient councils, with due examination of their interpretations and judgements; not differing from them but on just occasion, ·whereof good reason may be rendered by the means aforesaid.

The sixth and last is the knowledge of Greek and Latin histories, and chronicles, for the better understanding of the histories in the scriptures, and the reconciling of many places which otherwise might seem doubtful.

When every one of them by all these gifts, or so many as they could, hath diligently examined the text, two of them shall be appointed to deliver briefly in speech that which they are persuaded to be the meaning thereof, adding reasons for the proof of the same. The rest shall hear and judge, and then by objecting and answering in good order confer together of the interpretations till they depart. If they dissent in opinion they shall make it a 'question', and so determine it by disputation, as in questions of doctrine. And this to be the order of mutual conference, concerning the meaning of the Word.

196

The second means is disputation, which is profitable for defence of the truth, and the confutation of error, the manner whereof, to be according to the several customs practised in all universities.

In this disputation all the principal questions in controversy between us and the papists and other heretics shall be handled and determined in the aforesaid time of two years.

Finally, for the commodity and benefit of these and other students in divinity, and for the better remembrance of those good things which may come of these two exercises of private conference and disputation, two books are to be made. One to note such interpretations of hard and doubtful places, with the reasons thereof, as shall be thought necessary; the other, to write in all questions, objections and answers which shall be disputed and determined from time to time.

17 Extract from Knox's 'Book of Discipline'

Version from W. C. Dickinson (ed.) 'John Knox's History of the Reformation in Scotland', 2 vols (Nelson, 1949) ii 295-9. Addressed to 'The Great Council of Scotland'. The first edition of the 'History' was 1586/7, and contained part of the 'Book of Discipline'; the whole 'Book' was not published until 1621 (in Holland).

THE NECESSITY OF SCHOOLS

Seeing that God hath determined that his Church here in earth shall be taught not by angels but by men; and seeing that men are born ignorant of all godliness, and seeing also [that] God now ceaseth to illuminate men miraculously, suddenly changing them, as that he did his Apostles and others in the Primitive Church: of necessity it is that your Honours be most careful for the virtuous education and godly upbringing of the youth of this Realm, if either ye now thirst unfeignedly [for] the advancement of Christ's glory, or yet desire the continuance of his benefits to the generation following. For as the youth must succeed to us, so ought we to be careful that they have the knowledge and erudition to profit and comfort that which ought to be most dear to us, to wit, the Church and Spouse of the Lord Jesus.

Of necessity therefore we judge it, that every several church have a Schoolmaster appointed, such a one as is able, at least, to teach Grammar and the Latin tongue, if the town be of any reputation. If it be upland, where the people convene to doctrine but once in the week, then must either the Reader or the Minister there appointed, take care over the children and youth of the parish, to instruct them in their first rudiments, and especially in the Catechism, as we have it now translated in the Book of our Common Order, called the

198

Order of Geneva. And further, we think it expedient that in every notable town, and especially in the town of the Superintendent, [there] be erected a College in which the Arts, at least Logic and Rhetoric, together with the Tongues, be read by sufficient Masters, for whom honest stipends must be appointed: as also provision for those that be poor, and be not able by themselves, nor by their friends, to be sustained at letters, especially such as come from landward.

The fruit and commodity hereof shall suddenly appear. For, first, the youth-head and tender children shall be nourished and brought up in virtue, in presence of their friends; by whose good attendance many inconvenients may be avoided, in the which the youth commonly falls either by too much liberty, which they have in strange and unknown places, while they cannot rule themselves, or else for lack of good attendance, and of such necessities as their tender age requireth. Secondly, the exercise of the children in every church shall be great instruction to the aged.

Last, the great Schools, called Universities, shall be replenished with those that be apt to learning; for this must be carefully provided, that no father, of what estate or condition that ever he be, use his children at his own fantasy, especially in their youth-head; but all must be compelled to bring up their children in learning and virtue.

The rich and potent may not be permitted to suffer their children to spend their youth in vain idleness, as heretofore they have done. But they must be exhorted, and by censure of the Church compelled to dedicate their sons, by good exercise, to the profit of the Church and to the Commonwealth; and that they must do of their own expenses, because they are able. The children of the poor must be supported and sustained on the charge of the Church, till trial be taken whether the spirit of docility be found in them or not. If they be found apt to letters and learning, then may they not (we mean neither the sons of the rich, nor yet the sons of the poor), be permitted to reject learning but must be charged to continue their study, so that the Commonwealth may have some comfort by them. And for this purpose must discreet, learned, and grave men be appointed to visit all Schools for the trial of their exercise, profit, and continuance; to wit, the Ministers and Elders, with the best learned in every town, shall every quarter take examination how the youth hath profited.

A certain time must be appointed to Reading, and to learning of the Catechism; a certain time to the Grammar, and to the Latin tongue; a certain time to the Arts, Philosophy, and to the Tongues; and a certain [time] to that study in which they intend chiefly to travail for the profit of the Commonwealth. Which time being expired, we mean in every course, the children must either proceed to further knowledge, or else they must be sent to some handicraft, or to some other profitable exercise; provided always, that first they have the form of knowledge of Christian religion, to wit, the knowledge of God's law and commandments, the use and office of the same, the chief articles of our belief, the right form to pray unto God, the number, use, and effect of the sacraments, the true knowledge of Christ Jesus, of his office and natures, and such other [points] as without the knowledge whereof, neither deserveth [any] man to be named a Christian, neither ought any to be admitted to the participation of the Lord's table. And therefore, these principals ought and must be learned in the youth-head.

THE TIMES APPOINTED TO EVERY COURSE

Two years we think more than sufficient to learn to read perfectly, to answer to the Catechism, and to have some entry in the first rudiments of Grammar; to the full accomplishment whereof (we mean of the Grammar), we think three or four years, at most, sufficient. To the Arts, to wit, Logic and Rhetoric, and to the Greek tongue, four years; and the rest, till the age of twenty-four years, to be spent in that study wherein the learner would profit the Church or Commonwealth, be it in the Laws, or Physic or Divinity. Which time to twenty-four years being spent in the schools, the learner must be removed to serve the Church or Commonwealth, unless he be found a necessary Reader in the same College or University. If God shall move your hearts to establish and execute this order and put these things in practice, your whole Realm (we doubt not) within [a] few years shall serve the self of true preachers, and of other officers necessary for your Commonwealth.

200

The Grammar Schools and of the Tongues being erected as we have said, next we think it necessary there be three universities in this whole Realm, established in the towns accustomed. The first in Saint Andrews, the second in Glasgow, and the third in Aberdeen.

And in the first University and principal, which is Saint Andrews, there be three Colleges. And in the first College, which is the entry of the University, there be four classes or seiges: the first, to the new Supposts* shall be only Dialectics; the next, only Mathematics; the third, of Physics only; the fourth of Medicine. And in the second College, two classes or seiges: the first, in Moral Philosophy; the second in the Laws. And in the third College, two classes or seiges: the first, in the Tongues, to wit, Greek and Hebrew; the second, in Divinity.

OF READERS, AND OF THE DEGREES OF TIME, AND STUDY

Item. In the first College, and in the first class, shall be a reader of Dialectics who shall accomplish his course thereof in one year. In the mathematics, which is the second class, shall be a Reader who shall complete his course of Arithmetic, Geometry, Cosmography, and Astrology, in one year. In the third class shall be a Reader of Natural Philosophy, who shall complete his course in a year. And who, after these three years, by trial and examination, shall be found sufficiently instructed in these aforesaid sciences, shall be Laureate and Graduate in Philosophy. In the fourth class, shall be a reader of Medicine, who shall complete his course in five years: after the study of the which time, being by examination found sufficient, they shall be graduate in Medicine.

Item. In the second college, in the first class, one Reader only in the Ethics, Economics and Politics, who shall complete his course in the space of one year. In the second

* Members of the university, Knox means.

class, shall be two readers in the Municipal and Roman laws, who shall complete their courses in four years; after the which being by examination found sufficient, they shall be graduate in the Laws.

Item. In the third college, in the first class, a Reader of the Hebrew and another of the Greek tongue who shall complete the grammars thereof in half a year, and the remanent of the year the Reader of the Hebrew shall interpret a book of Moses, [or of] the Prophets, or the Psalms; so that his course and class shall continue one year. The Reader of the Greek shall interpret some book of Plato, together with some place of the New Testament. And in the second class, shall be two Readers in Divinity, that one in the New Testament, that other in the Old, who shall complete their course in five years. After which time, who shall be found by examination sufficient, shall be graduate in Divinity.

Item. We think expedient that none be admitted unto the first College, and to be Supposts of the university unless he have from the Master of the School, and the Minister of the town where he was instructed in the tongues, a testimonial of his learning, docility, age, and parentage; and likeways trial to be taken by certain Examinators, depute by the Rector and Principals of the same, and, if he be found sufficiently instructed in Dialectics, he shall incontinent, that same year, be promoted to the class of Mathematics.

Item. That none be admitted to the class of the Medicine but he that shall have his testimonial of his time well spent in Dialectics, Mathematics, and Physics, and of his docility* in the last.

Item. That none be admitted unto the class of the Laws, but he that shall have sufficient testimonials of his time well spent in Dialectics, Mathematics, Physics, Ethics, Economics, and Politics, and of his docility in the last.

Item, That none be admitted unto the class and seige of Divines but he that shall have sufficient testimonials of his time well spent in Dialectics, Mathematics, Physics, Ethics, Economics, Moral Philosophy, and the Hebrew tongue, and of his docility in the Moral Philosophy and the Hebrew tongue. But neither shall such as will apply them to hear the

* Dr Dickinson tells us that the word means 'aptitude to learning'.
202

Laws, be compelled to hear Medicine; neither such as apply them to hear Divinity be compelled to hear either Medicine or yet the Laws.

Item. In the second University, which is Glasgow, shall be two colleges only.* In the first shall be a class of Dialectics, another in Mathematics, the third in Physics, ordered in all sorts as [in] Saint Andrews.

Item. In the Second College, four classes; the first in Moral Philosophy, Ethics, Economics, and Politics; the second of the Municipal and Roman Laws; the third of the Hebrew tongue; the fourth in Divinity. Which shall be ordered in all sorts, conform to it we have written in the order of the university of Saint Andrews.

The third university of Aberdeen shall be conform to this university of Glasgow, in all sorts.

* 'alanerlie', in the text.

PART X

1589: Marprelate's Anti-episcopal Rhetoric

From October 1588 until September 1589 there were secretly printed seven pamphlets usually known together as 'the Marprelate Tracts'. The author of four of the seven was described as the reverend, worthy, famous and renowned Martin Marprelate; gentleman, clerk, Doctor in all the Faculties; primate and metropolitan of all the Martins in England; Martin Marprelate the Great. (One of the others was said to be edited by Martin Junior, 'a pretty stripling of his'; and another — from which my extract is taken — by Martin Senior, reverend and elder brother of the lad, son and heir to Martin Marprelate.) The authorship was, and remains, a mystery. (Lately computers have been at work on this literary problem.) The printing was largely done by Robert Waldegrave, 'one of the more reckless figures in Elizabethan puritan history' (1), who had printed in 1584 the first English edition of the Geneva Prayer Book. The printing press was kept on the move: from near Kingston-on-Thames, to Fawsley House, Northamptonshire, then to Coventry, then to nearby Wolston. After the sixth tract had appeared (July 1589) the press moved to Lancashire, and (after an accident with the type at Warrington) it was seized in Manchester in August, and the printers examined by the Earl of Derby. The seventh and final tract, probably printed at Wolston, came out in that September.

Marprelate's general theme was that of the usurping 'practice of prelates' (to borrow the words of the title of Tyndale's 1530 historical survey, published in Antwerp: a work commended by Marprelate). Marprelate said, quite rightly, that what many people objected to was not his

205

subject matter, but his 'form' (2); and the works fall into a tradition of English rhetoric which reminds one of Barnes, Tyndale, John Skelton, John Bale, Hugh Latimer, Thomas Becon and Field — and looks forward to John Milton. *The Act of Extravagant Abuse.* Marprelate's intention was 'to speak in plain English', and to tell 'pretty stories' (3). And though he had a good gift of succinct summary — as, for instance, in his exposition on whether the government of the church was prescribed in the New Testament (in the second tract) (4) — the general effect is throw-about; passionate, gossipy, racy, proverbs, puns and nicknames falling over each other, crammed with contemporary allusions. The bewildered reader feels he is on the receiving end of an extended monologue by Launcelot Gobbo; the tracts would be as difficult fully to annotate as say, the films of the Marx Brothers in their Paramount period. Marprelate was aware that many in the puritan establishment found him offensive — 'the Puritans are angry with me,' he wrote: 'I mean the puritan preachers. And why? Because I am too open, because I jest' (5). (Elsewhere he accepted the description 'puritan' without rancour' (6).) Thomas Cartwright, for instance, viewed the tracts with 'mislike and sorrow' (7) (so did C. S. Lewis) (8).

The present extract attacks Archbishop Whitgift and the 'usurping prelacy': 'usurpers and antichrists' (9). Seriously, in some ways: with a feel of 'the hungry sheep look up and are not fed', an appeal to the honour of Englishmen and (a loaded phrase!) 'the true doctrine of our church'. We are treated to attacks on the episcopal legal apparatus: chancellors and commissaries; and the Court of Faculties at Canterbury, which dealt with matters of marriage, discipline and tenure of benefices — grants of non-residence or plurality, for instance — and which really dated from April 1534, dispensations from Rome having been declared invalid in England from March. The new Canterbury system seemed to many not much quicker or cheaper than the old Roman one. 'I pray God send me little ado with any spiritual men', moaned someone involved in a marriage dispensation matter (10) — what most Tudor laymen thought, probably.

We also meet the idea that the prelates might be indicted under the old 'praemunire' statutes; a complex of four-teenth-century laws — meaning, really, an indictment for *offending against 'the prerogatives, liberties and pre-eminences of the imperial crown of this realm'. Some bishops and lower clergy had been so indicted in 1530; and in 1531 the entire clergy of all England were indicted (in rather a teasing way, one feels: they bought their way out). The attack on the 'spiritualty' in England was a leading theme of the years 1529 to 1532 (11); and it appears yet again here — the 'prelates' now being the Elizabethan bishops. The Whitgift-praemunire idea was to be common gossip by the autumn of 1590. And the idea falls into the related contro-versy within anglicanism since 1588 about the 'divine right' of episcopacy — 'by the early 1590's it is possible to detect a marked change in the character of the Anglican attitude to episcopacy': 'The jure divino movement' (12). In February 1589 Richard Bancroft, aged 43, canon of Westminster, attacked Marprelate in a sermon preached at Paul's Cross (the outdoor pulpit next to St Pauls Cathedral) — a sermon tradi-tionally cited as the first statement in anglican apologetic of the 'divine right of episcopacy'. In fact Bancroft was probably in line with John Whitgift and John Bridges, Dean of Salisbury. The first two of the Marprelate tracts were attacks on Bridges, and upon his 'Defence of the Government established in the Church of England' (against Cartwright and Walter Travers, published in 1587).*

But the reader of the extract will be more entertained by the stridency of the personal attack upon Whitgift.

Whitgift had been elected a Fellow of Peterhouse when he was 23, in 1555. The new Master of Peterhouse at the time was Andrew Perne, aged 36. Whitgift remained at Peterhouse until 1567, when he became Master of Trinity and Regius Professor of Divinity; he had originally gone up to Pembroke in 1550 (when Nicholas Ridley was Master of the College), and stayed in Cambridge in all for twenty-seven years, leaving in 1577 to be a Bishop of Worcester. It is typical of Mar-prelate's 'form' that a heavy insinuation is made in this extract (and elsewhere) that Perne and Whitgift had been homosexual lovers (13). (Both were bachelors.) Indeed, sexual references and puns abound in the tracts; and William Pierce, in his edition of 1911, discretely missed the signifi-cance of much of this. ('Vicar', for instance, is easily con-verted into the famous Anglo-Saxon four-letter word.) Perne

207

had died in 1586 while on a visit to Whitgift at Lambeth Palace. A generous, hospitable and academic man. But perhaps too 'applicable to every time, place and person', to use a phrase of Gabriel Harvey's He was Master of Peterhouse under Mary, and accepted the regime; indeed, while Vice-Chancellor (a post he was five times to hold) he preached a sermon at the condemnation of the corpses of Martin Bucer and Paul Fagius. During his next tenure of the office, in 1559, the university passed a grace restoring Bucer and Fagius to honour. The undergraduates invented a Latin word perno, 'to change often'; and the letters A.P.A.P. on the weathercock of a Cambridge church were said to mean Andrew Perne a papist (or protestant, or puritan). 'Old Andrew Turncoat', Marprelate elsewhere called him (14).

The passionate indignation of Marprelate springs from the relatively hard line pursued by Whitgift when he succeeded Grindal as Archbishop of Canterbury in 1583. In October 1583 all persons with ecclesiastical function were to 'consent and subscribe' to three articles: that the Queen has sovereignty over all persons; that the thirty-nine Articles are 'agreeable to the word of God'; and that the Book of Common Prayer 'containeth nothing in it contrary to the word of God', could be lawfully used, and was in fact exclusively to be used (15). So the 'subscription debate' began; and the present extract is a part of the story. (Note that Whitgift's articles merely made slightly more specific the details of clerical obedience dating from the 1559 Act of Uniformity.) In January 1584 — 'the woeful year of subscription' — sixty clergy were suspended in Suffolk and sixty in Norfolk. (Not too many were permanently deprived.) In all, in 1584, about 6 per cent of the clergy held out against Whitgift. And during the late 1580s about 10 per cent of the clergy in puritan regions were willing to stand up and be counted (16). (How many in more traditional areas? We may at any rate take it that 10 per cent was the maximum figure of clerical puritan allegiance).

A word more generally about the seven tracts. (The best to read in full is the so-called 'Theses Martinianae' of July 1589.) We may note Marprelate's repeated concern for 'the doctrine of the Church of England in the days of Henry VIII' — the doctrine of Christ and His apostles, upheld by Barnes,

208

Tyndale and Frith, then by John Hooper and John Foxe (and John Knox) (17). Marprelate's appeal to the godly situation in Scotland, France, Switzerland, Denmark, Saxony, the Low Countries, the Palatinate, Poland and Swabia was tempered by the fear that the puritan could be attacked as a man loving every country but his own — people apparently said 'it is the general disease of Englishmen to have in admiration the persons and states of other countries, and to loathe their own' (18). What was important, finally, was 'the cause of the church government which is now in controversy betwixt me and our prelates' (19). The basic imperative was that: 'our church government in England by lord archbishops and bishops is a government of maimed, unnatural and deformed members, serving for no use in the church of God' (20). Not, Marprelate hurriedly added, that we seek 'popularity' (i.e. government by the people). 'The government of the church of Christ is no popular government, but is monarchical in regard of our Head, Christ; aristocratical in the eldership; and democratical in the people. Such is the civil government of our Kingdom: monarchical in her Majesty's person; aristocratical in the higher house of Parliament, or rather at the council table; democratical in the body of the commons of the lower house of Parliament' (21). (Not unlike Thomas Cartwright in sober mood in the 1570s.)

To end on an approving note — Marprelate had an attractive contempt for 'muscular christianity'; the hearty Richard Bancroft was dismissed as a 'contemptible trencher-chaplain' (22) — it was also noted that he cheated at cards.

1. Collinson, 'The Elizabethan Puritan Movement', p. 273.
2. 'Theses Martinianae': Pierce ed., p. 304.
3. 'Oh read over Dr John Bridges: The Epistle': Pierce ed., pp. 85-6.
4. 'The Epitome': Pierce ed., p. 126.
5. 'Epitome': Pierce ed., p. 118.
6. For instance in 'The Epistle': Pierce ed., pp. 51, 53.

7. Quoted by Pierce, p. 238.

8. In 'English Literature in the 16th Century' (1954) pp. 405-7. See also Dover Wilson, 'The Marprelate Controversy' in 'Cambridge History of English Literature', iii (1909).

9. 'Epistle': Pierce ed., p. 43.

10. Quoted by D. S. Chambers, 'Faculty Office Registers 1534-1549' (1966) p. xxxi.

11. For the above, Elton, 'Tudor Constitution'.

12. W. D. J. Cargill Thompson, 'Anthony Marten and the Elizabethan Debate on Episcopacy', in 'Essays in Modern English Church History', ed. G. V. Bennett and J. D. Walsh (1966).

13. See also 'Epistle': Pierce ed., p. 69.

14. 'The Protestation': Pierce ed., p. 412. For Perne, see C. H. and T. Cooper, 'Athenae Cantabrigienses', II (1861) pp. 45-50.

15. The articles are in Elton, 'Tudor Constitution', no. 207.

16. See ibid., no. 173: Puritan 'Survey of the Ministry', Essex, 1586.

17. 'Theses Martinianae': Pierce ed., pp. 314, 326.

18. 'Mineral and Metaphysical Schoolpoints': Pierce ed., p. 192.

19. 'Protestation' (the last tract): Pierce ed., p. 401.

20. 'Theses Martinianae': Pierce ed., p. 309.

21. 'Hay Any Work For Cooper' (i.e. Thomas Cooper, Bishop of Winchester): Pierce ed., pp. 252-3.

22. Ibid., Pierce ed., p. 267.

18 Extract from 'The Just Reproof and Censure' by 'Martin Senior'

From 'The just Censure and Reproof of Martin Junior: wherein the rash and undiscreet headiness of the foolish youth is sharply met with, and the boy hath his lesson taught him, I warrant you, by his reverent and elder brother Martin Senior, son and heir unto the renowned Martin Marprelate the Great': printed July 1589; facsimile reprint, from a copy in the Bodleian Library, in 'The Marprelate Tracts' (a Scolar Press facsimile, Scolar Press, 1967) — a reprint of the seven tracts. Annotated edition, with modernised spelling and punctuation, by William Pierce, 'The Marprelate Tracts' (1911): here the extract is on pp. 364-8. Pierce had previously published 'An Historical Introduction to the Marprelate Tracts: a chapter in the evolution of religious and civil liberty in England' (1908).

The latest account (1967) is by Patrick Collinson, 'The Elizabethan Puritan Movement', pp. 391-7, 403-4.

I, Martin Senior, gentleman, son and heir to the reverend and worthy Metropolitan Martin Marprelate the Great, do protest, affirm, say, propound, and object against John Canterbury and his brethren, in manner and form following.

First, I protest and affirm that the foresaid John Whitgift, alias Canterbury, which nameth himself Archbishop of Canterbury, is no minister at all in the Church of God, but hath and doth wrongfully usurp and invade the name and seat of the ministry, unto the great detriment of the Church of God, the utter spoil of the souls of men, and the likely ruin of this commonwealth, together with the dishonour of her Majesty and the State. And in this case do I affirm all the lord bishops in England to be.

2. *Item.* I do protest that the entering in of this cursed man John Whitgift, and of all others our bishops in England, is not

211

an entering into the Church of God by the door Christ Jesus. Wherefore I affirm all of them to be thieves, robbers, wolves, and worriers of the flock, and therefore no true shepherds.

3. *Item.* I do proclaim the said John Canterbury, with the rest of our prelates, to be common simoniarcs, such as make merchandise of church livings and benefices by faculties, dispensations, etc, and make as common a gain of church censures, by absolutions and commutations of penance, etc, as any men in the land do of their lawful trades and occupations.

4. *Item.* I do propound and affirm that the said John Canterbury and his brethren do hinder and let with all their might the true knowledge of God amongst her Majesty's loving subjects, the inhabitants of this kingdom, and thereby, besides their own fore-provided damnation, are guilty of the blood of infinite thousands.

5. *Item.* I do proclaim that the said John Whitgift, with the rest of his brethren, doth spend and waste the patrimony of the church (which ought to be employed in the maintenance of true faithful ministers, and other church uses) in the persecuting the true members of Christ, her Majesty's most trusty and loving subjects; and also upon their own pomp and ambitious pride, in maintaining a rude ungodly train of vile men, and a company of lewd and graceless children.

6. *Item.* I do propound that the said John Whitgift and his brethren do, as much as in them lieth, sow sedition and discontentedness between her Majesty and her true loyal subjects, by pretending that their practices in avoiding subscription and in depriving men contrary to law (as for the surplice, denying to subscribe, etc) is at her Majesty's commandment. As though her Highness would command that which were contrary unto the true doctrine of our church, and contrary unto her lawful statutes and privileges; or, as though she would so delude her loving subjects as publicly to maintain that true doctrine, and these godly statutes, which privately she would have violated and trodden under feet.

7. *Item.* I, the said Martin Senior, do protest and affirm the said John Whitgift, with the rest of his brethren, to have incurred the statute of *praemunire facies*, for depriving of ministers for not subscribing, not wearing the surplice, and

212

for other their manifold proceedings against law and equity.

8. *Item.* I do propound all our bishops for their said practices to be *ipso facto* deprivable, and that her Majesty, if she will do them but right, may by law deprive them all tonight, before tomorrow.

9. I do also propound and avouch the said John Whitgift, and the rest of his wicked fraternity, though by outward profession they are in the church, yet to be none of the church; but to have, until they repent and desire to be received into the church, cut themselves (by the persecuting of the truth, and other their heinous sins) from the Church; and so, without their repentance, from the interest and inheritance of the kingdom of heaven.

Item. I do protest and affirm that the true church of God ought to have no more to do with John Canterbury, his brother,* and their synagogue — namely, with their anti-christian Courts of Faculties, etc, with their officers of commissaries, archdeacons, chancellors, officials, dumb ministers, etc — than with the synagogue of Satan. And that he their head and pope, together with his foresaid rabble, are not to be accounted for that church whose censures we are to reverence and obey, and in the unity whereof we are to remain.

Item. Particularly concerning John Canterbury himself, I do affirm, but yet no further than *quatenus probabile* (that is, by great likelihoods) that he is so finally hardened in his heinous sins against God and His church that as he cannot be reclaimed: for his mouth is full of cursing against God and His saints, his feet are swift to shed the blood of the holy ones, he teareth in pieces the churches which he ought to foster, wilfully pulling the shepherds from their sheep and so scattering them in a most lamentable sort, making much of wicked men that maintain his popedom and smiting the righteous for gainsaying his ways, bringing in daily into the church, either by himself or his hang-Johns, new errors not heard of before, blaspheming the way of truth. And being rooted in malice against that truth of Christ Jesus (who is blessed for ever) which he may see, if he did not hoodwink himself, he with all his power contrarieth and striveth against the going forward of the Gospel, lest by the light thereof his

* Martin means the Pope.

sins should be reproved. Finally, he hath in him too too many likely testimonies of an heir of the kingdom of darkness, where, without his true turning unto the Lord, he shall live in hell forever.

And, wicked man! if thou meanest to be elsewhere received, that is, into Christ's kingdom, turn thee from thy wickedness, and let men and angels be witnesses of thy conversion. Thy high place cannot save thee from His wrath, whose truth thou suppressest, and whose members thou dost persecute and imprison. And I would not wish thee to defer thy repentance, lest thou callest with the foolish virgins when there is no opening. Thou seest even here upon earth manifest tokens of God's anger towards thee. For thou seekest for honour; but, alas, I know none more contemptible than thyself, the poorest faithful minister in the Lord hath more true reverence in one day than thou hast had since the first time of thy popedom. There are almost none of God's children but had as lieve see a serpent as meet thee; not because they fear thy face, but inasmuch as it grieveth them that their eyes are forced to look upon so wicked an enemy of God and His church. Thine own creatures themselves, honour thee but as tyrants are commonly honoured of their parasites and sycophants. Thy brother the Pope hath the like honour unto thine, that is, an honour whose end will be shame and confusion of face for ever. The fearful and contemptible end that have been brought upon many of them ought to terrify thee. Nay, the message of death which the Lord sent lately even into thine own house, ought to move thee, and face thee to confess that thy years, also, yea, and days, are numbered. Doctor Perne, thou knowest, was thy joy, and thou his darling. He was the dragon from whose serpentine breasts thou didst first draw this poison wherewith now thou infectest the church of God, and feedest thyself unto damnation. He lived a persecutor, an atheist, an hypocrite, and a dissembler, whom the world pointed at, and he died, thou knowest, the death due unto such a life as he led; thou knowest he died suddenly even at thine own palace of Lambeth, when in thine own judgement he was likely, in regard of bodily strength, though not of age, to outlive thee. And take thou his death for a forewarning of thy destruction, except thou repent.

214

PART XI

Mid-1580s: Puritan Pleas

Dr Collinson has re-drawn attention to the historical 'register' of documents amassed by Field, from which come the three items in this section. This was a 'central' register — petitions, accounts of troubles and trials from many counties, surveys of the state of the ministry — probably gathered to influence M.P.s and other important sympathisers. 'The survival of this material from the early 'seventies is in itself tangible evidence of the web of correspondence spun from the London conference' (1). Very few items were added after Field's death in 1588. Bancroft's agents never discovered this material; though there is a contemporary manuscript catalogue of much of it, now in the British Museum. Some pieces were printed out of England (Edinburgh?) in 1593: 'A Parte of a Register', probably edited by Thomas Wilcox. The rest, which had come to Dr Williams's Library, Gordon Square, London, was not available in print until 1915, when Albert Peel published in two volumes his indispensable 'The Seconde Parte of a Register: being a Calendar of manuscripts under that title intended for publication by the Puritans', with wonderfully full indexes, and a preface by C. H. Firth. Sometimes these are summaries, not transcripts; and the transcripts often have unmarked omissions, and are not always accurate. But the volumes were of pioneer importance.

The Cornish 'Supplication' should be compared with 'The View of the state of the church in Cornwall', in Peel, vol. II, pp. 98-110. Over 170 ministers are named in that 'View'; only 24 were satisfactory (and some of these only marginally so). The 'Supplication' shows that 22 had more than one

215

benefice, and 3 were non-resident; there were 140 'unpreaching ministers', either beneficed or not. For all this, see Christopher Hill's best book: 'Economic Problems of the Church from Archbishop Whitgift to the Long Parliament' (1956).

1. 'The Elizabethan Puritan Movement', p. 134. See also pp. 90, 280, 388, 440, 500.

19 Cornish Supplication to Parliament

Dr Williams's Library, Morrice MSS 'B': 'The Seconde Parte of a Register', ff. 135-6. Transcript in A. Peel (ed.), 'The Seconde Parte of a Register', ii 174-6.

For as much as (right honourable assembly) by the Queen's Majesty's appointment you are gathered together to look to the wants, to behold the miseries, the ruins, decays, and desolations of the church of God and commonwealth of this realm of England, and to put your helping hand to the amendment of the same, your wonted clemency and duty to hear the complaints of the poor, and our miserable estate, do stir, provoke and compel us to bring our lamentable complaint to your ears, to lay our miserable estate before your eyes, and with all humble reverence to put this our sorrowful suit and petition into your hands, with hope that God will so bless and sanctify you to be means of comfort and relief to us.

We are in one of the farthest parts of this land, above the number of four score and ten thousand souls, which for want of the Word are in extreme misery. For the preaching of the Gospel being the beauty of Christ's spouse, the water of comfort, the bread of life, the immortal seed, we want the same and are therefore so far from that beauty and comfort wherewith God's church and children are adorned and do delight in, that we lie as men starved and pined with the famine of the Word; yea, which is most rueful, by the lack of that immortal seed we are as if we were not. And this is neither for want of maintenance nor of place, for, besides the impropriations in our shire, we do allow yearly above nine thousand and two hundred pounds, and we have about eight score churches. The greatest part of which maintenance and places is received and supplied by men which through

217

their ignorance and negligence are guilty of the sin of sins, namely of the sin of soul-murder. And yet, as if that were not enough, divers of them have added to the same such gross sins as the civil ethnics do abhor. For to say nothing that some of them are common gamesters (as well on the Sabbath as other days) some are fornicators, some adulterers, some felons, bearing the marks in their hands for the same offence.

Another part of the maintenance and places (which we take not fully to be the seventh part) is in the hand of preachers: but they are of sundry sorts; some are non-residents, some have divers benefices, some preach but their quarter sermons, so that between spring and spring, pasture and pasture, meal and meal, the silly sheep may starve; some drunkards, some quarrellers, some spotted with whoredom, and some with more loathsome and abominable crimes than these. So that, though the excellent dignity of the Word and Sacraments do not depend on the worthiness of the men, yet their infectious breath, which savoureth of carrion, maketh God's children to abhor them, and the uncleanness and filthiness of their hands maketh them unfit ministers to wait at the Lord's table, to deliver the bread of life, the food of the soul, to his little ones to feed on. And generally, though we allow so much and receive so little, yet these which sit not in the watch-tower, which feed not the Lord's flock, which are no light to his people, no pattern nor example to God's children, do fleece apace and will not lose one halfpenny offering day; the poor labourer must pay the tithe of his hand, the servant of his wages, the wife of her eggs, or else no sacrament can be had at their hands; nay, they shall be cited from court to court, yea, and if they do not satisfy these hungry men, which will never have enough, they shall be excommunicated.

A third sort of ministers we have, which do teach truly, labour painfully and faithfully in the Lord's husbandry, and watch diligently over the Lord's heritage, for whom we are to praise the name of our God for ever and ever. Yet these men are not suffered to attend their calling, for the mouths of the superstitious papists, of the godless atheists, and of the filthy livers, are open against them; and the ears of them that are called lords over them are sooner open to their accusations (though they be but for ceremonies) than to the others'

218

answers. Neither is it safe for us to go to hear them: for though our own pastures and fountains are withered and dried up, yet, if we seek for the bread and water of life elsewhere, we are called and cited to appear to their courts, where we are taunted, checked, reviled, and threatened with excommunications; so that we are worse dealt with than most merciless men deal with their beasts, for they will neither feed us at home nor suffer us to seek for food elsewhere, but will have us to perish in our ignorance and blindness.

Therefore from far we come and call unto you, most honourable assembly, for aid. Out of this sea of misery we lift up our hands, beseeching you to stretch out your helping hands for our relief, and in this famine to send us purveyors and stewards, stored both with old and new, furnished with skill rightly to divide the Word, and give everyone his portion in due season. And that these dumb dogs, ravenous wolves and dissolute persons which keep the place, and shut the door against the Lord's true ministers, being removed, and faithful ministers placed, such order may be taken as they may not be disquieted by every apparator, registrar, official, commissary, chancellor, etc (and that for every light occasion at the complaint of every lewd person): so that besides that we shall be bound to praise God for you, you shall build a most sure castle and fortress of defence for the safety and preservation of her Majesty, against the dangerous practices of all papists, atheists, and traitors whatsoever; and by this means you shall bring the blessing of God upon yourselves, your posterity, and upon this realm for ever.

20 Supplication to the Queen, in Verse

'A humble supplication to our sovereign Queen Elizabeth':
Dr Williams's Library, Morrice MSS 'B': 'The Seconde
Parte of a Register', pt i, ff. 164-5. Transcript (with some
errors) in A. Peel (ed.), 'The Seconde Parte of a Register', i
268-9.

Most gracious Queen Elizabeth, our liege lady
We, your poor subjects in great bondage through the land
With humbled hearts and souls are forced for to cry
Beseeching your good Grace our cause to understand.
    It is the food of life, God's word, which we do want
    Which makes us all for to lament good preaching scant.

We had of late dispersed abroad in each country
Some godly, learned, painful messengers indeed
Who with all diligence their office did apply
And taught the word of God whereon our souls did feed.
    But now those shining lamps are clean extinguished
    And we through want of food are almost famished.

In many places of this land it is most true
We have no preaching, of the Lord his holy day,
Save at the most some quarter sermons as our due
Wherewith we must content ourselves, there is no nay.
    For if we seek for food unto our soul elsewhere
    Then are we sure therefore to pay exceeding dear.

The bishops' sumners then do cite us all apace
And charge us very sore to make ourselves ready
With speed for to appear before their Lordships' grace
Where first we must pay fees, there is no remedy.
    The Bishops ask us then what subjects we have been
    For to refuse our Church commanded by the Queen.
220

We answer that our own curates they cannot preach
Which is the only cause why we do further seek.
We humbly crave to have such guides as can us teach
And will perform the same at least once every week.
    And for their diligence we promise for to give
    Good maintenance whereby they may the better live.

The bishops forthwith ask what shall our curates do
Or what allowance shall they have to live upon.
We say we think it best that out of hand they go
To their old trades or learn some occupation.
    Then did they storm with angry mood, saying that we
    Would have all vicars through the land beggars to be.

We answer no, but you, my lords, are merciless
In that you do prefer their state and standing here
Yea, smaller things as all your dealings do express
Before our souls their health which Christ hath brought so dear.
    Else would you not thrust forth good preachers out of place
    Else would you not but pity this our woeful case.

The bishops then with one consent did all agree
That we should keep our parish church and go to hell.
Or for default thereof in prison for to lie
O cruel men for to profess Christ his Gospel
    Thus with their children for to deal so extremely.
    God grant them true repentance here before they die.

Thus have we made a just report (most noble Queen)
Of that most lamentable state which we are in
Beseeching your Highness to hear when we complain
Lest that for want of food we perish in our sin.
    Remember how this want did force your Christ to weep
    When he beheld Jerusalem as wandering sheep.

And sith you have proclaimed now a Parliament
For to reform all things amiss in each degree
Good Queen with all your lords agree in one consent
That over every church a faithful guide may be.
    That with renowned Joshua your Majesty
    May say, O Lord, I and my folk will all serve thee.

Then shall God bless your reign with much felicity
Then shall all traitors soon be caught or flee the land
Then shall popery decay and all iniquity
Then shall you rule by Christ, and in his favour stand.
    Then shall we pray to God to guide your Majesty
    That you may live and die in Christ to reign eternally.

Your Highness' most bounden daily orators, the poor commons of your flourishing realm of England

21 Articles of Reformation of the Ministry

Dr Williams's Library, Morrice MSS 'B': 'The Seconde Parte of a Register', ff. 435-7. Partial transcript (some omissions) in A. Peel (ed.), 'The Seconde Parte of a Register', ii 199-202.

1. That no ministers be made or suffered in the ministry, but such as by the commandment of Christ, and precepts of the Apostle, are apt to teach; considering that the admitting or suffering of such is the ruin and destruction of the people touching the knowledge of God. For if it be true that the want of knowledge causeth destruction, and the blind cannot lead the blind but they must both fall into the pit, and the admission and sufferance of these ignorant and unlearned keepeth the learned out, it is not possible but ignorance must abound, and so destruction follow, unless this course be taken, which is the only way to avoid it.

It may seem at the first, the churches cannot be furnished with able men; though we have not to prescribe against God, let the best diligence be used in placing such as are already in 'esse' and are not bestowed, and so frame the ordering of shires (which will be easy) that within four miles' compass there may be one preaching minister, and to that one let all resort be made for ministration of the sacraments; and the rest that remain, and cannot be presently furnished, to have the most honest of the unlearned for reading only, but in no wise to meddle further with the word or sacraments; and those churches to resort to the place where is a minister for the sacraments.

That as fit men should from time to time be found, they may be placed, and the other put out, notwithstanding all former inductions, and so forth; as may be enacted by this present Parliament. For better it is for one man to be dis-

223

possessed of an unright possession, than that many souls should perish.

2. That, as well for the augmentation and perpetuity of the ministry, as also for the singular instruction of the people, there may be that exercise of prophecy and interpretation of the scriptures erected and placed in every shire in two or three places or more, as the commodity of the places will serve best for the people: which we find in the writings of the apostles.

3. That catechising be used in every church, with as great diligence and pain as may be, in all such places as we have fit ministers, and shall have, as by the order of the first article is desired.

4. That there be assemblies in every shire, at some place most convenient, wherein all ministers of the shire coming together may be examined both of their doctrine and diligence, and sounded therein, and also touching their conversations (as well touching themselves as their families); that upon such examination, correction may be used as the fault shall require.

5. That the universities render up yearly a just note unto her masters' Council of such learned ministers as they shall have yielded the commonwealth and church; and that such number be appointed to be yielded, as by view taken of the colleges may easily appear are to be yielded, if their time be well employed; as wherefore the Heads shall be answerable, if it be not performed, considering what good statutes they have for seeing to the same.

6. That all pluralities be utterly taken away, without exception or limitation; as a thing only tending to the enriching of the ministers, and manifest hurt of the people which is caused by having a hireling utterly unlearned: a thing procured by no one thing so much as by these pluralities.

7. That all licences 'De non residendo', 'non promonendo ad sacros ordines', and other suchlike given by authority from the archbishop, be taken away.

8. That the book of common prayer be amended in such points as it is faulty in; with cutting off of all the service of the holy-days, as a thing that cannot have any ground, besides the idleness that it bringeth into the realm and church.

224

9. That all such learned ministers that are not sound in doctrine be removed.

10. That no minister be made, but such as have been tried, either by sufficient exercise in one of the universities, or of the exercise of prophesying, from whence he shall be commended to the bishop, with good testimony of his honesty and good conversation, and as God shall have furnished with the gift of utterance.

11. That every cathedral church have an ordinary lecture of divinity at least thrice in the week, both for the instruction of such as shall be trained in the ministry, and for the benefit of the people.

12. That in all cathedrals and collegiate churches the stipends and rooms which have been, and are, given to a number of superfluous and needless chaplains and singing men and choristers, be turned to the maintenance of such as are to be employed in the ministry; appointing, according to the competency of the same living, a certain number of students in divinity, and certain lecturers both in the tongues and divinity.

13. That no sacrament be ministered without preaching the word: that the people may be instructed in the truth and true use of the sacraments, to the end they abuse not the sacraments, to their condemnation.

14. That diligent care be had, that the word be not despised and trodden underfoot; and therefore, according as it is preached, so it be executed, to the cutting off of sin and open rebellion against God, which is the only cause of disobedience to her Majesty. For this cause, that the commissaries and archdeacons be restrained, with severe punishment annexed, from redeeming sins with money; and therefore that they meddle not with the faults of any parish where there is a good minister placed, but leave them to be censured by him, and other honest men of his parish; or otherwise, that the archdeacon and commissary may in no wise punish any, without consent and counsel of the minister of the same place.

15. That such controversies of doctrine as shall fall out, be not determined in any wise, or meddled withal, by the archdeacon, commissary or chancellor, but by the bishop and so many godly ministers next adjoining to the place of the

225

offendant, as shall seem convenient to the ministers of an whole shire or exercise.

16. That there be quarterly in every shire, and every half year in every bishopric, and every year once in the whole province, an assembly of the ministers and other godly, to view and examine both the doctrine and manners of the ministers; and these doings at the end of the year to be presented to her Majesty or to the Council, as to the nurse of the church who ought to be watchful in that behalf; and to have ratification of their doings from her Majesty, for the better surety of obedience.

17. That the apparel of the ministry, which hath caused much trouble in the church, be left free for the use (so that there be a comeliness used in their apparel) as it is in all the churches reformed of the same profession that we are: with whom it is more seemly to agree than with the enemy, whose attire is rejected in all other churches, as well as their doctrine.

18. That none be cast out of the ministry, or kept from it, for any other cause than false doctrine and evil life; unless it be for schism stubbornly maintained and stood in against the whole church, without any good ground or warrant.

19. That excommunication be not used for money matters, but such sins and offences as we find by the word worthy such censure; if satisfaction be not made by the party offendant, before the congregation.

20. That papistry be condemned by law for heresy: that without further ambiguity of terms, if the law canon be now English, and not Romish, it may easily appear which part is comprehended within the compass of that law; and that accordingly they may be proceeded against, as sectaries that err in faith, and not remain.

21. That no papist be suffered to enjoy the benefit of the sacrament, before he have in open assembly renounced his heresy, and showed hearty repentance for the same. And in case they shall seem more willing to abstain from the said sacrament than to come, then they may be excommunicate; and as excommunicate persons not permitted to enjoy any commodity that may come by the company of the faithful, and be deprived of all action, both personal and criminal, whatsoever against any man, and so stand in the case of

226

outlaws, or, as the Scripture speaketh, as heathens and publicans, until they submit themselves, and renounce their heresies.

22. That no priest be suffered in the place of a minister, or to be admitted hereafter to be reputed and taken for a minister, unless publicly he renounce his priesthood as heretical and against the word, desiring the congregation to take him for a new man, and as one that never had entered unto so blasphemous and sacrilegious a function. Seeing the sin of idolatry is as the sin of witchcraft to the Lord, and so oftentimes among the people of God, as whatsoever sin can be greatest; being directly against the First Table, wherein the honour and dishonour of God immediately consisteth. And the Apostle precisely chargeth that none be chosen to this function of the ministry (to serve the Lord and his angels) and interpreter between him and his people, but such as have not through any gross fault fallen into the reprehension of men; concurring herein with the Prophet, forbidding the idolatrous priest to offer the Lord's sacrifices. Not that after repentance they may not; but that acknowledging their fault and renouncing their evil ways must first be publicly pronounced, to take away all offence from the church of Christ; and so only to be received. The words of the Apostle are of no small force: 'Probentur prius'.

PART XII

1587: Rev. Richard Rogers in Essex

Richard Rogers, a Cambridge graduate, was lecturer or 'preacher' at Wethersfield, Essex, from about 1572 until his death in 1618 (he was succeeded by his son). Some of his monthly journal has survived; and a section of it is printed here, as an early example of a puritan literary and psychological genre. William Perkins, in a treatise published in 1591 concerning the practical application of the doctrine of reprobation, was to advise the Christian to 'diligently try and examine himself whether he be in a state of damnation or a state of grace' (1). The obvious technique for the tradition was that of the diary: especially useful for reading back. And so we see Rogers pondering the pastoral calling, his 'weak ministry', concerned about his studies, his health and his peace of conscience, setting down his faults — an 'unstayed and unbridled mind'; depression; the world too much with him. Dennis Potter has written of 'the hidden tangles of the mind — the secret place where the words struggle out on the the page and the real hobgoblins of memory, fear, desire, fantasy and yearning stage their endless fight' (2) Rogers's journal is not terribly dramatic — not heroic, or devastating. For that, we must look to, say, the journal of the layman John Winthrop in Old and New England (3), or the diary kept in the 1650s in Massachusetts by Michael Wigglesworth (4). But the impetus was there — expressed in our own day by André Gide; 'I long ago looked at myself from all angles ... and have inventoried my spiritual furnishings' (5). The fatal lure of the abyss.

Rogers suffered from the hard discipline imposed in England by the Whitgift administration. 'I fear a fresh danger

229

from the Bishop', he wrote in the journal. He had been 'suspended a long time for not subscribing' — and named in a puritan survey of the 1580s as one of the thirty-eight 'sufficient, painful and careful preachers and ministers in Essex' (6) who were constantly molested by Authority. Twenty-seven Essex puritan parsons wrote to the Council in 1584, complaining that they had either been silenced or were living in fear because 'we refuse to subscribe that there is nothing contained in the Book of Common Prayer . . . contrary to the word of God' (7) (the second of Whitgift's 1583 three articles): Rogers was among the twenty-seven. On June 1587 — a month after my journal extract ends — Rogers and four others (including Ezekiel Culverwell) wrote a letter, which I have also printed, to their 'beloved brethren' of Dedham, Essex, in the name of 'the Israel of God' (8): 'at the time of the last Parliament order was taken by consent of many of our godly brethren and fellow labourers assembled at London that all the ministers which favoured and sought the reformation of our church should sort themselves together to have their meeting to confer about the matters of the church, besides such exercises as should most make for their profiting every way'. (Parliament had ended on 23 March 1587: one wonders whether Rogers's 'journey to London', mentioned in the journal, was in this connection.)

In the journal, Rogers was much concerned with his 'calling': 'I seek and desire such gifts as concern me in my ministry, to edify the church of God', gifts to help in the 'exercises of preaching and catechising' so vital for 'God's people'. He referred to 'many good brethren', makes much of his 'sweet journey with Mr Culverwell' (from Felstead) and seems to have established in Wethersfield a sort of little community within the parish. There is a passage of 31 March 1587 about a meeting of 'many together'; about 'meetings in the time past', with 'neighbour or brother', where there was 'conference about knowledge, attaining, or growing in godliness', and the members 'embraced Christian fellowship together' — a meeting 'such as were to be wished might be established universally in all congregations' (though risking 'likelihood of the displeasure of certain of our neighbours').

It is obvious that Rogers was at least on the fringe of that movement of the 1580s which is best illustrated by the

230

minute-book of the Essex 'Dedham classis' covering the years 1582 to 1589 (9). This was a self-styled 'conference', 'assembly' or 'exercise' of parsons, meeting during those years at about a dozen places in north Essex and south Suffolk, in the twenty or so miles around Colchester. The minute-book was kept by the Vicar of Dedham. There were eighty recorded meetings — about once a month — and there seem to have been, in all, about twenty or thirty members (including sixteen Cambridge graduates). (In the 1587 letter to the 'beloved brethren' of Dedham Rogers thought in terms of a maximum of ten.) The conference met from 8 a.m. till 3 p.m. There was prayer, and fasting; then a speech by one 'interpreter' of scripture (who, when done, left the room while his 'handling' was discussed: most important were points of 'controversy between the papists and us'); next there might be mutual admonition, 'touching their ministry, doctrine or life'; and finally, and most important, 'conference about other necessary matters for the furthering of the gospel', the 'cause of the church'.

From the pages of the minute-book arises the unmistakable odour of 'us'. 'None be brought in as one of this company without the general consent of the whole'. How did the members describe themselves? 'Preachers of the gospel', 'ministers of the word of God', 'the saints of God', 'the forward', 'the godly brethren': 'our company'. What mattered was 'the advice of the brethren'.

It is worth while considering the 'necessary matters' discussed in these meetings. Some were trivial — can lads of sixteen wear hats in church? who are the godliest clothiers? how can a witch be known? (not so trivial, maybe); how best to give thanks for the fate of the Armada (four months late). There is much on parish matters. How to deal with parishioners in doctrinal error — 'convent them before the whole church'. Discussion of divorce, baptism and the sacraments (the ideal was a monthly communion service). A lament for clerical penury — can we, like Paul, work with our hands: Calvin, said Richard Crick, 'I think is against it'. A feel, too, for a wider world; references (1586) to the state of affairs in France and the Low Countries, some advice to 'brethren in Lancashire' — and a judgement requested from 'the brethren at Cambridge' (it never came). More centrally, there is the

231

question of relations with the prelates. 'Whether we may use the bishops and come to their courts' (to be discussed at Cambridge by 'divers godly men', June 1585). Or, by 1588, 'whether the bishops were any longer to be tolerated or no: not dealt in'. Can there be a 'reconciliation' with the bishop? Since 'we profess one God and preach one doctrine' can we join with the bishop 'with better consent to build up the church' — this was 'not thought convenient of the most'. (That was in August 1584. In December Edmund Freke was succeeded as Bishop of Norwich by Edmund Scambler.) Then, from April 1584, there loom the issues of subscription (and suspension). How far may the Book of Common Prayer be used — one member was prepared to use it only if, decision-wise, 'he may be confirmed in it by the advice of the brethren'. 'How far a minister might go to the hazarding of his ministry for the surplice'.

Most sympathetic, perhaps (and this links Dedham with the Rogers journal) is the feel for the relationship of pastor and people. 'A pastor should have his own people': 'a near conjunction between the pastor and the people' (10). (On occasion, some member would submit for discussion a catechism 'that he had made for his people'.) Fear of the Bishop looms here, also. One member (one of ten who had no regular benefice, being 'teachers'): 'moved the brethren to advise him what he might do in a matter whereunto he was entreated and called by common consent, viz, to accept of a living: the brethren thought it very convenient he should accept the calling if his affection stood unto the people, and that he might have a lawful calling to them, and quietly pass through the bishop's hands'. This pastoral zeal was the motive force behind a survey (requested in July 1584) of local clergy — to name and inquire into those 'insufficient in learning and notoriously offensive in life'. Many such surveys survive from the 1580s (11). How, also, to make the gentry 'zealous for reformation'?

From the start, the word 'discipline' was stressed. In 1586 Edmund Chapman wished a letter to be written 'to the godly brethren in London', to make them yet 'more zealous' in 'furthering of discipline': 'some of them are of mind to ask a full reformation; and to accept of none if they had not all. But the judgement of the brethren was that some reforma-

232

tion might be accepted, if it were granted.' (This was on 7 November 1586: Parliament had met at the end of October.) In March 1587 a judgement was wanted on 'the Book of Discipline set down by the brethren'. But judgement was deferred — the members hadn't got hold of a manuscript copy yet (12). (Matters are always being 'deferred'; 'nothing done' — a general inclination to postpone things till the next meeting.)

And, finally, the terror. In August 1583 'it was said our meetings were known and threatened'. So: send for some 'godly lawyer', to advise 'how we may meet by law'. 'The time present threatened much misery to come' (1586). The last recorded meeting was on 2 June 1589. The secretary, Richard Parker, Vicar of Dedham, had been called up to London and examined by the Bishop (John Aylmer), 'complaints against us' having been made. Ranks had been depleted by 'the death of some of our brethren, and their departure from us to other places'. So this 'blessed meeting' was now 'ended, by the malice of Satan'. Rogers's 'beloved brethren' of Dedham had lost their way.

Wethersfield was twenty-five miles west of Dedham — not in the 'neighbourhood'. But we have certain proof that there was in the area some sort of 'meeting' and 'exercises'. Proof in the Rogers letter written on 7 June 1587 to the brethren of Dedham which is my second extract in this section: 'we your brethren, whose names are underwritten, have had our meeting so often as our troubles would give us leave'. The five signatories badly needed another member, as they are upset by the 'smallness of our number, and distance of place'. The four besides Rogers were: Culverwell; Carr, parson of Raine, Essex; Huckle, minister of Aythorp Roding, Essex; and Whiting, parson of Panfield, Essex. All five (said a contemporary account) among the 'painfullest ministers in Essex, whom the Bishop threateneth to deprive, saying we shall be white with him, or he will be black with us' (13). The group wanted 'our beloved brother Mr Newman', prominent in the Dedham classis, to join them. Laurence Newman was Vicar of Coggeshall, Essex, between Colchester and Braintree.

But this request 'from the brethren of another company' was deferred, and then declined.

233

1. 'Works', i 361.

2. 'The Times', 'Saturday Review', 16 August 1969.

3. Extracts in 'The Puritans', ed. Miller and Johnson.

4. E. S. Morgan (ed.), 'The Diary of Michael Wigglesworth' (Harper Torchbook, 1965).

5. 'The Journal of André Gide', trans. Justin O'Brien, iv 231: January 1944.

6. A. Peel (ed.), 'The Seconde Parte of a Register', ii 163.

7. Ibid., i 225.

8. R. G. Usher (ed.), 'The Presbyterian Movement in the Church of England' (Camden Society, 1905) p. 98.

9. First printed by R. G. Usher, ibid. Text on pp. 25-74: all my quotations from here.

10. There had been debate on whether a pastor might resign: 'we are not so straitly tied to his flock in these confused days wherein we have no discipline or good order', said some (ibid., p. 45).

11. Some printed or calendared by A. Peel in 'The Seconde Parte of a Register', no. 205 (ii 88-174).

12. For the various (easily confused) Books of Discipline, see Patrick Collinson, 'The Elizabethan Puritan Movement', esp. pt 6, ch. 1.

13. Peel, 'The Seconde Parte of a Register', ii 261; cf. 163-5.

22 Rogers's Monthly Journal, February to April 1587

Dr Williams's Library MSS, no. 61, 13. The full manuscript runs to 82 folios. In the seventeenth century it belonged to Roger Morrice, literary executor of Richard Baxter. M. M. Knappen gave Dr Williams's Library a typed transcript in 1933, 176 folios (with some notes). I have printed here the first five folios of the manuscript (or what remains: the first 8 folios are defective at the bottom of each folio). This corresponds to the first 9 folios of the Knappen transcript. Knappen printed only about one folio of this section in his extracts from the journal — published in 'Two Elizabethan Puritan Diaries' (1933). The manuscript is anonymous, though a cover note describes the author as 'a puritan minister of Cambridge'. Knappen thought it 99 per cent certain that Rogers was the author.

February 28th: The comfort of study, and what hindered from it
If I might see continuance at my study with such willingness and breaking through lets as this first week I have done, being wholly carried this way, I can see what comfort I should find in my life. But this continuance is a small time obtained, what with unsettledness from home, or time-spending with one or other, though to good ends, and with what unfitness of mind and faintness of body. And thus my good course hath been at this time interrupted. And though such things fall out not very oft, yet indeed I must say, they are hardly taken; and perhaps half a day or more shall be passed in unprofitableness and unfitness before I shall enjoy my former freedom again. Of things worth the remembrance in this month this was one: a most sweet journey with Mr. Culverwell* two days, and much time bestowed in the way

* Ezekiel Culverwell: 'preacher' at Felstead, Essex, eight miles south of Wethersfield.

about our Christian estate, of God's mercy in our calling to the fellowship of the Gospel, of the true testimonies of faith, and of the great comfort which by continuing herein doth come unto God's people. I may further say, one time except, my mind hath little been roving after the world: wherein I crave continuance also, and that when greater trials shall come I may find strength not to be overcome. Sickness hath been much kept from me; and I, being so full of self love, do fear that such times will not be gone under of me as I may find joy therein. For being now holden with a sore cough, I saw that it much unsettled me in duty, and some relic of unwillingness to go under it, in the continuance of it, through sensible impatience, as I could judge of it, I felt not, but for that at some time it stayed my study, and that I do hardly bear, knowing mine own wants in knowledge of good things. And one time this month it fell out with me very hardly, for I could not for a time apply myself to anything; which came to pass after I had cast many things too and fro in my mind about mine wants in gifts, etc. And although I desire of my God that I be not unthankful for his kindness to me, to me infinite ways (as I have many times noted), yet I fear, knowing best myself, mine own estate, that I may dishonour the Lord. . . . [Section missing in MS.]

*(Meditation small one, sweet one: then I accused myself that they were so few. . . . Sweet thinking of our departure, with a true valuation of things below, by Mr. Leaper's death, March 12th.)**

. . . But herein, to the pulling down of pride in me, the Lord will be fulfilled (though I be thereby abased amongst men) so as I may have this witness, that I seek and desire such gifts as concern me in my ministry, to edify the church of God. I am stayed (though hardly), when I consider that God has brought many to the knowledge of his truth by my weak ministry, and that he doth increase his gifts in me in some measure. For though I ought to have known that which I know many years agone, yet seeing I behold that daily, whereof I have been ignorant, I am much comforted. But I

* Written in at the top of the page, as supplement to the main entry. William Leaper (1518-87) had been Vicar of Braintree, Essex, and was a former Fellow of St John's College, Cambridge (B.A. 1538).

236

would not choose to be partaked of all knowledge (as some excell others therein) without the comfortable use of it through love.

March 31st

He that is to live in our calling had needs (for the manifold occasions of being occupied both at home and abroad in doing good) to furnish himself before with necessary gifts of knowledge, seeing one way or other, partly as I have said, and partly through infirmity of body and mind, and other hindrances by court officers, etc, there fall out many unsettlednesses from our study. For mine own part, I can say, as I see that so it falleth out with me, that (with exceeding grief I speak of it) I seem in mine own judgement to go slenderly forward in my study; although in mine exercises of preaching and catechising I have peace to my conscience by that which I do. I am much cast down oftimes in consideration of my wants. And yet I know, as many good brethren have faithfully told me, that therein I may easily fall into unthankfulness for the grace which I have received. But yet I wonder oftimes at that which the Lord hath done by mine unworthy ministry, ten, yea twelve years agone, when my judgement was raw and almost unsettled. . . . [Section missing in MS.]

25th March: I have seen great outward peace here this twelve month. So beginning to take much comfort in joy, lest I should stay on so weak grounds, behold much breach. Pasfield [and others: illegible] with me, and many together. Not unsettled by this. *

And this I say, that I have never enjoyed the like with any neighbour or brother at any time; for it is not out of season at any time, to be occupied either in conference about knowledge, attaining, or growing in godliness. We have made small use of our meetings in time past, for either of these almost, before his coming; only I have seen a continuance of love thereby. And this shall be one of the greatest stays unto mine heavy heart if it may please the Lord to continue this benefit unto us. Mine heart hath been much occupied in

* Entry at top of page.

237

thinking of the uncertainty of our life, and the momentary brittleness of things below, by occasion of the death of Mr. Leaper. I find myself at great liberty by this means, when I find a sensible contempt of this world, and a joyful expectation of departure from hence. And the contrary is an estate full of uncomfortableness and anguish. And although since my last restoring I confess the Lord hath given me a goodly time of liberty, with much outward peace; whereby we have with more diligence sought knowledge and embraced Christian fellowship together, and such as were to be wished might be established universally in all congregations, and to continue with us, yet because there is no warrant of the long enjoying of my outward benefit, I have thus carefully endeavoured myself not to set mine heart upon it; yet being somewhat desirous of it, perhaps more than I should, lest I should be too much carried away with the same, the Lord hath tried me with the likelihood of the displeasure of certain of our neighbours. But I will wait for a good issue of it, as I have seen of greater than these. (Mark how these troubles end and be confirmed in hope by experience.)* Also I fear a fresh danger from the bishop: but I trust God will also turn it to the best. I am also oft times much troubled with rising of heart and frowardness, when it hath not been warily watched against; and hardly brought to shame myself with it. . . . [Section missing in MS.]

Methinks sometimes I am sour countenanced to the godly, when somewhat is in my mind against them that I misliked, especially they not having offended. I misliked it.†

April 29th
Mine estate this latter part of the month (for the former thoughts break order, and shall be set down after) hath been as much to my misliking as any this long time. And yet, seeing it not to be good, I have had no ability either by meditation or to read these my writings, that thereby I might recover my strength. Particularly that which I complain of is this: my mind hath run upon commodity, to my shame, ever

* Marginal note.
† Entry at top of page.

since this journey to London, wherein, for that I did not at my setting forth settle myself against all evil, and, at the first, season mine heart with good communications and covenants, I say God's just dealing towards me when I came there; that occasion was offered me of the trial by commodity, which I, not wisely foreseeing, was carried away with, by little and little; and mine heart so occupied ever since in thinking upon increase, that I have been punished with those thoughts which have made me, to mine opinion and judgement, more barren and unsavoury both public and privately. Since that I misliked myself exceedingly, both for the unprofitableness at my study which it brought to me, and also for such an unsettling of my mind as I have felt; yet, behold by no means I could expel this poison, though I had prayed and meditated. The means which I used were too weak, and I slid again forth into the same pit. But as I have ever seen that my merciful God hath not suffered me to be overwhelmed in such distress (wherein I would gladly have found release, but I knew no way how) so now the Lord hath brought such tidings to me which wakened me; (although I must say this, that even when it was opened unto me I was in a profitable meditation). But though it was like to turn to my discommodity, and that greatly, yet I, knowing that I had dealt uprightly in that in which I was charged, I was not for the outward danger troubled, but grieved for his cause who judged me; whom I hoped better of; rejoicing that for no just cause given to the party I sustained this, but that the Lord would awake me from sloth, and earthly mindedness. And surely I see how hardly I should take it if for any wilful offence, I should bring any cross, as reproach, upon me. And I thank my God, who hath kept me from many dangerous evils. [Section missing in MS.]

(25th April: *Too much minding the earth this month, that I am ashamed of it, and idle unprofitable study*).*

And saw that I must needs use fasting against it as a remedy. I did not, and many an accusation I have had for that since; and thus will out of hand perform it. Thus it may appear how hardly I use prosperity well, any long time. And I

* Entry at top of page.

239

pray God I may ever fear it, as in some measure even in this sottish estate I did. To this I may add how I have through this month walked in much unprofitableness, and not following my study. The earth also hath been too much in my mind. And although as a deceivable bait it hath enticed me, and carried my mind in fond deceivableness about it; yet the truth is that such an estate is to me very unwelcome and tedious. Another fruit of an unstayed and unbridled mind is this: that the weather falling not out according to expectation fair and warm, but contrary, my mind rose troubled, and frowardness did much accuse me, to see storming against the Lord's doings. But the grossness of it would not suffer me to dwell in it, but forsooth I called it back with shame, and purged mine heart of the same. As I sensibly felt it odious to my heart, and shame to myself for it, so I saw in the continuance of the weather, mine heart to be constant: and received much comfort and patience after it for unsettledness and unprofitableness before.

23 Letter from Rogers and Others, June 1587

Copy by Richard Parker (of the Dedham Classis) attached to the Dedham minutes in a private manuscript collection in Norfolk: printed 1905 by R. G. Usher, 'The Presbyterian Movement in the Reign of Queen Elizabeth', p. 98. The letter was addressed to 'our beloved brethren' Edmund Chapman, Richard Crick, Robert Lewis 'and the rest': Robert Lewis, former fellow of St John's, Cambridge, had a parish in Colchester; Richard Crick was a former fellow of Magdalen, Oxford, and sometime chaplain to the Bishop of Norwich (deprived); Dr Edmund Chapman, former fellow of Trinity, Cambridge, then Canon of Norwich (deprived 1576), was the 'virtual head and director' of the Dedham classis (A. Peel, 'The Seconde Parte of a Register', p. xxxvii), and 'preacher' at Dedham.

Whereas (beloved brethren) at the time of the last Parliament order was taken by consent of many of our godly brethren and fellow labourers assembled at London that all the ministers which favoured and sought the reformation of our church should sort themselves together to have their meeting to confer about the matters of the church, besides such exercises as should most make for their profiting every way; it was further advised that none should assemble above the number of ten, and therefore they which exceeded that number should sort themselves with others of their brethren next adjoining, where defect was. According hereunto, we your brethren, whose names are underwritten, have had our meeting so often as our troubles would give us leave; but find, in regard to the smallness of our number, and distance of place, that we stand in need of further aid of some to be adjoined unto us. Whereupon, understanding that God hath blessed you with store, we are constrained to make suit unto you that you would of your abundance supply our want. And namely, considering that our beloved brother Mr Newman is one who may be profitable unto us, and in place most fit, in respect of you and us, our earnest desire is that you would yield this benefit unto us, which we shall receive as a pledge of your love with thankfulness, and so remain in unfeigned love indebted to you. The lord our God and merciful father multiply His graces upon us that, according to the manifold wants of His church, and the times wherein we may live, we may be enabled unto that high and mighty service He hath called us unto. June 7, 1587.

Yours in the truth,
Richard Rogers, Ezekiel Culverwell, Roger Carr, John Huckle, Giles Whiting

PART XIII

1593: Richard Hooker's Analysis of the Sectarian Mind

In February 1585 Whitgift appointed a new Master of the Temple (that is, chaplain to two Inns of Court: the Inner and Middle Temple). On the advice of Edwin Sandys, the appointment was given to a relatively obscure country parson, aged 30, former Fellow of Corpus, Oxford: Richard Hooker. This was a blow to the existing Reader (second-in-command) at the Temple, Walter Travers, who was six years older than Hooker. Travers was one of the two dons who had been expelled from Trinity, Cambridge, under the Mastership of Whitgift. The other was Thomas Cartwright. Cartwright and Travers had gone to Geneva in 1571 – a sort of Burgess and Maclean act. At Geneva Travers wrote his book 'de Disciplina Ecclesiastica' (1574, preface by Cartwright) (1). And he was ordained at Antwerp, in the Reformed fashion, in 1578. For one year (1585-6) Hooker and Travers both used the Temple pulpit; in the famous phrase of Thomas Fuller, 'the pulpit spake pure Canterbury in the morning, and Geneva in the afternoon' (2). By March 1586 Travers was complaining to the Council about the shocking opinions of the new Master. Hooker found himself compelled to defend those opinions (which were supported by Whitgift). And although he remained in London until July 1591, the controversy compelled Hooker from 1585 to look into his conscience, at the scriptures and at the Law (comparatively easy to do at the Inns of Court). And so, from 'irksome strifes' and 'tedious contentions' (3) there arose 'Of the Laws of Ecclesiastical Polity', written as a 'burdensome labour' (4). Hooker, inspired by Whitgift's example, 'thought it convenient to wade through the whole cause' (5). He resisted the

243

temptation to prefer his 'private ease' (6)—the constant pull, as in so many of his seventeenth-century admirers, to a 'private kind of solitary living' (7). He attempted to avoid — what was a natural lure for him — 'the gall' of 'bitterness' (8). 'It sometimes cometh to pass, that the readiest way which a wise man hath to conquer, is to fly' (9). And so in 1591, when he was 37, Hooker went to live in Salisbury, as Sub-Dean of the cathedral, and Rector of Boscombe. He lived much of the time in the Close; and worked in the cathedral library, which contained the bequeathed books of his old benefactor, Bishop Jewel. By 1593, when he was 38, he had finished the preface and the first four books. These were printed in March. The plan was for eight books. Book V appeared in 1597, by which time Hooker had moved to be Rector of Bishopsbourne, near Canterbury. His death was hastened — he reminds us here of Proust — by the rush to finish his epic; but the final three books were still in manuscript when he died in 1600, aged 46. The work did not, at first, sell very well.

Hooker put his cards on the table at the beginning of the preface (10): 'The wonderful zeal and fervour wherewith ye have withstood the received orders of this church, was the first thing which caused me to enter into consideration, whether ... every Christian man, fearing God, stand bound to join with you for the furtherance of that which ye term the Lord's discipline.' The preface as a whole is addressed to the men of the 'Book of Discipline' (Hooker never once uses the word 'puritan'). 'The order of your Discipline': traced in the preface from Calvin at Geneva (a ten-page sketch), through the reigns of Edward and Mary, the controversies of the 1560s and the 'Admonitions to Parliament' of 1572. Chapter 8 (a late addition to the preface) has a rather Cranmerian bit about the extremists (the 'newfangled'?): 'they must endeavour to purge the earth of all manner evil, to the end there might follow a new world afterward'. (He was thinking of Cartwright: 'this is no innovation, but a renovation, and doctrine not new, but renewed, no stranger, but born in Zion' (10).) The argument of the chapter is directed against those who mask their errors 'under the cloak of divine authority'; the mind 'imagining itself to seek the execution of God's will', by proposing imperatives 'which are not the

244

commandments of God, but your own erroneous collections'. 'That which you are persuaded of, ye have it no otherwise than by your own only probable collection' (11). The phrase brings Hobbes to mind: 'For if a man pretend to me, that God hath spoken to him supernaturally and immediately, and I make doubt of it, I cannot easily perceive what argument he can produce, to oblige me to believe it' (12). And Elizabeth herself had attacked in 1585 (in her speech at the closing of Parliament) those who were 'over-bold with God' — it being 'dangerous to a kingly rule, to have every man according to his own censure to make a doom of the validity and privity of his prince's government, with a common veil or cover of God's word, judged by private men's expositions'. Elizabeth could not 'tolerate new-fangleness' (13). In book V, Hooker considered the tension between 'singularity' and 'common peace'. We must instinctively suspect what 'God is likely to have revealed to some special person', there being a 'strong presumption' that 'God hath not moved their hearts' (14). Whitgift in the 1570s had said to Cartwright that 'it is singularity to divide yourself from that church which doth profess the name of God truly' (15). John Fisher, in his 1526 St Paul's Cathedral sermon against Barnes and Luther, had linked (as 'the ground of all heresy') 'singularity' and 'pride' (16) And we remember that Lady Russell in 'Persuasion' was to state it to be 'singularity which often makes the worst part of our suffering, as it always does of our conduct'. And chapter 8 of the preface develops wonderfully into a brilliant piece, both perceptive and unfair, expounding the marks of the 'sectarian mind'. The sort of thing Ben Jonson might have read when he was preparing Ananias or Zeal-of-the-Land-Busy. 'When they and their Bibles were alone together, what strange fantastical opinion soever at any time entered into their heads, their use was to think the Spirit taught it them': 'Nothing more clear unto their seeming, than that a new Jerusalem being often spoken of in scripture, they undoubtedly were themselves that new Jerusalem'. So, with 'restless levity', they 'every day broach some new thing, not heard of before'. The aim — 'establishing the kingdom of Christ with perfect liberty'. The purpose 'herein is to show, that when the minds of men are once erroneously persuaded that it is the will of God to have those things done which

245

they fancy; their opinions are as thorns in their sides, never suffering them to rest till they have brought their speculations into practice'. And not men only. Hooker (like Grindal) thought that women were especially liable to succumb to puritanism (17). The ultimate result of these persuasions? '. . . all must come by devolution at the length, even as the family of Brown will have it, unto the godly among the people; for confusion unto the wise and the great, the poor and the simple, some Knipperdoling with his retinue, must take the work of the Lord in hand; and the making of church laws and orders must prove to be their right in the end' (18). (Bernard Knipperdollinck was an anabaptist politician of Münster, active in the 1530s.)

In this (rushed?) chapter, Hooker is sharp and not always very stylish. Not the 'judicious Hooker' of legend (the phrase was invented by James I). One feels that he was happier in satirical repartee than he usually allowed himself to be, or than his later admirers have admitted. Here he is his natural self. The tone of much of his whole vast work is rather cautious and conditional – subtle, unruffled, complex (even contorted): and melancholy. Even the most devoted Hooker fan must admit that the book, in its 1350 pages, does drag at times. (Hooker admitted that many would find it 'perhaps tedious, perhaps obscure, dark and intricate' (19): two remedies – read all of it; or don't read any of it (20). By the 'sweet sound of your melodious style', said an anti-Hooker broadsheet in 1599 (21), we are 'almost cast into a dreaming sleep'; the work is 'long and tedious, in a style not usual', very unlike 'the simplicity of holy scripture' – and quite outside the plain tradition of Cranmer, Latimer, Ridley, Hooper, Bradford, Jewel, Whitgift and Foxe. (It was typical of Hooker to begin a discussion of Festival Days, in book V, with a six-page essay on the nature of Time.)

Hooker begins the chapter by inventing a speech for a 'foolish Barrowist'. Henry Barrow, of Clare College, Cambridge, and Gray's Inn, had been imprisoned in 1588. In 1587 he had written his 'Four Causes of Separation' (22). This was two years after Robert Browne had made his submission to Whitgift (October 1585). But Barrow we may think of here as in the Browne tradition. And Hooker intended to show that a move away from the prelatica

246

discipline logically involves Brownism. If puritans separate themselves, it is because they are putting into execution the ideas of Travers and Cartwright; the Barrowist 'deriveth his schism by way of conclusion, as to him it seemeth, directly and plainly out of your principles'. Hooker maintains, at the end of the chapter, that the puritan movement is divided between 'the warier sort' and the 'forwarder in zeal' (another echo of Cranmer). Question: 'whether the people and their godly pastors that way affected, ought not to make separation from the rest, and to begin the exercise of discipline without the licence of civil powers'. The theme of the initial Barrowist speech, addressed to the conservative puritans, is: we got it all from you in the first place.

Henry Barrow was executed on 6 April 1593. In March — the month of the publication of Hooker — he was being tried for sedition at the Old Bailey.

1. See S. J. Knox, 'Walter Travers: Paragon of Elizabethan Puritanism' (1962).

2. Quoted by Arthur Pollard, 'Richard Hooker' (British Council pamphlet, 1966). (Good bibliography.)

3. Hooker, 'Of the Laws of Ecclesiastical Polity': Everyman ed., i 117-18.

4. Ibid., i 79.

5. Ibid., ii 4.

6. Ibid., ii 12.

7. Ibid., i 198.

8. Ibid., i 143.

9. Ibid., i 87-8.

10. In Whitgift, 'Works', i 17.

11. Hooker, 'Of the Laws of Ecclesiastical Polity': Everyman ed., i 118.

12. 'Leviathan', ch. xxxii: Oakeshott ed., p. 243.

13. D'Ewes, 'Journals', p. 329. D'Ewes worked from a copy in the handwriting of John Stow; Neale also used a copy in Stow's hand ('Elizabeth I and her Parliaments', ii 99-101).

14. Hooker, 'Of the Laws of Ecclesiastical Polity': Everyman ed., ii 37.

15. Whitgift, 'Works', i 42.

16. Sermon (in English) printed 1528.

17. Hooker, 'Of the Laws of Ecclesiastical Polity': Everyman ed., i 103.

18. Bk viii, ch. 6: Keble ed. (1874) iii 416.

19. Hooker, 'Of the Laws of Ecclesiastical Polity': Everyman ed., i 148.

20. Ibid., i 148-9.

21. 'A Christian Letter of Certain English Protestants' (Middelburg, 1599) pp. 4-5, 45.

22. Henry Barrow, 'Writings 1587-90', ed. Leland E. Carlson (1962); 'Writings 1590-91', ed. Carlson (1966): being vols iii and v of the series 'Elizabethan Nonconformist Texts'. 'Four Causes of Separation' was first printed in 1906.

24 Chapter 8 of the Preface to 'Of The Laws of Ecclesiastical Polity'

Text from the 1604 edition, pp. 30-40: that second edition (the first edition of the preface and books i-iv was March 1593) had a preface by John Spencer hoping for 'an end to the calamities of these our civil wars'.

Spelling and capitalisation modernised. 1604 punctuation retained (apart from my modern use of quotation marks). I have omitted all Hooker's marginal references and 'footnote' material. Among the works cited by Hooker is Marprelate's March 1589 'Hay any Work for Cooper': the Marprelate phrase which caught Hooker's eye was, 'whether her Majesty and our state will or no'.

John Keble, whose edition of Hooker first appeared in 1836, amended Hooker's punctuation with some — he admitted it — liberty. An exact reprint of the original would not appeal, he felt, to the general reader. He also broke the text up into numbered paragraphs; and added a large number of footnotes. All this (as later revised: final version, 1888) was taken over by the Everyman Library edition of Hooker (though this is nowhere stated in the edition). The Everyman two volumes, apart from the introductory essays (1907, Ronald Bayne; replaced by Christopher Morris, 1954) and the convenience of their being in print, are unsatisfactory and off-putting.

There are plans for a new edition of Hooker, in six volumes, by the press of Casè Western Reserve University (Cleveland, Ohio), sponsored by the Folger Library. W. Speed Hill, executive editor, has pointed out to me that an early draft of chapter 8 of the preface was printed anonymously at Oxford in 1642: 'The Dangers of New Discipline, to the State and Church Discovered, Fit to be Considered by them who Seek (as they term it) the Reformation of the Church of England'. Hill also thinks that chapters 8 and 9 of the preface (the final two chapters) were

249

originally an addition to the preface, which Hooker at first intended to conclude with chapter 7.

The case so standing therefore my brethren as it doeth, the wisdom of governors ye must not blame, in that they further also forecasting the manifold strange and dangerous innovations, which are more than likely to follow if your discipline should take place, have for that cause thought it hitherto a part of their duty to withstand your endeavours that way. The rather, for that they have seen already some small beginnings of the fruits thereof, in them who concurring with you in judgement about the necessity of that discipline, have adventured without more ado, to separate themselves from the rest of the Church, and to put your speculations in execution. These men's hastiness the warier sort of you doth not commend, ye wish they had held themselves longer in and not so dangerously flown abroad before the feathers of the cause had been grown; their error with merciful terms ye reprove, naming them in great commiseration of mind, your 'poor brethren'. They on the contrary side more bitterly accuse you as their 'false brethren', and against you they plead saying:

'From your breasts it is that we have sucked those things, which when ye delivered unto us, ye termed that heavenly, sincere, and wholesome milk of God's word, howsoever ye now abhor as poison that which the virtue thereof hath wrought and brought forth in us. Ye sometime our companions, guides and familiars, with whom we have had most sweet consultations, are now become our professed adversaries. Because we think the statute-congregations in England to be no true Christian Churches; because we have severed ourselves from them; and because without their leave or licence that are in civil authority, we have secretly framed our own Churches according to the platform of the word of God. For of that point between you and us there is no controversy. Alas what would ye have us to do? At such time as ye were content to accept us in the number of your own, your teachings we heard, we read your writings: and though we would, yet able we are not to forget with what zeal ye
250

have ever professed, that in the English congregations (for so many of them as be ordered according unto their own laws), the very public service of God is fraught, as touching matter, with heaps of intolerable pollutions, and as concerning form, borrowed from the shop of Antichrist; hateful both ways in the eyes of the most holy: the kind of their government by bishops and archbishops, Antichristian, that discipline which Christ hath essentially tied, that is to say, so united unto his Church, that we cannot accompt it really to be his Church which hath not in it the same discipline, that very discipline no less there despised, than in the highest throne of Antichrist, all such parts of the word of God as do any way concern that discipline, no less unsoundly taught and interpreted by all authorized English pastors, than by Antichrist's factors themselves; at baptism crossing, at the Supper of the Lord kneeling, at both a number of other the most notorious badges of antichristian recognisance usual. Being moved with these and the like your effectual discourses, whereunto we gave most attentive ear, till they be entered even into our souls, and were as fire within our bosoms; we thought we might hereof be bold to conclude, that sith no such antichristian synagogue may be accompted a true Church of Christ, ye by accusing all congregations ordered according to the laws of England as Antichristian, did mean to condemn those congregations, as not being any of them worthy the name of a true Christian Church. You tell us now it is not your meaning. But what meant your often threatenings of them, who professing themselves the inhabitants of mount Sion, were too loth to depart wholly as they should out of Babylon? Whereat our hearts being fearfully troubled, we durst not, we durst not continue longer so near her confines, lest her plagues might suddenly overtake us, before we did cease to be partakers with her sins: for so we could not choose but acknowledge with grief that we were, when they doing evil, we by our presence in their assemblies seemed to like thereof, or at leastwise not so earnestly to dislike, as became men heartily zealous of God's glory. For adventuring to erect the discipline of Christ without the leave of the Christian magistrate, happily ye may condemn us as fools, in that we hazard thereby our estates and persons, further than you which are that way more wise think necessary: but of

251

any offence or sin therein committed against God, with what conscience can you accuse us, when your own positions are, that the things we observe should every of them be dearer unto us than ten thousand lives; that they are the peremptory commandments of God, that no mortal man can dispense with them, and that the magistrate grievously sinneth in not constraining thereunto? Will ye blame any man for doing that of his own accord, which all men should be compelled to do that are not willing of themselves? When God commandeth, shall we answer that we will obey, if so be Caesar will grant us leave? Is discipline an ecclesiastical matter or a civil? If an ecclesiastical, it must of necessity belong to the duty of the minister. And the minister (ye say) holdeth all his authority of doing whatsoever belongeth unto the spiritual charge of the house of God, even immediately from God himself, without dependency upon any magistrate. Whereupon it followeth, as we suppose, that the hearts of the people being willing to be under the sceptre of Christ, the minister of God, into whose hands the Lord himself hath put that sceptre, is without all excuse if thereby he guide them not. Nor do we find that hitherto greatly ye have disliked those churches abroad, where the people with direction of their godly ministers, have even against the will of the magistrate brought in either the doctrine or discipline of Jesus Christ. For which cause we must now think the very same thing of you, which our Saviour did sometime utter concerning false-hearted scribes and pharisees, 'They say and do not'.'

Thus the foolish Barrowist deriveth his schism by way of conclusion, as to him it seemeth, directly and plainly out of your principles. Him therefore we leave to be satisfied by you from whom he hath sprung. And if such by your own acknowledgement be persons dangerous, although as yet the alterations which they have made are of small and tender growth; the changes likely to ensue throughout all states and vocations within this land, in case your desire should take place, must be thought upon. First concerning the supreme power of the highest, they are no small prerogatives which now thereunto belonging the form of your discipline will constrain it to resign, as in the last book of this treatise we have showed at large. Again it may justly be feared, whether

252

our English nobility, when the matter came in trial, would contentedly suffer themselves to be always at the call, and to stand to the sentence of a number of mean persons, assisted with the presence of their poor teacher, a man (as sometimes it happeneth) though better able to speak, yet little or no whit apter to judge them than the rest: from whom, be their dealings never so absurd (unless it be by way of complaint to a Synod) no appeal may be made unto anyone of higher power, inasmuch as the order of your discipline admitteth no standing inequality of courts, no spiritual judge to have any ordinary superior on earth, but as many supremacies as there are parishes and several congregations. Neither is it altogether without cause that so many do fear the overthrow of all learning, as a threatened sequel of this your intended discipline. For if the world's preservation depend upon the multitude of the wise; and of that sort the number hereafter be not likely to wax over great, when (that wherewith the son of Syrach professeth himself at the heart grieved) men of understanding are already so little set by: how should their minds whom the love of so precious a jewel fills with secret jealousy even in regard of the least things which may any way hinder the flourishing estate thereof, choose but misdoubt lest this doctrine, which always you match with divine doctrine as her natural and true sister, be found unto all kinds of knowledge a stepmother; seeing that the greatest worldly hopes, which are proposed unto the chiefest kind of learning, ye seek utterly to extirpate as weeds; and have grounded your platform on such propositions, as do after a sort undermine those most renowned habitations, where through the goodness of almighty God all commendable arts and sciences are with exceeding great industry hitherto (and so may they for ever continue) studied, proceeded in, and professed. To charge you as purposely bent to the overthrow of that wherein so many of you have attained no small perfection, were injurious. Only therefore I wish that yourselves did well consider how opposite certain your positions are unto the state of collegiate societies, whereon the two universities consist. Those degrees which their statutes bind them to take, are by your laws taken away; yourselves who have sought them ye so excuse, as that you would have men to think ye judge them not allowable, but tolerable only, and

253

to be borne with for some help which you find in them unto the furtherance of your purposes, till the corrupt estate of the Church may be better reformed. Your laws forbidding ecclesiastical persons utterly the exercise of civil power, must needs deprive the Heads and Masters in the same colleges of all such authority as now they exercise, either at home, by punishing the faults of those, who not as children to their parents by the law of nature, but altogether by civil authority are subject unto them; or abroad, by keeping courts amongst their tenants. Your laws making permanent inequality amongst ministers a thing repugnant to the word of God, enforce those colleges, the seniors whereof are all or any part of them ministers under the government of a master in the same vocation, to choose as oft as they meet together a new president. For if so ye judge it necessary to do in Synods, for the avoiding of permanent inequality amongst ministers, the same cause must needs even in these collegiate assemblies enforce the like. Except peradventure ye mean to avoid all such absurdities, by dissolving those corporations, and by bringing the universities unto the form of the School of Geneva. Which thing men the rather are inclined to look for, inasmuch as the ministry, whereinto their founders with singular providence have by the same statutes appointed them necessarily to enter at a certain time, your laws bind them much more necessarily to forbear, till some parish abroad call for them. Your opinion concerning the law civil is, that the knowledge thereof might be spared, as a thing which this land doth not need. Professors in that kind being few, ye are the bolder to spurn at them, and not to dissemble your minds as concerning their removal: in whose studies although myself have not much been conversant, nevertheless exceeding great cause I see there is to wish that thereunto more encouragement were given, as well for the singular treasures of wisdom therein contained, as also for the great use we have thereof both in decision of certain kinds of causes arising daily within ourselves, and especially for commerce with nations abroad, whereunto that knowledge is most requisite. The reasons wherewith ye would persuade that scripture is the only rule to frame all our actions by, are in every respect as effectual for proof that the same is the only law whereby to determine all our civil controversies. And then what doth let, but that as

254

those men may have their desire, who frankly broach it already that the work of reformation will never be perfect, till the law of Jesus Christ be received alone; so pleaders and counsellors may bring their books of the common law, and bestow them as the students of curious and needless arts did theirs in the Apostle's time? I leave them to scan how far those words of yours may reach, wherein you declare, that whereas now many houses lie waste through inordinate suits of law, 'This one thing will show the excellency of Discipline for the wealth of the realm, and quiet of subjects, that the church is to censure such a party who is apparently troublesome and contentious, and without reasonable cause upon a mere will and stomach doth vex and molest his brother and trouble the country.' For mine own part I do not see but that it might very well agree with your principles, if your discipline were fully planted, even to send out your writs of surcease unto all courts of England besides, for the most things handled in them. A great deal further I might proceed and descend lower. But for as much as against all these and the like difficulties your answer is, that we ought to search what things are consonant to God's will, not which be most for our own case; and therefore that your discipline being (for such is your error) the absolute commandment of almighty God, it must be received although the world by receiving it should be clean turned upside down; herein lieth the greatest danger of all. For whereas the name of divine authority is used to countenance these things, which are not the commandments of God, but your own erroneous collections; on him ye must father whatsoever ye shall afterwards be led, either to do in withstanding the adversaries of your cause, or to think in maintenance of your doings. And what this may be, God doth know. In such kinds of error, the mind once imagining itself to seek the execution of God's will, laboureth forthwith to remove both things and persons which any way hinder it from taking place; and in such cases if any strange or new thing seem requisite to be done, a strange and new opinion concerning the lawfulness thereof, is withal received and broached under countenance of divine authority. One example herein may serve for many, to show that false opinions touching the will of God to have things done, are wont to bring forth mighty and violent practices

255

against the hindrances of them; and those practices new opinions more pernicious than the first, yea most extremely sometimes opposite to that which the first did seem to intend. Where the people took upon them the reformation of the church by casting out popish superstition, they having received from their pastors a general instruction that whatsoever the heavenly father hath not planted must be rooted out, proceeded in some foreign places so far, that down went oratories and the very temples of God themselves. For as they chanced to take the compass of their commission stricter or larger, so their dealings were accordingly more or less moderate. Amongst others there sprang up presently one kind of men, with whose zeal and forwardness the rest being compared, were thought to be marvellous cold and dull. These grounding themselves on rules more general; that whatsoever the law of Christ commandeth not, thereof Antichrist is the author; and that whatsoever Antichrist or his adherents did in the world, the true professors of Christ are to undo; found out many things more than others had done, the extirpation whereof was in their conceit as necessary as of anything before removed. Hereupon they secretly made their doleful compaints everywhere as they went, that albeit the world did begin to profess some dislike of that which was evil in the kingdom of darkness, yet fruits worthy of a true repentance were not seen; and that if men did repent as they ought, they must endeavour to purge the earth of all manner evil, to the end there might follow a new world afterward, wherein righteousness only should dwell. Private repentance they said must appear by every man's fashioning his own life contrary unto the custom and orders of this present world, both in greater things and in less. To this purpose they had always in their mouths those greater things, Charity, Faith, the true fear of God, the Cross, the mortification of the flesh. All their exhortations were to set light of the things in this world, to count riches and honours vanity, and in token thereof not only to seek neither, but if men were possessors of both, even to cast away the one and resign the other, that all men might see their unfeigned conversion unto Christ. They were solicitors of men to fasts, to often meditations of heavenly things, and as it were conferences in secret with God by prayers, not framed according to the frozen manner

256

of the world, but expressing such fervent desires as might
even force God to harken unto them. Where they found men
in diet, attire, furniture of house, or any other way observers
of civility, and decent order, such they reproved as being
carnally and earthly minded. Every word otherwise than
severely and sadly uttered, seemed to pierce like a sword
through them. If any man were pleasant, their manner was
presently with deep sighs to repeat those words of our
Saviour Christ, 'Woe be to you which now laugh, for ye shall
lament'. So great was their delight to be always in trouble,
that such as did quietly lead their lives, they judged of all
other men to be in most dangerous case. They so much
affected to cross the ordinary custom in everything, that
when other men's use was to put on better attire, they would
be sure to show themselves openly abroad in worse: the
ordinary names of the days in the week they thought it a
kind of profaneness to use, and therefore accustomed themselves to make no other distinction than by numbers, the
first, second, third day. From this they proceeded unto
public reformation, first ecclesiastical, and then civil.
Touching the former, they boldly avouched, that themselves
only had the truth, which thing upon peril of their lives they
would at all times defend; and that since the Apostles lived,
the same was never before in all points sincerely taught.
Wherefore that things might again be brought to that ancient
integrity which Jesus Christ by his word requireth, they
began to control the ministers of the Gospel for attributing
so much force and virtue unto the scriptures of God read,
whereas the truth was, that when the word is said to
engender faith in the heart, and to convert the soul of man,
or to work any such spiritual divine effect, these speeches are
not thereunto applicable as it is read or preached, but as it is
engrafted in us by the power of the Holy Ghost opening the
eyes of our understanding, and so revealing the mysteries of
God, according to that which Jeremy promised before should
be, saying, 'I will put my law in their inward parts, and I will
write it in their hearts.' The book of God they notwithstanding for the most part so admired, that other disputation
against their opinions than only by allegation of scripture
they would not hear; besides it, they thought no other
writings in the world should be studied; in so much as one of

257

their great prophets exhorting them to cast away all respects unto humane writings, so far to his motion they condescended, that as many as had any books save the Holy Bible in their custody, they brought and set them publicly on fire. When they and their Bibles were alone together, what strange fantastical opinion soever at any time entered into their heads, their use was to think the Spirit taught it them. Their frenzies concerning our Saviour's incarnation, the state of souls departed, and such like, are things needless to be rehearsed. And for as much as they were of the same suite with those of whom the Apostle speaketh, saying, 'They are still learning, but never attain to the knowledge of truth', it was no marvel to see them every day broach some new thing, not heard of before. Which restless levity they did interpret to be their growing to spiritual perfection, and a proceeding from faith to faith. The differences amongst them grew by this mean in a manner infinite, so that scarcely was there found any one of them, the forge of whose brain was not possessed with some special mystery. Whereupon, although their mutual contentions were most fiercely prosecuted amongst themselves; yet when they came to defend the cause common to them all against the adversaries of their faction, they had ways to lick one another whole, the sounder in his own persuasion, excusing 'the dear brethren', which were not so far enlightened, and professing a charitable hope of the mercy of God towards them notwithstanding their swerving from him in some things. Their own ministers they highly magnified as men whose vocation was from God: the rest their manner was to term disdainfully scribes and pharisees, to account their calling an humane creature, and to detain the people as much as might be from hearing them. As touching sacraments; baptism administered in the church of Rome, they judged to be but an execrable mockery and no baptism; both because the ministers thereof in the papacy are wicked idolaters, lewd persons, thieves, and murderers, cursed creatures, ignorant beasts; and also for that to baptise is a proper action belonging unto none but the Church of Christ, whereas Rome is Antichrist's synagogue. The custom of using godfathers and godmothers at christenings they scorned. Baptising of infants, although confessed by themselves to have been continued even sithens the very apostles'

own times, yet they altogether condemned: partly because
sundry errors are of no less antiquity; and partly for that
there is no commandment in the Gospel of Christ which
saith, 'Baptise infants', but he contrariwise in saying, 'Go
preach and baptise', doth appoint that the minister of
baptism shall in that action first administer doctrine, and
then baptism, as also in saying, 'whosoever doth believe and is
baptised', he appointeth that the party to whom baptism is
administered shall first believe, and then be baptised; to the
end that believing may go before this sacrament in the
receiver, no otherwise than preaching in the giver, sith
equally in both, the law of Christ declareth not only what
things are required, but also in what order they are required.
The Eucharist they received (pretending our Lord and
Saviour's example) after supper: and for avoiding all those
impieties which have been grounded upon the mystical words
of Christ, 'This is my body, this is my blood'; they thought it
not safe to mention either body or blood in that sacrament,
but rather to abrogate both, and to use no words but these,
'Take, eat, declare the death of our Lord: drink, show forth
our Lord's death.' In rites and ceremonies their profession
was hatred of all conformity with the Church of Rome: for
which cause they would rather endure any torment than
observe the solemn festivals which others did, in as much as
Antichrist (they said) was the first inventor of them. The
pretended end of their civil reformation, was that Christ
might have dominion over all, that all crowns and sceptres
might be thrown down at his feet, that no other might reign
over Christian men but he, no regiment keep them in awe but
his discipline, amongst them no sword at all be carried
besides his, the sword of spiritual excommunication. For this
cause they laboured with all their might in overturning the
seats of magistracy, because Christ hath said, 'Kings of
nations'; in abolishing the execution of justice, because Christ
hath said, 'Resist not evil'; in forbidding oaths the necessary
means of judicial trial, because Christ hath said, 'Swear not at
all'; finally in bringing in community of goods, because Christ
by his Apostles hath given the world such example, to the
end that men might excel one another, not in wealth the
pillar of secular authority, but in virtue. These men at the
first were only pitied in their error, and not much withstood

259

by any; the great humility, zeal, and devotion which appeared to be in them, was in all men's opinion a pledge of their harmless meaning. The hardest that men of sound understanding conceived of them was but this, 'O quam honesta voluntate miseri errant?: With how good a meaning these poor souls do evil.' Luther made request unto Frederick Duke of Saxony, that within his dominion they might be favourably dealt with and spared, for that (their error exempted) they seemed otherwise right good men. By means of which merciful toleration they gathered strength, much more than was safe for the state of the commonwealth wherein they lived. They had their secret corner-meetings and assemblies in the night, the people flocked unto them by thousands. The means whereby they both allured and retained so great multitudes were most effectual; first a wonderful show of zeal towards God, wherewith they seemed to be even rapt in everything they spake: secondly an hatred of sin, and a singular love of integrity, which men did think to be much more than ordinary in them, by reason of the custom which they had to fill the ears of the people with invectives against their authorized guides, as well spiritual as civil: thirdly the bountiful relief wherewith they eased the broken estate of such needy creatures, as were in that respect the more apt to be drawn away: fourthly, a tender compassion which they were thought to take upon the miseries of the common sort, over whose heads their manner was even to pour down showers of tears in complaining that no respect was had unto them, that their goods were devoured by wicked cormorants, their persons had in contempt, all liberty both temporal and spiritual taken from them, that it was high time for God now to hear their groans, and to send them deliverance: lastly a cunning slight which they had to stroke and smooth up the minds of their followers, as well by appropriating unto them all the favourable titles, the good words, and the gracious promises in scripture; as also by casting the contrary always on the heads of such as were severed from that retinue. Whereupon the people's common acclamation unto such deceivers was, these are verily the men of God, these are his true and sincere prophets. If any such prophet or man of God did suffer by order of law condign and deserved punishment; were it for felony,

260

rebellion, murder, or what else, the people (so strangely were their hearts enchanted) as though blessed Saint Stephen had been again martyred, did lament that God took away his most dear servants from them. In all these things being fully persuaded, that what they did, it was obedience to the will of God, and that all men should do the like; there remained after speculation practice, whereby the whole world thereunto (if it were possible) might be framed. This they saw could not be done, but with mighty opposition and resistance: against which to strengthen themselves, they secretly entered into a league of association. And peradventure considering, that although they were many, yet long wars would in time waste them out; they began to think whether it might not be that God would have them do for their speedy and mighty increase, the same which sometime God's own chosen people, the people of Israel did. Glad and fain they were to have it so: which very desire was itself apt to breed both an opinion of possibility, and a willingness to gather arguments of likelihood that so God himself would have it. Nothing more clear unto their seeming, than that a new Jerusalem being often spoken of in scripture, they undoubtedly were themselves that new Jerusalem, and the old did by way of a certain figurative resemblance signify what they should both be and do. Here they drew in a sea of matter, by applying all things unto their own company, which are anywhere spoken concerning divine favours and benefits bestowed upon the old commonwealth of Israel; concluding that as Israel was delivered out of Egypt, so they spiritually out of the Egypt of this world's servile thralldom unto sin and superstition; as Israel was to root out the idolatrous nations, and to plant instead of them a people which feared God, so the same Lord's goodwill and pleasure was now, that these new Israelites should under the conduct of other Joshuas, Samsons, and Gideons, perform a work no less miraculous in casting out violently the wicked from the earth, and establishing the kingdom of Christ with perfect liberty: and therefore as the cause why the children of Israel took unto one man many wives, might be lest the casualties of war should any way hinder the promise of God concerning their multitude from taking effect in them; so it was not unlike that for the necessary propagation of Christ's kingdom

261

under the Gospel, the Lord was content to allow as much. Now whatsoever they did in such sort collect out of scripture, when they came to justify or persuade it unto others, all was the heavenly father's appointment, his commandment, his will and charge. Which thing is the very point in regard whereof I have gathered this declaration. For my purpose herein is to show, that when the minds of men are once erroneously persuaded that it is the will of God to have those things done which they fancy; their opinions are as thorns in their sides, never suffering them to take rest till they have brought their speculations into practice; the lets and impediments of which practice their restless desire and study to remove, leadeth them every day forth by the hand into other more dangerous opinions, sometimes quite and clean contrary to their first intended meanings: so as what will grow out of such errors as go masked under the cloak of divine authority, impossible it is that ever the wit of man should imagine, till time have brought forth the fruits of them: for which cause it behoveth wisdom to fear the sequels thereof, even beyond all apparent cause of fear. These men in whose mouths at the first, sounded nothing but only mortification of the flesh; were come at the length to think they might lawfully have their six or seven wives apiece: they which at the first thought judgement and justice itself to be merciless cruelty; accompted at the length their own hands sanctified with being imbrued with Christian blood: they who at the first were wont to beat down all dominion, and to urge against poor constables, 'kings of nations'; had at length both consuls and kings of their own erection amongst themselves: finally they which could not brook at the first that any man should seek, no not by law, the recovery of goods injuriously taken or witheld from him; were grown at the last to think they could not offer unto God more acceptable sacrifice, than by turning their adversaries clean out of house and home, and by enriching themselves with all kind of spoil and pillage; which thing being laid to their charge, they had in a readiness their answer, that now the time was come, when according to our Saviour's promise, 'The meek ones must inherit the earth', and that their title hereunto was the same which the righteous Israelites had unto the goods of the wicked Egyptians. Wherefore sith the world hath had in these

262

men so fresh experience, how dangerous such active errors are, it must not offend you though touching the sequel of your present mispersuasions much more be doubted, than your own intents and purposes do happily aim at. And yet your words already are somewhat, when ye affirm that your pastors, doctors, elders, and deacons, ought to be in this Church of England, 'whether her Majesty and our state will or no'; when for the animating of your confederates ye publish the musters which ye have made of your own bands, and proclaim them to amount I know not to how many thousands; when ye threaten, that sith neither your suits to the Parliament, nor supplications to our Convocation house, neither your defences by writing, nor challenges of disputation in behalf of that cause are able to prevail, we must blame ourselves if to bring in discipline some such means hereafter be used as shall cause all our hearts to ache. That 'things doubtful are to be considered in the better part', is a principle not safe to be followed in matters concerning the public state of a commonweal. But howsoever these and the like speeches be accompted as arrows idly shot at random, without either eye had to any mark, or regard to their lighting place: hath not your longing desire for the practice of your discipline, brought the matter already unto this demurrer amongst you, whether the people and their godly pastors that way affected, ought not to make separation from the rest, and to begin the exercise of discipline without the licence of civil powers, which licence they have sought for, and are not heard? Upon which question as ye have now divided yourselves, the warier sort of you taking the one part, and the forwarder in zeal the other; so in case these earnest ones should prevail, what other sequel can any wise man imagine but this, that having first resolved that attempts for discipline without superiors are lawful, it will follow in the next place to be disputed what may be attempted against superiors which will not have the sceptre of that discipline to rule over them? Yea even by you which have stayed yourselves from running headlong with the other sort, somewhat notwithstanding there hath been done without the leave or liking of your lawful superiors, for the exercise of a part of your discipline amongst the clergy thereunto addicted. And lest examination of principal parties therein should bring

263

those things to light, which might hinder and let your proceedings; behold for a bar against that impediment, one opinion ye have newly added unto the rest even upon this occasion, an opinion to exempt you from taking oaths which may turn to the molestation of your brethren in that cause. The next neighbour opinion whereunto, when occasion requireth, may follow for dispensation with oaths already taken, if they afterwards be found to import a necessity of detecting ought which may bring such good men into trouble or damage, whatsoever the cause be. O merciful God, what man's wit is there able to sound the depth of those dangerous and fearful evils, whereinto our weak and impotent nature is inclinable to sink itself, rather than to show an acknowledgement of error in that which once we have unadvisedly taken upon us to defend, against the stream as it were of a contrary public resolution! Wherefore if we anything respect their error, who being persuaded even as ye are, have gone further upon that persuasion than ye allow; if we regard the present state of the highest governor placed over us, if the quality and disposition of our nobles, if the orders and laws of our famous universities, if the profession of the civil, or the practice of the common law amongst us, if the mischiefs whereinto even before our eyes so many others have fallen headlong from no less plausible and fair beginnings than yours are: there is in every of these considerations most just cause to fear, lest our hastiness to embrace a thing of so perilous consequence, should cause posterity to feel those evils, which as yet are more easy for us to prevent, than they would be for them to remedy.

PART XIV

William Perkins: 1558-1602

In 1599 Hooker, in discussing predestination, emphasised that Augustine had a 'first opinion' and (when driven to extremes by a British optimist) a 'second opinion', expressed in the later works upon which Calvin drew. Hooker thought the first opinion more akin to the general sense of the Fathers(1). In the sweep of Tudor theology Hooker was less 'augustinian' than Colet: he did not stress that the body of mankind was a mass of corruption, he thought that the elect were 'no small number', and he based his discussion of the will of God on Colet's abhorred Aquinas. But on at least four points Colet and Hooker were jointly opposed to the 'calvinist' exegesis: their belief in a concurrence of God's grace and man's endeavour, in reprobation occasioned by a refusal of grace, in a Christian assurance far short of 'inexpugnabilis securitas', and in an emphasis that God would 'all should be saved'. Hooker's views he expressed in London sermons from 1581.

For expressing them, he ran into trouble. (We know from Ben Jonson that 'pronouncing reprobation' was a mark of the 'holy brethren'.) For from about the 1570s there was a hardening of lines of opinion about predestination and related points — the last great Tudor theological debate, coming to full fruition in the 1590s. The 'Tableau de l'oeuvre de Dieu' (1569) of the Spaniard de Corro was attacked by the minister of the French Church as unsound on predestination and free will. Further blows to the high calvinists were Peter Baro's lectures at Cambridge from 1574, Sam Harsnett's Paul's Cross sermon of 1584, Lancelot Andrewes's teaching at Cambridge in the 1580s, and John Overall's *appointment there as Regius Professor of Divinity in 1595 (when Richard Montague, to be the most outspoken 'arminian' of the 1620s, was a Fellow of King's)(2).*

On the calvinist side, the great intellectual figure was Perkins: with his aim to 'clear the truth, that is (as they call it) the 'Calvinist's' doctrine' especially in his Treatise of Predestination (1598). Arminius was prompted to begin a reply to his work: and in the last eight years of Elizabeth's reign academic theological discussion centred around the points to be known as 'arminian' — though the English discussion antedated the Dutch. The elect are those foreknown to believe; Christ died for all men; grace is not irresistible; a total and final fall from grace is possible. Those arminian points of 1610, and others, were raised in England after a 1595 Cambridge sermon by William Barrett, which occasioned an attempt by Whitaker, Some and the Cambridge calvinists to add to the Thirty-nine Articles a detailed statement on these matters. The bid to extend the minimum of substantial doctrine was frustrated by Whitgift (and later by the Hampton Court Conference).

No one could have been technically more 'Elizabethan' than Perkins, born in 1558, dying in 1602. His adult life was spent in Cambridge. He went up to Christ's in 1577, when he was 18, and became a Fellow in 1582, and lectured at St Andrew's Church (opposite Christ's) from 1584. He married (thus resigning his Fellowship) in 1595. His intention — he wrote when he was 33 — was to 'cast my mite into the treasury of the Church of England'. His first work was published about 1585; there followed two dialogues, about 1588; and (Cambridge 1590) 'Armilla Aurea', 'A Golden Chain'; the Latin version being four times printed at Basle in the 1590s. Before his death nearly thirty titles had appeared, the majority at Cambridge: after, the flow continued, supervised by at least six editors (including William Crashaw, father of the poet Richard), until the definitive English edition of his works (Cambridge, 1608-9; reprinted 1612-13, 1616-18), containing nearly forty works. Of these sermons, lectures and treatises, the first thing to impress is their variety: formal treatises of calvinist theology — 'Predestination' (1598); 'God's Free Grace and Man's Free Will' (1602); clerical aids such as 'The Art of Prophesying: or, a Treatise

266

concerning the sacred and only true method of preaching' (1592), or two lecture courses on 'The Calling of the Ministry'; practical Reformed advice — 'Christian Economy: or a short survey of the right manner of erecting and ordering a family according to the scriptures'; works of comfort, such as the 1595 'Salve for a sick man: or, a treatise containing the nature, differences, and kinds of death, as also the right manner of dying well', or the 1601 'How to live and that well, in all estates and time: specially when helps and comforts fail'; works of casuistry, heralded by the 'Discourse of Conscience: wherein is set down the nature, properties, and differences thereof, as also the way to get and keep good conscience' (1596) (3), and announced in his 'treatise of case divinity', posthumously published in 1606, based on sermons — 'Cases of Conscience', a 'form of relieving and rectifying the conscience' with 'special and sound direction' for 'particular cases'. The best of all his works, perhaps, is 'A Reformed Catholic: or, a declaration shewing how near we may come to the present church of Rome in sundry points of religion, and wherein we must for ever depart from it': though Richard Baxter thought that Perkins's 'choicest piece' was 'Declaration of Christ Crucified' (1597). During Perkins's lifetime 'A Reformed Catholic' appeared in Latin, German, French and Spanish; his complete works were to be published in Latin at Geneva; at least twenty four of his works were translated into Dutch in the first half of the seventeenth century; and various works appear in Irish, Welsh, Czech and Hungarian. Perkins himself made an eclectic use of continental Reformed theology, and his influence was in turn to be felt in Europe — for nearly a century now his contribution to German theology has been a discussed point.

What of his use of earlier English theology? He found in manuscript in the library of Corpus Christi College, Cambridge, a treatise 'De Causa Dei' by Thomas Bradwardine (1290-1349), and used it to prove that 'free will being tempted cannot overcome any temptation by itself without the assistance and grace of God' (4). He used also the 'sweet and savoury writings' of Tyndale and Bradford: 'my meaning is not to add thereto, or to teach another doctrine, but only to renew and revive the memory of that which they have taught'. And he acknowledged his debt to Jewel, and to his

Cambridge colleagues Fulke and Whitaker.

Variety, then, and great appeal. Also clarity and concision, a theological artist in full control, and with the developed technique of the populariser. He was one of the earliest Reformed theologians to make extensive use of charts, diagrams and visual aids: the best being the 'Table declaring the order of the causes of salvation and damnation according to God's word' — a 'catechism' in 'the chief points of religion' for 'them which cannot read': irresistibly reminiscent of the map of the New York City subway. I have placed the table at the end of this book. Perkins was very fond of diagrams, and logical synopses; they were indeed fairly common in the 1590s, partly derived from medieval precedent. And with all this, rhetoric and use of imagery which place him in the tradition of Tyndale and Latimer, and made him the most read of Elizabethan theologians in Europe and New England. 'A master of music hath his house furnished with musical instruments of all sorts; and he teacheth his own scholars artificially to use them, both in right tuning of them, as also in playing on them: there comes in strangers, who admiring the said instruments, have leave given to them of the master to handle them as the scholars do: but when they come to practise, they neither tune them aright, neither are they able to strike one stroke as they ought, so as they may please the master and have his commendation. This world is a large and sumptuous palace, into which are received, not only the sons and daughters of God, but also the wicked and ungodly men: it is furnished with goodly creatures in use more excellent than all musical instruments: the use of them is common to all: but the godly man taught by God's spirit, and directed by faith, so useth them, as that the use thereof is acceptable to God' (5). And an appeal, also, that those who 'keep purity of heart in a good conscience' should not be 'branded with vile terms' — such as 'puritan'. Perkins attacked, from 1592, those 'that make a separation from our church' (6); though he never, in his writings, discussed the details of church government. We may also note that he was fond of music, laughter, food and drink (7).

Perkins's editor in 1604 made the point that the Cambridge man's commentary in Galatians was as good as

268

Luther's — for Luther, after all, was 'but a foreigner' (8).

Rather than giving short extracts from Perkins's thirty-eight works (as published in the three-volume Cambridge edition), I have chosen to give, in full, ten of his letters — being prefaces to some of his works. The first is concerned with 'this our English nation', now happily under the gospel for forty years — but unthankful: the theme is, England repent! The second lists thirty-two popular misconceptions — 'common opinions' of poor, ignorant people (including, 'it was a good world when the old religion was, because all things were cheap'). The third deals with the dignity of preaching. Nos 4, 5 and 6 link with the Richard Rogers journal. Many people 'not once in all their lifetimes' have examined themselves 'whether they be in the estate of grace'; 'it is the duty of every Christian to try and examine himself whether he be in the faith or not' — by searching his heart. Perkins attempts to combat 'secret pangs and terrors', the 'gulf of desperation', springing from 'the benumbed and drowsy conscience'. This letter (6) is an essay on anguish. And Perkins determines to give 'particular examples', 'rules and precepts of conscience': because 'general doctrine in points of religion is dark and obscure'. Next (7) we have, written for the 'common Protestant', a definition of the 'Reformed Catholic'. Letter 8 is on similar ground, though much more technically theological: but the general points emerge — the papist as an 'enemy of the grace of God', depriving 'God of his honour' and 'sovereignty'. No. 9, about predestination, is also very technical: 'that I might clear the truth, that is (as they call it) the 'Calvinist's' doctrine'. And, in letter 10, Perkins, very much on form, gives an incredibly succinct account of four differing opinions on predestination: he himself adhering to the fourth.

I give as the first extract in this section the editorial preface (written at Emmanuel in 1603) to one of the first of Perkins's works to be posthumously published. This is a brief survey of the puritan 'world picture'; of 'the whole frame of the heavens and the earth', 'the law of creation', the nature of men and 'the right use and exercise of their callings'. Of particular interest is the attack on fugitive and cloistered virtue, on those 'living apart from the common societies of men' (monks, for example). Tyndale had said in 1528 that

269

the merchant is a better christian than the monk (9). Richard Holdsworth, Master of Emmanuel, was to refer, in a lecture at Gresham College (founded 1596) to Christ as 'the good merchant' (10). The theme had a future. And it is really part of 'the great Renaissance debate over the Active and Contemplative lives' (11).

1. Hooker's manuscript reply (in the Library of Corpus Christi College, Oxford) to the 1599 'Letter of certain English Protestants'. Printed by Keble (and in the Everyman edition) as an appendix to bk v: Everyman ed. II 490-543. The 'Letter' attacked Hooker's exposition of the subject, as showing that God was capable of mutability: 'the witty schoolmen have seduced you': 'Reason is highly set up against Holy Scripture': 'your position of the light of nature'. Hooker had been in trouble about this matter since a sermon preached in London in 1581, when he was 27; he based his arguments there on the ideas of Thomas Aquinas. Calvin took the mystical insights of Paul together with the meditations of the elderly Augustine (driven to extremes of controversy by the British optimist Pelagius) — and let the mind of a French lawyer play on them: the result has the fascination of a fugue.

2. I dealt with all this at length in part three of 'Reformation and Reaction in Tudor Cambridge' (1958).

3. Reprinted in 1966 in 'William Perkins, English Puritanist', ed. Thomas F. Merrill (B. De Graaf, Nieuwkoop, Netherlands). Merrill has a good introduction, paying tribute to Perkins's 'pioneer effort to develop a uniquely Protestant science of casuistry' (p. x). Thomas Wood made a similar point: 'English Casuistical Divinity during the 17th Century' (1952). The most attractive essay on Perkins is by Louis B. Wright, 'Huntington Library Quarterly' (Jan 1940).

4. 'Perkins, Works' (1612-13) ii 518.

5. Ibid., i 416.

6. Ibid., iii 389. Cf. p.425: 'Our church doubtless is God's cornfield, and we are the corn-heap of God: and those

270

Brownists and sectaries are blind and besotted who cannot see that the Church of England is a godly heap of God's corn' (though, he admits, 'full of chaff').

7. Ibid., i 503-4; ii 131; iii 62-3.

8. Rudolph Cudworth of Emmanuel: ibid., ii 156.

9. Tyndale, 'Works' (Parker Society) i 280: from 'Obedience of a Christian Man'.

10. Quoted by Christopher Hill, 'Intellectual Origins of the English Revolution' (1965) p. 124.

11. Brian Vickers (ed.), 'Essential Articles for the Study of Francis Bacon' (1968) p. xix.

25 An Editor's 1603 Preface to a Perkins Work

Preface to 'A Treatise of the Vocations, or Callings of Men', with 'the Sorts and Kinds of them, and the right use thereof', by T. P. (Thomas Pickering or Thomas Pierson, both of Emmanuel). Dated Cambridge, 16 February 1602 (i.e. 1603): Perkins had died on the previous 22 October. 'Works' (1612-13) i 747-8.

Experience teacheth, and it is a true conclusion propounded and proved in the scriptures of the Old and New Testament, that as God in the beginning by his omnipotent power established the whole frame of the heavens and the earth, so he hath in his wisdom directed them, and all things contained in them, unto one main end, the manifestation of his glory. Whereunto, though everything created, by his appointment, according to the law of creation and the principles of its own entire nature is, and ought to be, referred; yet amongst the works of God, some do more principally and directly make for that purpose, as namely, man, whom God hath endued with the gifts of understanding and knowledge, and in whom he hath engraven his own image in righteousness and true holiness.

Now if the question be, how man being fallen from that integrity wherein he was created, and having brought a confusion upon the whole world by the fall, should yet be fitted and framed for such an end: The answer is, that God, who is able to draw light out of darkness, and to rectify things that are confounded, hath in great wisdom set an order in mankind, which by certain degrees tendeth directly to the advancement of his own glory. For in the first place, he would have man to acknowledge him his sovereign Lord, and to serve him immediately in the duties of faith and obedience. Secondly, it is his will that man, being made a sociable creature, apt to converse with his own kind, should do service unto himself by serving of man in the duties of love. Thirdly, he would not that men conversing each with other should be as wandering Rechabites tied to no certain place or calling; and therefore bindeth all men, both by special assignment unto Adam in his innocency and by particular commandment to him and all his posterity, to be confined within some certain state and condition of life, in the family, in the commonwealth, or in the church. Lastly, that man should use the place and office assigned unto him by God, in a holy manner, performing the duties annexed unto it in faith and obedience, and eschewing those vices that usually attend upon it, with all care and circumspection. In this manner hath God disposed the whole estate of mankind, for the accomplishment of the foresaid end, the honour and glory of his name.

Against this order do offend two sorts of men. The first, are such as live in the bosom of the church, and are not ranged within the compass of any calling or condition of life wherein they might gain glory unto God, or good unto men. Under these are comprehended all popish votaries: as monks, friars, etc, who have been justly condemned of ancient times for thieves and robbers because, living apart from the common societies of men they are neither the members of any body, nor maintainers of any of the three states before named. And to them may be referred all wandering and straggling persons, who, having no settled place of abode and being neither members of any civil society, not annexed to any particular church, have no personal calling wherein to live, and therefore cannot either glorify their creator, or do the least good unto men. The lives of these persons are so much the more odious because they are like the unprofitable drone, that bringeth nothing into the hive, and yet feeds of the honey that is brought in by the labours of others. Another sort of men are they who indeed are called unto some certain condition and trade of life wherein they do walk and yield some benefit unto others; and yet they are greatly to be blamed, in respect of their want in the right use and exercise of their callings. For though they may be skilful and expert in their kind, yet they err in the main point, in that they do not practise their personal callings in, and with, the general. Whereas on the contrary, the principal scope of their lives ought to be the honouring of God in the service of men; and the rule of direction for the attainment of that end is nothing else but a constant performance of the duties of the moral law in that very calling wherein they be placed.

A remedy for these and sundry more corruptions incident unto the lives of men, as also a warning to those that offend in this kind, the author hereof, whose memory is blessed, hath presented unto our view in the discourse following; wherein are handled at large, out of the word of God, the differences and right use of all callings whatsoever.

In publishing whereof, I have thought good to make choice of your worship,* to whose protection I might commend the same, and that upon these considerations. First, because you are and have been an ancient favourer and well-willer to learning and learned men, whereof amongst the rest of our college hath already had very sufficient testimony, for which it doth acknowledge you by the name of a loving and liberal benefactor. Secondly, for that (in my knowledge) you were very lovingly affected unto the author of this treatise whilst he lived, having always a reverent opinion of his gifts and wishing him encouragement in all his proceedings. Beside these respects, it is my desire by this dedication to give unto you some testimony of a thankful mind for your love and kindness toward me. And thus craving your acceptation hereof, I take my leave, and commend you, with all your affairs, to the grace and favour of God.

* Robert Taylor.

1. To Henry Grey, Earl of Kent: preface to 'A Warning against the Idolatory of the last Times; and touching religious or divine Worship' (first published 1601): 'Works' (1612-13) i 670.
2. To 'All Ignorant People that Desire to be Instructed': preface to 'The Foundation of Christian Religion, gathered into six Principles (written 1590): 'Works', i A2.
3. To 'the faithful ministers of the gospel; and to All that Are Desirous of and Do Labour for the Knowledge of Holy Learning': preface to 'Prophetica' (1592): English translation by Thomas Tuke (1607): 'The Art of Prophesying: or, a sacred Treatise concerning the sacred and only true Manner and Method of preaching': 'Works', ii 645.
4. To Valentine Knightly, J. P.: letter before 'A Treatise tending unto a Declaration whether a Man be in the Estate of Damnation or in the Estate of Grace; and if he be in the first, how he may in time come out of it; if in the second, how he may discern it, and persevere in the same to the end' (1586; first printed 1588): 'Works', i 354.
5. To the Christian Reader: 1595 preface to 'A Treatise tending unto a Declaration': 'Works', i 355.
6. To Sir William Piryam, Baron of the Exchequer: 1596 preface to 'A Discourse of Conscience: wherein is set down the Nature, Properties, and Differences thereof; and also the way to get and keep good Conscience': 'Works', i 516.
7. To the Christian Reader: 1597 preface to 'A Reformed Catholic: or, a Declaration showing how near we may come to the present Church of Rome in sundry points of Religion; and wherein we must for ever depart from them': 'Works', i 555.
8. To Sir Edward Denny: preface to 'A Treatise of God's free Grace and Man's free Will' (published 1602): 'Works', i 718-19.
9. Epistle to the Reader: 1598 preface to 'De Praedestina-

tione Modo et Ordine', trans. Francis Cacot and Thomas Tuke (1607): 'A Christian and plain Treatise of the Manner and Order of Predestination and of the Largeness of God's Grace': 'Works', ii 605.

10. To the Christian Reader: 1592 preface to second edition of 'A Golden Chain: or the Description of Theology; containing the Order of the Causes of Salvation and Damnation, according to God's Word; a view whereof is to be seen in the Table annexed; hereunto is adjoined the Order which Theodore Beza used in comforting afflicted Consciences' (first ed. Latin 1590, English 1591): 'Works', i B2.

Letter No. 1, To Henry Grey, Earl of Kent

Right Honourable,etc. Great hath been the mercy of God to this our English nation, in that beside peace and protection he hath bestowed on us the treasure of his gospel now more than forty years, and that under the government of a most gracious Queen. It is a benefit unspeakable; and England (as I think) never had the like before.

For this great mercy we owe to God all thankfulness that heart can think or tongue can speak. Our thankfulness must show itself in the fruit of obedience to the gospel. And obedience is to turn even unto God from every evil way, to believe in Christ, and to walk in newness of good life.

But alas, in respect of the greatest number we are a nation very unthankful; yielding small obedience to the gospel of life. If the things which have been done in England had been done in Barbary, or Turkey, or America, it may be they would have repented in sackcloth and ashes, and have turned more earnestly unto God than we have done. And, for this cause, we have deserved that God should take away his gospel from us and give it to a nation that will bring forth the fruits thereof. For the preventing of this evil which we have deserved, it stands us in hand to repent of our unthankfulness, to embrace the gospel more than we have done, and to walk worthy of it in holiness of life.

For the furthering of this good work I have penned this small Treatise of Idols, and the true worship of God. For this is the right practice of the gospel, to put from us all manner of idols and to sanctify God in our hearts, that is, to serve

276

him in mind and spirit, namely, with a pure heart, a good conscience, and faith unfained.

And having penned this Treatise I now present it to your Honour, and presume to publish it in your name. First, because God hath made you Honourable, not only by civil dignity but also by an unfained love and obedience to the Gospel of Christ. Again, my desire is to give some testimony of a thankful mind for favour undeserved. Thus I take my leave, praying God to establish the heart of your Honour, and all his people, without blame in holiness before him, even our Father, against the coming of our Lord Jesus Christ with all the Saints.

Your Honour's in all duty to command
W. Perkins

Letter No. 2, to All Ignorant People that Desire to be Instructed

Poor people, your manner is to sooth up yourselves, as though you were in a most happy estate: but if the matter come to a just trial it will fall out far otherwise, for you lead your lives in great ignorance, as may appear by these your common opinions, which follow:

1. That faith is a man's good meaning and his good serving of God.

2. That God is served by the rehearsing of the ten commandments, the Lord's Prayer and the Creed.

3. That ye have believed in Christ ever since you could remember.

4. That it is pity that he should live which doth any whit doubt of his salvation.

5. That none can tell whether he shall be saved or no certainly; but that all men must be of a good belief.

6. That howsoever a man live, yet if he call upon God on his deathbed and say, 'Lord have mercy upon me', and so go away like a lamb, he is certainly saved.

7. That if any be strangely visited, he is either taken with a planet, or bewitched.

8. That a man may lawfully swear when he speaks nothing but the truth, and swears by nothing but that which is good, as by his faith or troth.

9. That a preacher is a good man no longer than he is in

the pulpit. 'They think all like themselves'.

10. That a man may repent when he will, because the Scripture saith, 'At what time soever a sinner doth repent him of his sins, etc.'

11. That it is an easier thing to please God than to please our neighbour.

12. That ye can keep the commandments, as well as God will give you leave.

13. That it is the safest to do in religion as most do.

14. That merry ballads and books, as Scoggin,* Bevis of Southampton, etc, are good to drive away the time and to remove heart qualms.

15. That ye can serve God with all your hearts, and that ye would be sorry else.

16. That a man need not hear so many sermons, except he could follow them better.

17. That a man which cometh at no sermons may as well believe as he which hears all the sermons in the world.

18. That ye know all the preacher can tell you; for he can say nothing but that every man is a sinner, that we must love our neighbours as ourselves, that every man must be saved by Christ, and all this ye can tell as well as he.

19. That it was a good world when the old religion was, because all things were cheap.

20. That drinking and bezelling in the ale-house or tavern is good fellowship, and shows a good kind nature, and maintains neighbourhood.

21. That a man may swear by the Mass, because it is nothing now, and by Our Lady, because she is gone out of the country.

22. That every man must be for himself, and God for us all.

23. That a man may make of his own whatsoever he can.

24. That if a man remember to say his prayers every morning (though he never understand them) he hath blessed himself for all the day following.

25. That a man prayeth when he saith the ten commandments.

26. That a man eats his Maker in the Sacrament.

* 'Gests of Scoggin' (1566). Also rather disliked by C. S. Lewis, 'English Literature in the Sixteenth Century', pp. 427-8.

† Bevis of Hampton (1500, etc.; 4 editions by 1582).

278

27. That if a man be no adulterer, no thief, no murderer and do no man harm, he is a right honest man.

28. That a man need not have any knowledge of religion because he is not book-learned.

29. That one may have a good meaning when he saith and doeth that which is evil.

30. That a man may go to wizards, called wise men, for counsel; because God hath provided a salve for every sore.

31. That ye are to be excused in all your doings, because the best men are sinners.

32. That ye have so strong a faith in Christ that no evil company can hurt you.

These and suchlike sayings, what argue they but your gross ignorance? Now where ignorance reigneth there reigns sin, and where sin reigns there the devil rules, and where he rules men are in a damnable case.

Ye will reply unto me thus: that ye are not so bad as I would make you. If need be you can say the Creed, the Lord's Prayer and the ten commandments, and therefore ye will be of God's belief, say all men what they will, and you defy the devil from your hearts.

I answer again that it is not sufficient to say all these without book unless ye can understand the meaning of the words and be able to make a right use of the commandments, of the Creed, of the Lord's Prayer, by applying them inwardly to your hearts and consciences, and outwardly to your lives and conversations. This is the very point in which you fail.

And for a help in this your ignorance, to bring you to true knowledge, unfained faith and sound repentance, here I have set down the principal points of Christian religion in six plain and easy rules; even such as the simplest may easily learn; and hereunto is adjoined an exposition of them word by word. If ye do want other good directions then use this my labour for your instruction. In reading of it first learn the six principles; and when you have them without book, and the meaning of them withal, then learn the exposition also; which being well conceived, and in some measure felt in the heart, ye shall be able to profit by sermons, whereas now ye cannot; and the ordinary parts of the Catechism, namely, the ten commandments, the Creed, the Lord's Prayer, and the institution of the two sacraments, shall more easily be understood.

Thine in Christ Jesus
William Perkins

Letter No. 3, To the Faithful Ministers of the Gospel: and to All that are Desirous of and Do Labour for the Knowledge of Holy Learning

That common-place of divinity which concerneth the framing of sermons is both weighty and difficult, if there be any other throughout all that sacred science. For the matter which is to explicate and treat on is Prophecy: an excellent gift indeed, whether we consider it in respect of dignity or of use. The dignity thereof appeareth in that, like a Lady, it is highly mounted and carried aloft in a chariot; whereas all other gifts, both of tongues and arts, attend on this like handmaids aloof off. Answerable to this dignity there is also a twofold use. One, in that it serveth to collect the Church, and to accomplish the number of the elect. The other, for that it driveth away the wolves from the folds of the Lord, for this is indeed that *Flexanima,* that allurer of the soul, whereby men's froward minds are mitigated and moved from an ungodly and barbarous life unto Christian faith and repentance. This also is that Engine which, as it hath shaken the foundation of ancient heresies, so it has in these few by-past years cut as under the sinews of that great Antichrist. Wherefore it be demanded which is the most excellent gift of all, doubtless the praise must be given to Prophesying. Now by how much the more excellent every thing is, by so much the more diligently it ought to be adorned with variety and plenty of precepts. Therefore, when I saw this common-place so handled of many as that it would remain naked and poor, if all other arts should call for those things which are their own, I perused the writings of divines, and having gathered some rules out of them, I have couched them in that method which I have deemed most commodious; that they might be better for use and fitter for the memory. I do also publish them, that they might be approved if they bring with them that which is good; if any evil, that they may receive their deserved punishment. And whosoever thou art that pleaseth to read them, where thou art persuaded of this order

280

of Preaching which here I handle, walk on with me; where thou standest at a stay, inquire with me; where thou perceivest thine own errors, return to me; where thou seest mine, call me back to thee. For that which now liketh me shall dislike me if it like not godly and moderate minded men. But if any man shall carp at this my travail, though very small, let him know that my only meaning is to benefit the church of God, and that the conscience of my fact is a sufficient muniment against all calumnies. I do now betake you to God; and this tractate of the Art of Prophesying both to you and to God.

Anno 1592 December 12

William Perkins

Letter No. 4, To Valentine Knightly, J. P.

Sir, I pray you consider with me an especial point of God's word, carefully to be weighed. It is this: Many professors of Christ, in the day of grace, persuade themselves that they are in the estate of grace, and so the true church esteemeth of them too; yet when the day of grace is past, they contrariwise shall find themselves to be in the estate of damnation, remediless. A doleful case, yet a most resolute truth, and the reason is plain. Men that live in the Church are greatly annoyed with a fearful security and deadness of heart, by which it comes to pass that they think it enough to make a common protestation of the faith, not once in all their lifetimes examining themselves whether they be in the estate of grace before the eternal God or not. And indeed it is a grace peculiar to the man elect, to try himself whether he be in the estate of grace or not.

The further opening of the truth of this point, as also the danger of it, I have enterprised in this treatise; which I am willing to bestow on you, both for the profession of the faith which you make, as also for that Christian friendship you have showed to me. Accept of it I pray you, and use it for your edification. Thus I commend you to God, and to the word of his grace, that is able to build you up further, and give you an inheritance among them which are sanctified. From Cambridge this 24th of November, 1586.

Your Worship's to command
William Perkins

281

Letter No. 5, to the Christian Reader

Good Reader, it is a thing to be considered, that a man may seem both unto himself and to the church of God to be a true professor of the Gospel, and yet indeed be none. All professors that be of this sort are excellently described in these words; 'And they which are upon the stony ground are they which, when they shall hear, receive the word with joy, but, having no root, believe for a time, and in the time of temptation go away'. (Luke 8:13) Where are to be noted three things. I, their faith, in that they are said to believe for a season. II, the fruits of that faith, in that they are said to receive the word preached with joy. III, their unsoundness, in that they are compared to stony ground, and in time of temptation go away.

Concerning their faith, whereas the spirit of God saith that they do believe, these things are to be considered. First, that they have the knowledge of God's word. Secondly, that they both can and do give assent unto God's word, that it is most true. Thirdly, in more special manner they give assent unto the covenant of grace made in Christ, that it is most certain and sure; and they are persuaded, in a general and confused manner, that God will verify the same covenant in the members of his church. This is all their faith; which indeed proceedeth from the Holy Ghost but it is not sufficient to make them sound professors. For albeit they do generally believe God's promises, yet herein they deceive themselves, that they never apply the same to their own souls. An example of this faith we have (John 2:24) when our Saviour came to Jerusalem at the feast of Easter: 'many believed in his name, and yet he would not commit himself unto them, because he knew them all, and what was in them'.

To come to the second thing. Those professors which are endued with thus much faith as to believe in Christ in a confused manner go yet further, for this their faith; though it be not sufficient to salvation yet it showeth itself by certain fruits which it brings forth; for as a tree or a branch of a tree that has no deep rooting but either is covered with a few mouls or else lies in the water, at the season of the year brings forth leaves and blossoms and some fruit too; and that for one or two more years; so one that is an hearer of the word may receive the word, and the word as seed, by this

282

general faith may be somewhat rooted in his heart, and settled for a season, and may bring forth some fruits in his life, peradventure very fair in his own and other men's eyes; yet indeed neither sound, nor lasting, nor substantial. What these fruits are, it may be gathered forth of these words where it is said 'that they receive the word with joy' when they hear it. For here may be gathered, first, that they do willingly subject themselves to the ministry of the word. Secondly, that they are as forward as any, and as joyful in frequenting sermons. Thirdly, that they reverence the ministers whom they so joyfully hear. Lastly, they condemn them of impiety which will not be hearers or be negligent hearers of the word.

Now, of these and suchlike fruits this might be added: though they are not sound, yet they are void of that gross kind of hypocrisy. For the minds of those professors are in part enlightened, and their hearts are endued with such a faith as may bring forth these fruits for a time; and therefore herein they dissemble not that faith which they have not, but rather show that which they have. Add hereunto, that a man being in this estate may deceive himself and the most godly in the world which have the greatest gifts of discerning, how they and their brethren stand before the Lord; like as the fig-tree with green leaves deceived our Saviour Christ, as he was man, for when in his hunger he came unto it to have had some fruit, he found none.

If this be so, it may be then required how these unsound professors differ from true professors. I answer, in this they differ, that they have not sound hearts to cleave unto Christ Jesus for ever. Which appeareth in that they are compared to stony ground. Now stony grounds mingled with some earth are commonly hot, and therefore they have, as it were, some alacrity and hastiness in them, and the corn as soon as it is cast into this ground it sprouteth out very speedily, but yet the stones will not suffer the corn to be rooted deeply beneath, therefore when summer cometh the blade of the corn withereth with roots and all. So it is with these professors; they have in their hearts some good motions of the Holy Ghost to that which is good; they have a kind of zeal to God's glory, they have a liking to good things, and they are as forward as any other for a time, and they do

283

believe. But these good motions and graces are not lasting, but like the flame and flashing of straw and stubble; neither are they sufficient to salvation.

With true professors it is far otherwise; for they have upright and 'honest hearts before the Lord, and they have faith which worketh by love'. And that Christian man which loves God, whatsoever shall befall, yea though it were a thousand deaths, yet his heart can never be severed from the Lord, and from his Saviour Christ; as the spouse speaketh unto Christ of her own love, 'Set me as a seal on thy heart, as a signet upon thy arm, for love is as strong as death, jealousy is as cruel as the grave, the coals thereof are fiery coals and a vehement flame. Much water cannot quench love, neither can the floods drown it; if a man should give all the substance of his house for love, they would greatly contemn it.' (Song of Solomon 8:6-7).

Wherefore (good Reader) seeing there is such a similitude and affinity between the temporary professor of the Gospel and the true professor of the same, it is the duty of every Christian to try and examine himself whether he be in the faith or not. And whereas it is an hard thing for a man to search out his own heart, we are to pray unto God that he would give us his spirit to discern between that which is good and evil in us. Now when a man hath found out the estate of his heart by searching it 'he is further to observe and keep it with all diligence' (Proverbs 4:23) that when the hour of death or the day of trial shall come he may stand sure, and not be deceived of his hope.

And for this purpose I have described the most of these small treatises which follow, to minister unto thee some help in this examining and observing of thine own heart. Read them, and accept of them, and by the blessing of God they shall not be unprofitable to thee. And if they shall any whit help thee, help me also with thy prayer.
1595

Letter No. 6, To Sir William Piryam, Baron of the Exchequer
Right Honourable, it cannot be unknown to yourself, or to any man of a day's experience, that it is thought a small matter to commit a sin, or to lie in sins against a man's own conscience. For many, when they are told of their duty in

this point, reply and say, 'What tell you me of conscience? Conscience was hanged long ago.' But unless they take better heed, and prevent the danger by repentance, hanged conscience will revive and become both gibbet and hangman to them either in this life or the life to come. For conscience is appointed of God to declare and put in execution his just judgement against sinners, and as God cannot possibly be overcome of man, so neither can the judgement of conscience, being the judgement of God, be wholly extinguished. Indeed Satan for his part goes about by all means he can to benumb the conscience; but all is nothing. For as the sick man, when he seems to sleep and take his rest, is inwardly full of troubles, so the benumbed and drowsy conscience wants not his secret pangs and terrors, and when it shall be roused by the judgement of God it waxeth cruel and fierce like a wild beast. Again, when a man sins against his conscience, as much as in him lieth, he plungeth himself into the gulf of desperation; for every wound of the conscience, though the smart of it be little felt, is a deadly wound; and he that goes on to sin against his conscience stabs and wounds it often in the same place; and all renewed wounds (as we know) are hardly or never cured. Thirdly, he that lieth in sins against his conscience cannot call upon the name of God; for a guilty conscience makes a man fly from God. And Christ saith, 'God heareth not sinners'; understanding by sinners, such as go on in their own ways against conscience; and what can be more doleful than to be barred of the invocation of God's name? Lastly, such persons after the last judgement shall have not only their bodies in torment, but the worm in the soul and conscience shall never die; and what will it profit a man to gain the whole world by doing things against his own conscience, and lose his own soul.

Now, that men on this manner careless touching conscience may see their folly and the great danger thereof and come to amendment, I have penned this small treatise; and according to the ancient and laudable custom, as also according to my long intended purpose, I now dedicate and present the same to your Lordship. The reasons which have emboldened me to this enterprise (all by-respects excluded) are these: general doctrine in points of religion is dark and

285

obscure, and very hardly practised without the light of particular examples; and therefore the doctrine of conscience by due right pertains to a man of conscience, such an one as your Lordship is who (others of like place not excepted) have obtained this mercy at God's hand, to keep faith and good conscience. Again, considering that justice and conscience have always been friends, I am induced to think that your Lordship, being publicly set apart for the execution and maintenance of civil justice, will approve and accept a treatise propounding rules and precepts of conscience. Thus therefore craving pardon for my boldness, and hoping of your Lordship's good acceptance, I commend you to God and to the word of his grace.

1596 June 14

> Your Lordship's to command
> W. Perkins

Letter No 7, To the Christian Reader

By a 'Reformed Catholic' I understand anyone that holds the same necessary heads of religion with the Roman Church; yet so, as he pares off and rejects all errors in doctrine whereby the said religion is corrupted. How this may be done I have begun to make some little declaration in this small treatise; the intent whereof is to show how near we may come to the present Church of Rome in sundry points of religion; and wherein we must ever dissent.

My purpose in penning this small discourse is threefold. The first is, to confute all such politicks as hold and maintain that our religion and that of the Roman Church differ not in substance, and consequently that they may be reconciled. Yet my meaning is not here to condemn any pacification that tends to persuade the Roman Church to our religion. The second is, that the papists which think so basely of our religion may be won to a better liking of it, when they shall see how near we come unto them in sundry points. The third, that the common Protestant might in some part see and conceive the points of difference between us and the Church of Rome, and know in what manner and how far forth we condemn the opinions of the said Church.

I crave pardon, for the order which I use in handling the
286

several points; for I have set them down one by one as they came to mind, not respecting the laws of method. If any papist shall say that I have not alleged their opinions aright, I answer that their books be in hand, and I can justify what I have said.

Thus craving thine acceptation for this my pains, and wishing unto thee the increase of knowledge, and love of pure and sound religion I take my leave and make an end.

The places of doctrine handled are: of free will, of original sin, assurance of salvation, justification of a sinner, of merits, satisfactions for sin, of traditions, of vows, of images, of real presence, the sacrifice of the mass, of fasting, the state of perfection, worshipping of saints departed, intercession of saints, implicit faith, of purgatory, of the Supremacy, of the efficacy of the sacraments, of faith, of repentance, the sins of the Roman Church.

Letter No. 8, to Sir Edward Denny

Right worshipful, it is a thing most evident that the present religion of the Church Of Rome is an enemy to the grace of God two ways. First, because it exalts the liberty of man's will and exterminates the grace of God: and this it doth in five respects.

For first of all, it teacheth that natural free will of man hath in it not only a passive or potential but also an active power, or imperfect strength, in duties of godliness; and so much the less power is ascribed to the grace of God. This doctrine of theirs is flat against reason. For the will of man in itself is a natural thing; and therefore it is neither fit nor able to effect any supernatural action (as all actions of godliness are) unless it be first of all (as they say) elevated above his condition by the impression of a supernatural habit. And the scripture is utterly against this doctrine when it saith: 'Ye were once darkness' (Ephesians 5,8); 'We are not sufficient of ourselves to think anything of ourselves' (2 Corinthians 3,5); 'The natural man' (that is, he that wants the spirit of God) 'cannot perceive the things of God' (1 Corinthians 2,14); 'Ye were dead in sins and trespasses' (Ephesians 2,1); 'without Christ and without God in the world' (verse 12). Again, scripture saith further: that the 'heart of man is slow' (Luke 24,25)

287

and 'vain' (Psalm 59) and 'hard that cannot repent' (Romans 2,5) and 'stony' (Ezekiel 36,26), and that 'the Jews were obstinate, their neck as an iron sinew and their brow brass' (Isaiah 48,4), and that it is God 'who gives eyes to see and an heart to understand' (Deuteronomy 29,4). By these testimonies it is manifest that grace doth not only help and assist our weak nature, but altogether change the perverse quality thereof and bring it from darkness to light (Acts 28,18) and from death to life (Ephesians 2,1). Which grace, whosoever doth not so far forth acknowledge, never yet knew what the Gospel meant, neither did he ever consider the word of our Saviour Christ: 'No man comes unto me unless the Father draw him' (John 6,44). Prosper, the scholar of Saint Augustine, hath a notable saying, which I marvel the papists of our time do not consider. 'We have' (saith he) 'free will by nature, but for quality and condition it must be changed by our Lord Jesus Christ.'

Secondly, some of the Romish religion avouch that the efficacy of God's preventing grace depends upon the co-operation of man's will, and they affirm that the Council of Trent is of this mind. But then to the question of Paul, (1 Corinthians 4,7) 'Who hath separated thee?', the answer may be made: I myself have done it by mine own will. And that shall be false which Paul teacheth, that beside *posse velle*, the power of well-willing, *ipsum velle*, that is, the act of well-willing, is of God (Philippians 2,13). Others therefore place the efficacy of grace in the congruity of fit objects and persuasions; as though it were sufficient to stir up the heart and to incline the will in spiritual matters, and our weakness might be cured with so easy a medicine. But God is further said 'to soften the heart' (Ezekiel 36,26), 'to turn the heart' (Luke 1,17), 'to open the heart' (Acts 16,14). And because our hearts are over hard 'he wounds them' (Song of Solomon 4,9), 'he circumciseth them' (Deuteronomy 30,6), nay, 'he bruiseth them' (Ezekiel 6,9). And when nothing will do good, at length God is said 'to take away the stony heart' (Ezekiel 11,19), 'to quicken them that are contrite' (Isaiah 57,15; Ephesians 2,5), 'to give a new heart' (Ephesians 4,23; Ezekiel 36, 26), nay, 'to create a new heart' (Ephesians 2,10 and 4,28.)

Thirdly, they give unto God in all contingent actions a depending will, whereby God wills and determines nothing but according as he foresees that the will of man will determine itself. And thus to maintain the supposed liberty of the will, that is, the indifferency and indetermination thereof, they deprive God of his honour and sovereignty. For by this means not God but the will itself is the first mover and beginner of her own actions. And there are even of the Papists themselves that condemn this doctrine as a conceit.

Fourthly, they teach that the grace which makes us acceptable and grateful to God stands in the inward gifts of the mind, specially in the gifts of charity. But this is most false which they teach; for charity is the fulfilling of the law. And Paul saith: 'we are not under the law but under grace' (Romans 6,14). And again: 'as many as are justified by the law are fallen from grace' (Galatians 5,4). Now the grace that doth indeed make us grateful to God is the free favour and mercy of God, pardoning our sins in Christ, and accepting us to eternal life, and not any quality in us, as Paul signifieth when he saith: 'we are saved not according to our works but according to his purpose and grace, which is given to us in Christ before all times' (2 Timothy 1,9).

Lastly, they teach that the renewed will of man, by the general direction and co-operation of God, can perform the duties of godliness without any special help from God by new grace. But the scripture speaks otherwise. 'By the grace of God I am that I am. I have laboured, yet not I, but the grace of God which is with me' (1 Corinthians 15,10). 'No man can say that Jesus is the Lord, but by the Holy Ghost' (1 Corinthians 12,3). 'Without me ye can do nothing' (John 15,5). 'After ye believed ye were sealed with the spirit' (Ephesians 1,13). 'He which hath begun this good work in you will finish it until the day of Christ' (Philippians 1,6). 'That ye may abound with hope by the virtue of the spirit' (Romans 15,13). 'It is God that works in you the will and the deed' (Philippians 2,13). 'Though the righteous fall, he shall not be cast off, for the Lord puts under his hand' (Psalm 37,24). 'Incline mine heart to thy testimonies, turn away mine eyes from beholding of vanity, and quicken me in thy way' (Psalm 119,37). 'Teach me to do thy will, because thou art my God; let thy good spirit lead me in the land of righteousness' (Psalm 143,10). 'Create in me a new heart, renew a right

289

spirit in me, and stablish me by thy free spirit' (Psalm 51,12). 'Draw me and I will run after thee.' By these and many other places it is evident that God, after he hath endued us with his spirit doth not leave us to be guided by ourselves (for then we should fall again to our former misery) but he directs us, he lifts us up, he leads us, he confirms and sustains us by the same grace and by the same spirit dwelling in us, that walking in the way of his commandments we may at length attain to everlasting happiness.

The second way whereby the Papist shows himself to be an enemy of the grace of God, is that he joins the merit of works as a con-cause with the grace of God, in that which they call the second justification, and in the procurement of eternal life. Whereas on the contrary Paul, in the article of justification, opposeth grace to works, yea to such as are the gifts and fruits of the spirit. For Abraham did good works not by natural free will but by faith (Hebrews 11,8). And Paul opposeth justifying grace to the works of Abraham when he saith: 'to him that worketh the wage is not imputed according to grace'. And (Titus 3,5) 'not of the works of righteousness which we have done, but of his mercy, he saved us'; (Romans 11,6). 'If by grace, then not of works, or else were grace no more grace.' Augustine said well, that grace is no way grace unless it be freely given every way.

Thus then, all things considered, it is the best to ascribe all we have or can do that is good, wholly to the grace of God. Excellent is the speech of Augustine: 'Only hold this as a sure point of godliness, that no good thing can come either to the sense or mind, or be any way conceived, which is not of God.' And Bernard: 'The church shows herself to be full of grace when she gives all she hath to grace, namely by ascribing to it both the first and last place, Otherwise, how is she full of grace, if she have anything which is not of grace?' Again: 'I tremble to think anything mine own, that I may be mine own.' This doctrine is the safest and the surest in respect of peace of conscience and the salvation of our souls. So much the Papists themselves (betraying their own cause) say and confess. Bellarmine the Jesuit saith: 'By reason of the uncertainty of our own justice, and for fear of falling into vain glory, it is the safest to put our whole confidence in the alone mercy and goodness of God.' Cassander — in his book

290

called the Consultation of Articles in question: to Maximilian the Emperor — cites a saying of Bonaventure, which is on this manner: 'It is the duty of godly minds to ascribe nothing to themselves, but all to the grace of God. Hence it follows that how much soever a man gives unto grace, though in giving many things to the grace of God he takes something from the power of nature and free will, he departs not from godliness; but when anything is taken from the grace of God, and given to nature, which pertains to grace, there may be some danger.' Thus then to hold and maintain justification by faith without works, and to ascribe the whole work of our conversion to God without making any division between grace and nature, is the safest.

These things I show more at large in this Treatise following, which I now present to your Worship as a small testimony of mine humble duty and love, desiring you to accept the mind of the giver, and to peruse it at your leisure. And thus I commend your Worship to the protection and grace of God in Christ.

> Your Worship's in the Lord
> William Perkins

Letter No. 9, Epistle to the Reader

The doctrine of predestination and God's grace is to be founded upon the written word of God, and not upon the judgements of men. For as Hilary saith well, God cannot be understood but by God; and again, we must learn of God that we are to understand of God, because he is the only author of our knowledge of him. It is also requisite that this doctrine agree with the grounds of common reason, and of that knowledge of God which may be obtained by the light of nature; and such are these which follow.

1. God is always just, albeit men do not understand how he is just.

2. God is not governed of, much less does he depend upon, second causes; but doth justly order them, even then when they work unjustly.

3. God worketh wisely, to wit, propounding unto him a certain end. He is ignorant of nothing; he doth not will or decree that which he cannot effect; he doth not idly behold

291

what shall be, or what may be done, but he disposeth all things unto his glory; and therefore he hath decreed to do so.

4. God is not changed; and those things which are changed are not changed without his unchangeable decree, all circumstances being certain and sure.

5. The secret and unsearchable judgements of God are to be honoured and acknowledged. Augustine. It moveth me (thou sayst) that he perisheth and another is baptized, it moveth me, it moveth me as a man. If you wilt hear the truth, it also moveth me, because I am a man. But if you be-est a man, I am also a man. Let us both hear him that saith: O man! Verily, if we be therefore moved because we are men, the apostle speaks to human nature itself being weak and feeble, saying: O man, who art thou which pleadest against God! Shall the thing formed say to him that formed it, Why hast you made me thus? If a beast could speak and did say to God, Why have you made him a man and me a beast?; mightest thou not justly be angry, and say, O beast, who are you? And thou are a man, but in comparison with God, thou are a beast.

6. No good thing can be done unless God doth absolutely will and work it; and we do that which is good so far forth as God doth work in us more or less.

7. No evil can be avoided unless God do hinder it; and we avoid evil so far forth as God doth more or less hinder it.

8. The will of God is known not only by the written word or by revelation, but also by the event. For that which cometh to pass doth therefore come to pass because God hath willed that it should come to pass.

9. A man doth not that good thing which by grace he is able to do unless God make him do it, as he hath made him able to do it if he will.

10. Not a part only, but the whole government of the world, and the execution of justice, is to be ascribed to God, as to the Author.

I do now exhibit unto thee a view and picture of this doctrine, composed of these principles, and do publish the same that I might to my power help out those that stick in the difficulties of this doctrine of Predestination, and that I might clear the truth, that is (as they call it) the 'Calvinist's' doctrine, of those reproaches which are cast upon it; and that

I might mitigate and appease the minds of some of our brethren which have been more offended at it than was fit. For I do willingly acknowledge and teach universal redemption and grace, so far as it is possible by the word. My mind is to pursue after peace, which is departing from us; and I would have all men so interpret my fact.

I allege the testimonies of the ancient everywhere, not but that even one evident and perspicuous sentence of sacred scripture concerning any point of doctrine and faith is of more value and force than all the testimonies of the doctors and schoolmen, but because I hold it necessary that there should be had an example of consent and concord in that doctrine which is expounded in holy books and is propagated to all posterity. And I hope I shall sufficiently persuade an indifferent judge that these things have not been lately hatched at home which we deliver in our congregations and Schools, but that we have also derived and fetched them from the Fathers themselves.

William Perkins

Letter No. 10, to the Christian Reader

Christian Reader, there at this day four several opinions of the order of God's predestination.

The first is of the old and new pelagians, who place the causes of God's predestination in man; in that they hold that God did ordain men either to life or death according as he did foresee that they would by their natural free will either reject or receive grace offered.

The second of them, who (of some) are termed Lutherans; which teach that God foreseeing how all mankind, being shut up under unbelief, would therefore reject grace offered, did hereupon purpose to choose some to salvation of his mere mercy, without any respect of their faith or good works, and the rest to reject; being moved to do this because he did eternally foresee that they would reject his grace offered them in the gospel.

The third, semi-pelagian papists, which ascribe God's predestination partly to mercy and partly to men's foreseen preparations and meritorious works.

The fourth, of such as teach that the cause of the execu-

293

tion of God's predestination is his mercy in Christ in them which are saved, and in them which perish, the fall and corruption of man, yet so as that the decree and eternal counsel of God concerning them both has not any cause beside his will and pleasure.

Of these four opinions, the three former I labour to oppugn as erronious; and to maintain the last, as being truth which will bear weight in the balance of the sanctuary.

A further discourse whereof here I make bold to offer to thy godly consideration; in reading whereof regard not so much the thing itself, penned very slenderly, as mine intent and affection, who desire among the rest to cast my mite into the treasury of the Church of England, and, for want of gold, pearl and precious stone to bring a ram's skin or twain and a little goat's hair to the building of the Lord's tabernacle (Exodus 35,23).

The Father of our Lord Jesus Christ grant that, according to the riches of his glory, thou mayest be strengthened by his spirit in the inner man, that Christ may dwell in thy heart by faith, to the end that thou being rooted and grounded in love mayest be able to comprehend with all saints what is the breadth and length and height thereof, and to know the love of Christ which passeth knowledge, that thou mayest be filled with all fulness of God. Amen. Farewell, July 23, the year of the last patience of Saints 1592.

Thine in Christ Jesus
William Perkins

27 A Chart of Salvation and Damnation

'A Survey or Table declaring the Order of the Causes of Salvation and Damnation, according to God's Word. It may be read instead of an ocular Catechism to them which cannot read: for by the pointing of the Finger they may sensibly perceive the chief Points of Religion, and the Order of them': inserted before *The Foundation of Christian Religion, gathered into six principles; and it is to be learnt of ignorant People, that they may be fit to hear Sermons with Profit, and to receive the Lord's Supper with Comfort.* (written 1590): at beginning of 'Works' i (1612).

'To the Reader. *The White line sheweth the order of the causes of salvation from the first to the last. The black line sheweth the order of the causes of damnation. The lines A. A. A. shew how faith doth apprehend Christ and all His benefits, and applieth them to the person of every believer for his justification and sanctification. The lines B. B. B., descending, likewise shew the tentation of the godly and their remedies. The wide spaces C. C. C. shew the communication of the Godhead from the Father to the Son, and from them both to the Holy Ghost.*'

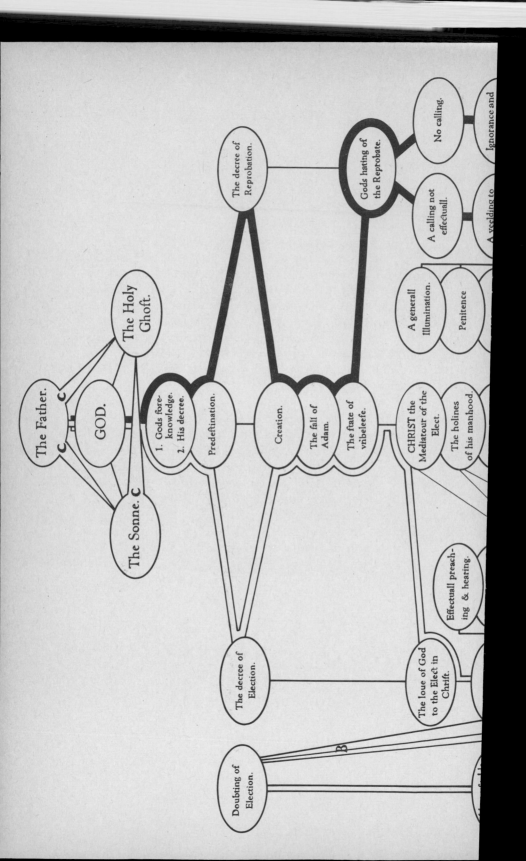

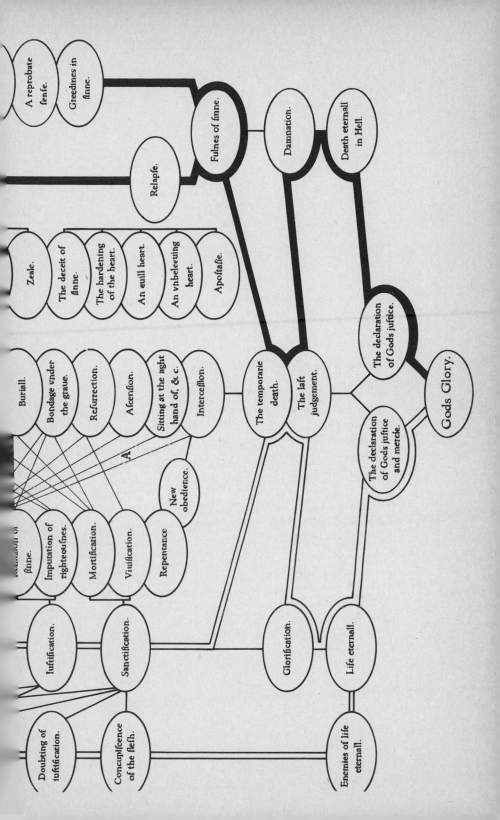

A. The communication of the Godhead from the Father to the Son and from them both to the Holy Ghost
 God
 The Father
 The Son
 The Holy Ghost

B. Christ
 Christ the meditator of the elect
 The holiness of His manhood
 The fulfilling of the Law
 His accursed death
 Burial
 Bondage under the grave
 Resurrection
 Ascension
 Sitting at the right hand
 Intercession

C. The order of the causes of salvation
 God's foreknowledge
 His decree
 The decree of election
 Creation
 The fall of Adam
 Christ the mediator of the elect
 The love of God to the elect in Christ
 Effectual calling
 Justification
 Sanctification
 The temporary death
 The last judgement
 Glorification
 Life eternal
 The declaration of God's justice and mercy
 God's glory

D. How faith doth apprehend Christ and all His benefits, and applieth them to the person of every believer for his justification and sanctification
    Effectual preaching and hearing
    The mollifying of the heart
    Faith
    Remission of sin
    Imputation of righteousness
    Vivification
    Repentance
    New obedience

E. The temptations of the godly
    Doubting of election
    Unprofitable hearing
    Despair
    Doubting of faith
    Doubting of justification
    Concupiscence of the flesh
    Enemies of life eternal

F. The order of the causes of damnation
    God's foreknowledge
    His decree
    Predestination
    The decree of reprobation
    Creation
    The fall of Adam
    The state of unbelief
    God's hatred of the reprobate
    No calling
    A calling not effectual
    A yielding to God's calling — but relapse
    Ignorance and vanity of mind
    The hardening of the heart
    A reprobate sense
    Greediness in sin
    Fullness of sin
    The temporary death

The last judgement
Damnation
Death eternal in hell
The declaration of God's justice
God's glory

Suggested Further Reading

This is not intended to be a full bibliography. I have merely noted books which I happened to find most useful, and which I like to have by me. A comprehensive list of books and articles (up to 1967) can be found in Patrick McGrath, 'Papists and Puritans under Elizabeth I' (London, 1967; available in paperback). I also like the select bibliography (with comments) in William M. Lamont, 'Godly Rule: Politics and Religion 1603-60 (London, 1969; Papermac).

Albert Camus, 'L'Homme Revolté' (Paris, 1951): English translation, 'The Rebel' (London, 1952; Peregrine paperback 1962).

Patrick Collinson, (ed.), 'Letters of Thomas Wood, Puritan, 1566-1577 (Bulletin of the Institute of Historical Research', Special Supplement no. 5, London, Nov 1960).

Patrick Collinson, 'John Field and Elizabethan Puritanism', in 'Elizabethan Government and Society: essays presented to Sir John Neale', ed. S. T. Bindoff, J. Hurstfield and C. H. Williams (London, 1961).

Patrick Collinson, 'A Mirror of Elizabethan Puritanism: the life and letters of 'godly Master Dering'' (Friends of Dr Williams's Library Lecture, London, 1963).

Patrick Collinson, 'The Elizabethan Puritan Movement (London, 1967).

Claire Cross, 'The Royal Supremacy in the Elizabethan Church' (London, 1969: UU paperback, H 8).

Horton Davies, 'The Worship of the English Puritans (London, 1948).

A. G. Dickens, 'Lollards and Protestants in the Diocese of York 1509-1558 (London, 1959).

A. G. Dickens, 'The English Reformation' (London, 1964; rev. paperback ed. London, 1967).

W. H. Frere, and C. E. Douglas (eds), 'Puritan Manifestoes: a

301

study of the origin of the puritan revolt' (London, 1907; reprinted, with a preface by Norman Sykes, 1954).

Christina H. Garrett, 'The Marian Exiles: a study in the origins of Elizabethan puritanism' (Cambridge, 1938; reprinted 1966).

C. H. George, 'Puritanism as History and Historiography', 'Past and Present,' no. 41 (Dec 1968); see the 'further thoughts' on this by William M. Lamont, 'Past and Present', no. 44 (Aug 1969).

C. H. and K. George, 'The Protestant Mind of the English Reformation 1570-1640' (Princeton, 1961).

M. M. Knappen, 'Tudor Puritanism: a chapter in the history of idealism' (Chicago, 1939; paperback, with a new preface, Phoenix Books, Chicago, 1965).

William Haller, 'The Rise of Puritanism: or, the way to the new Jerusalem as set forth in pulpit and press from Thomas Cartwright to John Lilburne and John Milton, 1570-1643' (New York, 1938; paperback, Harper Torchbooks 22, 1957). 'et al'.,

William Haller, 'John Foxe and the Puritan Revolution', in R. F. Jones 'et al'., 'The Seventeenth Century: studies in the history of English thought and literature from Bacon to Pope' (Stanford, 1951; paperback, SP 93, Stanford, 1965).

William Haller, 'Foxe's Book of Martyrs and the Elect Nation' (London, 1963).

William P. Haugaard, 'Elizabeth and the English Reformation: the struggle for a stable settlement of religion' (Cambridge, 1968).

Christopher Hill, 'Economic Problems of the Church from Archbishop Whitgift to the Long Parliament' (Oxford, 1956).

Christopher Hill, 'Puritanism and Revolution: studies in interpretation of the English Revolution of the 17th century' (London, 1958; paperback, Mercury Books, London, 1962).

Christopher Hill, 'Society and Puritanism in Pre-Revolutionary England' (London, 1964; available in paperback).

Christopher Hill, 'Reformation to Industrial Revolution: a social and economic history of Britain, 1530-1780' (London, 1967).

W. P. Holden, 'Anti-Puritan Satire 1572-1642' (New Haven, Conn., 1954; reprint 1968).

S. J. Knox, 'Walter Travers: Paragon of Elizabethan Puritanism' (London 1962).

Ronald A. Marchant, 'The Puritans and the Church Courts in the Diocese of York 1560-1642' (London, 1960).

Perry Miller, 'Orthodoxy in Massachusetts 1630-1650' (Cambridge, Mass., 1933; paperback, with new preface, Beacon BP 89, Boston, Mass., 1959).

Perry Miller, 'The New England Mind', I: 'The Seventeenth Century' (New York, 1939; paperback, with new preface, Beacon BP 127, Boston Mass., 1961).

Edmund S. Morgan, 'Visible Saints: the history of a puritan idea' (New York, 1963; Cornell paperback, 1965).

Edmund S. Morgan, (ed.), 'Puritan Political Ideas 1558-1794' (New York, 1965; American Heritage paperback 33).

Edmund S. Morgan, 'The Puritan Family: religion and domestic relations in seventeenth-century New England', new ed. (Harper Torchbooks 1227 L, New York, 1966).

J. E. Neale, 'Elizabeth I and her Parliaments', I: (1559-1581) (London, 1953); II: '1584-1601' (London 1957). Now in paperback (1965).

A. F. Scott Pearson, 'Church and State: political aspects of 16th century puritanism' (Cambridge, 1928).

A. Peel (ed.), 'The Seconde Parte of a Register: being a calendar of manuscripts under that title intended for publication by the puritans about 1593 and now in Dr Williams's Library, London', 2 vols (London, 1915).

A. Peel (ed.), 'The Notebook of John Penry 1593' (Camden Society, London 1944).

A. Peel (ed.), 'Tracts ascribed to Richard Bancroft 1584' (Cambridge, 1953).

A. Peel and L. H. Carlson (eds.), 'Cartwrightiana' (London, 1951): being vol I of the series 'Elizabethan Nonconformist Texts'; further volumes have appeared devoted to Robert Harrison, Robert Browne, Henry Barrow and John Greenwood.

Norman Pettit, 'The Heart Prepared: grace and conversion in puritan spiritual life' (New Haven, Conn., 1966).

Rainer Pineas, 'Thomas More and Tudor Polemics' (Bloomington, Ind., 1968) (for Robert Barnes).

Alan Simpson, 'Puritanism in Old and New England' (Chicago, 1955).

Werner Stark, 'The Sociology of Religion: a study of Christendom', II: 'Sectarian Religion' (London, 1967).

R. G. Usher (ed.), 'The Presbyterian Movement in the Church of England as illustrated by the minute book of the Dedham classis 1582-89' (Camden Society, London, 1905).

Michael Walzer, 'The Revolution of the Saints: a study in the origins of radical politics' (London, 1966).

A. S. P. Woodhouse (ed.), 'Puritanism and Liberty' (London, 1934; 2nd ed. 1951).

Three books should be noted which were published after the completion of my manuscript:

Ian Breward (ed.), 'The Work of William Perkins' (extracts, with a long introduction) (Abingdon, Courtenay Library of Reformation Classics, 1970).

Martin Bucer, 'De Regno Christi', English translation by W. Pauck, and L. J. Satre and P. Larkin, in 'Melanchthon and Bucer' (Library of Christian Classics, London, 1969).

Paul Seaver, 'The Puritan Lectureships: the politics of religious dissent, 1560-1662' (Stanford, 1970).

Index to Editorial Material

307

308

Index to Documents

309

310

311

78255